"*Richard Hart Bread* ... ...en by one
of the world's ... ... advice
for you: Buy it ... ...he usual
suspects—a ba... ...f—now
it's time to earn ... ...ook will
guide you to ba...

—**Nancy Silverto...**

"Richard is the bread whisperer. Having been in the trenches
with him, I've seen it firsthand. Next to his family, I don't think
there's anything in the world Richard cares more about than
bread—it's more than a job; breadmaking courses through
his veins. So when diving into the pages of this book, you're
getting a piece of his soul. Each word, each method, is steeped
in his essence. The passion, the meticulous care—it's all here.
This book isn't just about bread; it's a type of manifesto of
Richard's lifelong quest for that fleeting (life-affirming) moment
of a perfect bake. It is a testament to the art and craft of baking.
Trust me, you can taste the difference."

—**René Redzepi**

"Even if you have shelves and shelves of bread books, you'll still
want this one!"

—**Nigella Lawson**

"This book is for all the dreamers. For people who aren't afraid of
making mistakes. We need more touch and feel and smell and
taste. This book will provide a path of love and misery in trying,
but if we don't try, we will never know, so it's worth it! Break your
brain or bake your heart."

—**Matty Matheson**

"Richard Hart restores the heart to bread baking. He urges us to
trust our senses over strict science. Like learning an instrument,
baking bread demands patience, practice, precision, but above
all, passion. We're all safe in Hart's hands."

—**Yotam Ottolenghi**

Richard Hart Bread

Richard Hart

and Laurie Woolever with Henrietta Lovell

Photographs by Maureen Evans

Clarkson Potter/Publishers
New York

Intuitive Sourdough Baking

Richard Hart Bread

Library of Congress Cataloging-in-Publication Data
Names: Hart, Richard (Writer on cooking) author.
    | Woolever, Laurie, author. | Lovell, Henrietta,
    contributor. | Evans, Maureen, photographer.
Title: Richard Hart Bread: Intuitive Sourdough Baking
    / Richard Hart and Laurie Woolever; with
    Henrietta Lovell; photographs by Maureen Evans.
Description: New York: Clarkson Potter, 2024 |
    Includes index.
Identifiers: LCCN 2023043869 (print) | LCCN
    2023043870 (ebook) | ISBN 9780593234297
    (hardcover) | ISBN 9780593234303 (e-book)
Subjects: LCSH: Cooking (Bread) | Bread. | LCGFT:
    Cookbooks.
Classification: LCC TX769 .H344 2024 (print) | LCC
    TX769 (ebook) | DDC 641.81/5—dc23/eng/20231122
LC record available at https://lccn.loc
    .gov/2023043869
LC ebook record available at https://lccn.loc
    .gov/2023043870

ISBN 978-0-593-23429-7
Ebook ISBN 978-0-593-23430-3

Printed in China

Editors: Francis Lam and Susan Roxborough
Editorial assistant: Darian Keels
Designer: Robert Diaz
Art director: Ian Dingman
Production editor: Christine Tanigawa
Production manager: Kim Tyner
Compositors: Merri Ann Morrell and Hannah Hunt
Copyeditor: Deri Reed
Proofreaders: Rachel Holzman, Kim Lewis, Erica Rose
Indexer: Barbara Mortensen
Publicist: Kristin Casemore
Marketer: Andrea Portanova

10 9 8 7 6 5 4 3 2 1

First Edition

This book is dedicated to my boys,
Bodhi, Indy, Jude, and Remy.

And to Henrietta for telling them that I'm the best baker
in the world, and again to them for believing her.

Contents

Bread Baking Techniques

Creating a Starter

Rye Breads & Pan Loaves

City Loaf & Variations

Wheat Loaves Flavored with Other Grains

Flatbreads Plus Focaccia & Ciabatta

Mixed Bag

Baking with Sourdough Discard

Sweet Breads

Panettone

Good Bread

There are a million bread books and bakers out there. Why pick this one by me?

I can easily be outgeeked. I meet a lot of bakers who want to talk to me about bread baking in a very scientific way, but to be honest, my eyes glaze over in seconds. There are plenty of books that go deep into this stuff, if you want to go there. It's quite easy to find online forums where you can argue about the effect of a half-degree temperature difference on a specific flour's storage protein glass phase. Looking to compare the phylogenetic distribution patterns of wheat species between Asia and North America? Fuck me—I'll be in my bakery, mixing together flour, water, and salt.

I understand and respect the science, I admire the enthusiasm, but that's not the kind of baker I am. I look at the dough, I put my hands in it, I smell it. I see how it behaves when I touch and stretch and shape it. I watch how it rises in the oven. I assess the baked bread. And I compare it to what I've done before. I go by my experience and my senses. I'm more of a sensualist than a scientist, and in this book, I'll show you exactly what I look for, so you can see, smell, touch, and taste your way to your own great bread.

I've been baking bread professionally for fifteen years. I still get nervous every morning, waking up with my first thought being, "How did my dough do overnight?" I worry every single day about how well my bread will turn out. There are only two or three days a year when I can honestly say I've baked a perfect loaf. I can make great bread, but each new day brings the possibility of *perfect* bread. It's never not exciting. I truly love being a bread baker, and I'm so lucky that I can make a living out of this.

In my late twenties I left behind a career as a chef and the clean-shaven, regimented precision of London fine dining kitchens. I started baking bread in California, in a rustic barn with two wood-burning ovens. The first time I walked into that bakery, Della Fattoria, I was completely gobsmacked.

I couldn't believe that people still made bread like that. It felt so old school, so honest. I'd imagined that professional bakeries were full of modern machinery, all stainless steel and white tile. At Della, if you took away the one big mixer, it could have been a bakery from a thousand years ago. Here was an ancient art that I could still explore, as relevant and as important to human happiness as it has always been.

When I first quit working as a chef, my mum said, "You're going to be so bored. You've gone from working with tons of different ingredients to just a few."

But the truth is, I've never been more engaged. After all these years, I still can't wait to get up in the morning (or even the middle of the night) and start baking. A lot of what makes me a good baker is how much I care. I really do give a shit. Giving people freshly baked bread, as good as you can possibly make it—bread that you've made with your own hands, and put all your heart into—is magical.

And there is something profoundly humbling about making bread. You can't get cocky about it. (Well, you can, but the minute you do, it kicks you in the arse, and you're back to being humbled.)

There are so many tiny variables. You fed your starter ten minutes later today, or your dough was half a degree warmer last night. Maybe there was a storm and the air pressure changed. Perhaps the flour was milled from wheat that came from a higher-elevation field on the farm. Trying to account for and adjust to all the variables—it's endlessly challenging, fascinating, and rewarding, and no one day is exactly like any other.

There will be days when you make your best bread ever, and then the next day, something intangible changes, and the dough just isn't the same. The trick is to embrace the changes, not get freaked out, and you'll still learn how to make bread that's just as good.

Absolute devotion to consistent methods and exact recipes is useful when you're running a fast-food franchise or a fine dining kitchen, but when you're baking bread, the most important thing is to understand your dough and be ready to make adjustments.

When I first started baking, my day was managed through increments of time. We'd mix and shape the dough and bake bread strictly according to the recipes and the clock, with no variations, and sometimes the quality of the bread suffered because of that.

But when I joined the team at Tartine in San Francisco, I was amazed by the way Chad Robertson, the founder, made bread by reading the dough. For me, it was a chance to dive deeper into understanding why things happened. It wasn't about following recipes. We made bread using our intuition and collective experience, to do with it what *it* wanted. I started to appreciate that the dough is a living thing; *it's alive,* constantly changing, and like all living things, it wants to be taken care of, and treated with love and respect.

When I set up my own bakery in Copenhagen, Denmark, I faced new challenges that have deepened my understanding of breadmaking. The flour in Europe is so different from the flour in the US. And I know that you and I won't necessarily be baking in the same climate, with the same ingredients, but don't worry. Whether you're a home baker or a professional, wherever you are in the world, the way to make good bread remains the same if you learn how it behaves and you learn to develop an intuition for it.

Learning to take care of your dough requires a bit of dedication and work. You're unlikely to get it spot-on straightaway. You need to form an intimate relationship with the craft, and the only way to improve is through practice, repetition, and learning through your experience—your successes and your mistakes.

You'll need to start asking questions of your environment, your ingredients, and the dough. Is it humid outside, or dry? How hot or cold is it? How does the flour feel in your fingers— dry and powdery, or slightly damp? What can you smell in the starter, the flour, the dough? How big are the bubbles in the fermenting dough? How sticky is it? How does the dough react when you touch it? What does it look like when you divide it? How does it act when you shape it, score it, and bake it?

You probably do this kind of intuitive, observational caretaking and problem-solving all the time. If you're a parent, you can often tell what's going on with your kids just by looking at their faces, or the way they're sitting. You can tell when your bike needs a tune-up by how it rides. You know when your knives need to be sharpened by how they cut, without having to touch the blade. We all have examples of an intuition developed through experience, repetition, and some trial and error.

I have written this book to share everything I have learned about baking bread, and all the experience I have gained. I'm not going to hold anything back. I believe it's good to give away all your knowledge, to help others and not be afraid of their successes. Everyone who knows me knows I can't keep a secret anyway. It doesn't stop me from growing. I'm always thinking and evolving.

I want to help you develop your intuition and become a baker of great bread that has amazing flavor and texture. It will look beautiful, too. I want us all to make good bread—and this book is about how to do that.

Cast of Characters

You'll see a number of shout-outs in this book; it's important to credit the people whose work, recipes, mentorship, ideas, and kindness helped me become the baker and the person I am today.

You'll also see a few chapters that you could well skip if, for instance, you just want to know about bread but don't care about how I got to be a baker. But reading this bit will help you understand who the people are who helped me along the way, and so that I don't have to keep introducing them every time if you see their names again later on.

Karishma Sanghi was interning at restaurant 108, part of the Noma group, when I met her. I was helping out there for a couple of weeks, making bread, when I first arrived in Copenhagen. I started at four in the morning, and she came in every day at the same time as me, before her shift started, to learn.

I liked her. I liked her work ethic. I liked her enthusiasm. I've grown to love her. She is so dedicated. She's a fantastic cook. And she makes some of the best Indian food I've ever eaten.

After her internship, Karishma asked me for a job. Of course it was a yes. We have worked together since then. She keeps pushing me to be better, to think outside the box, to keep evolving. Karishma has really helped me in the research and development of this book, and I wanted to say a massive thank-you.

Aris Albiñana has worked with me since my days at Della Fattoria. He moved to Tartine with me, and then to Hart Bageri in Copenhagen, where he's still baking. He's a lovely man whom everyone loves, even though he misses his alarm way too often and drives us all crazy.

Talia Richard-Carvajal is the person I trust to run Hart in my place. She gets it. She gets me. She gets everything. She's so damn smart, super funny, and super talented and is married to the future prime minister of Denmark, Hans Peter. He said he'd pose naked for this book but chickened out. I love him anyway.

Laurie Woolever, my cowriter and organizer extraordinaire, loves the sentence "We're in great shape." She put up with a lot of shit from me when I was freaking out about getting this book right. She talked me down with her calm demeanor and is always chill and brilliantly cynical. Laurie really kept us on track and became a great baker along the way. Thanks, love.

Kathleen Weber was my first bread mentor, at Della Fattoria. She is the reason I became a baker. I'm so grateful for this fantastic lady and am so sad she is no longer alive. I wish I could share my stories and my bread with her. I think she would be proud.

Chad Robertson was my second bread mentor. Chad founded Tartine in San Francisco. He is basically Yoda, just taller and less green. He changed the world of baking. I would, in no way, be the baker I am today if it weren't for Chad.

Monika Walecka is a fantastic baker whom I met when we both lived in California and talked about everything bread. She has her own bakery now, in Warsaw, Poland, and I promise I'll visit someday soon.

Michael Schulze, a German baking legend, has a bakery in Freiburg called Brotbruder. He is an amazing baker and a lovely man.

Wendy Williams and I worked together at Tartine, and then she came to join me at Hart Bageri. She is a fantastic baker and now has a bakery in San Francisco in the Sunset District, called Day Moon.

Matt Jones is another friend I met working at Tartine. Before that, he was baking at a restaurant called Outerlands in San Francisco, making some of the most beautiful bread ever, baked in a Dutch oven. He proved what you can do with passion, rather than equipment. Matt now lives in North Carolina, where he's setting up his next great thing. He's someone to keep your eye on.

Doug McMaster is a good friend and brilliant revolutionary. He founded a restaurant in London called Silo. It's zero waste. These are very easy words to write, and very hard principles to live by. He has a small box of all the rubbish that has come into Silo over the last four years. Go there; he'll show you. He intends to make a beautiful art piece with it. Even the glass bottles are ground down into sand, to make ceramics. Doug is a legend. His book, *Silo: The Zero Waste Blueprint,* is essential reading for every human being.

Danny Mariani is an Italian farmer and miller. He opened my eyes to the real craft of milling, and upended many of my preconceptions, showing me that technology can be used for the right reasons. He's got a lovely family: three generations of millers all still working together, including his father, Paulo, and his nonna Lucia, who is still bustling about, making sure everything is shipshape.

Gabriele Bonci is a baking and pizza legend in Italy and around the world. He has a killer place in Rome called Pizzarium. The minute you meet Bonci, you are embraced by his warm, charismatic, enthusiastic spirit. He's wonderful to be around; a beautiful human, and my friend. I always look forward to the next time we bake together.

Maureen Evans takes amazing pictures, even of my hero, Nick Cave. She is so brilliant, I forgive her for not getting his address so I could send him bread.

Lars and Anne Batting are the owners of Copenhagen's best bakery (aside from mine). They are my much-loved Danish family.

René Redzepi is one of the most important chefs in the world today, with his restaurant Noma, as well as many other projects. He has a huge presence, like a superpower. What he has already achieved blows my mind, and I'm bloody older than him. René is my business partner in Denmark and took a huge leap of faith to help me set up Hart Bageri, which I'm forever grateful for, but his take on a British accent is truly terrible.

Jeremy Fox is a chef with a fantastic restaurant in Santa Monica called Birdie G's. He was the best chef I ever worked for in my cooking days. He gave me a job at his old restaurant in Napa, Ubuntu. After my first service, he said, "Wow, for an Englishman, you really don't suck at this." I loved working with Jeremy, but he also does a terrible British accent.

Rosio Sanchez owns and runs Mexican restaurants in Copenhagen: Hija de Sanchez and Sanchez. I first met Rosio when she ran pastry at Noma, and she came to hang out with me at Tartine. We've been friends ever since. She made me drink wine shots at her wedding. Who drinks wine shots?

Cannelle Deslandes worked with me at Hart, and she's been part of my family ever since. Whenever we were in the shit, she came to help out. Whenever there was a party, she was there. And she tells the best lurid stories of anyone I've ever met.

Ezra Kedem is a famous chef in Israel. I was invited to Jerusalem to do an event with him. We'd never met before, but working with him was really wonderful. He took us under his wing and took great care of me. His food is so good, and I can't wait to see him again.

Brooks Headley owns Superiority Burger, hands down my favorite restaurant in New York. Whenever Henrietta and I are in Manhattan, we eat there every day if we can. He is a genuinely kind soul, and makes unfeasibly good food that also happens to be vegetarian/vegan. His cooking is dirty and delicious.

Darina Allen founded Ballymaloe Cookery School just outside Cork, in Ireland. Her first champion was Julia Child. She is such a firecracker, full of vigor, joy, and love.

Cameron Wallace was a bread baker at Tartine before I started there. His cool, calm, chill self was lovely to be around in the bakery. For a gringo from San Diego, he makes some of the best Mexican food I've ever had.

Ben Liebmann is the former COO of Noma, and he now lives back in his native Australia. He helped me move from California to Copenhagen. Since then, he has supported me in everything I've done. He's a good friend, and I'm super grateful to have him in my life.

Manuel Avila Solis is a filmmaker who shot all the video for this book. He came all the way from Mexico City, with his young family, to help me. I've only hung out with him for a week, but I feel we've started a friendship that will last a lot longer.

Francis Lam is an award-winning writer and editor who, lucky for me, wanted to be *my* editor. Any chance you can win me an award, mate? Cheers in advance.

Henrietta Lovell is my love, my partner, my wife. Henrietta is the Tea Lady. A lot of you out there already know her and the amazing work she does. She is the founder and head of the brilliant Rare Tea Company. She's also *my* lady and has helped me for countless hours on the text of this book. She knows me so well that she can reshape my ramblings and terrible grammar but still keep it sounding like me. She also helped make this old Cockney sound a little poetic here and there.

Bodhi, Indy, Jude, and Remy Lovejoy-Hart are my children. And my life. They are wonderful humans, kind, good-natured. They take great care of each other. I'm so proud of them.

How I Became a Baker

If you just want to get started baking bread, by all means, skip ahead to the next chapter (page 24). But I reckon if you want to go on this lifelong bread journey with me, you might want to know who I am, where I came from, and how I fell in love with bread baking. If so, read on.

I don't know where my work ethic came from, but I have it. Well, I found it along the way.

It was the '90s, and I was heavily into the rave scene. This was Essex, suburban East London. I dropped out of college and got a job with my best friend, Dean, flipping ready-made burgers at a bowling alley diner. I loved working in a kitchen—the banter, the craziness—but I knew nothing about food; I was just working to get money, to party.

Then one of my friends took a job at a restaurant in Selfridges, the iconic department store in the very center of the city. They needed more hands, and he got me in. To me, as a young kid, this was where all the music, all the fashion, all the cool stuff was happening. Any amazing thing could be right around the corner.

Cooking wasn't a big part of our family life. I don't have many food memories from childhood, but I do remember getting fresh, hot bread from the supermarket. The feel of it in your hands, the fresh crust, the warmth, the smell: I think we all feel it. And my nan made the best steak and kidney pies, which were famous in our family.

I don't want to put my mum and dad down, because they were, and still are, amazing. They both worked full-time, with three kids to look after, and all the washing, cleaning, and organizing that entails. They did a great job taking care of us. It was just that good food, for us, as for most of the families we knew, bore no resemblance to what came out of the kitchens at Selfridges.

I didn't yet know what rocket (arugula) was. I didn't know that tomatoes weren't only red. The only herbs I knew were the desiccated herbes de Provence on my mum's shelf. I think she put them in her sautéed potatoes. I had never seen chives or basil—none of it. It was like learning a new language, and it was delicious.

In the beginning, though, I was terrible. I was lazy, and I would bullshit my way through each day, doing just enough to keep me out of trouble. I'd cross off things from my mise en place list that I hadn't actually done. I was fucking around like I was still in school.

But it was my first band; I had a *crew.* There were two guys called James, and there was Lee, Trevor, Joe, and Matt. There was Luke, who got taken away by the police in the middle of service one day. We never did find out what happened to him. There was Hendrick, Dave on pot wash, and me, at the bottom. Oh, and Daryll, who never actually worked with us but used to come by to hang out and talk about DJing. These guys liked me and stuck up for me.

Eventually, I realized that I had to pull my weight if I wanted to be as good as the rest of the gang, who *were* good. They all taught me something. Cooking is a make-or-break kind of job, and if you're no good, you don't last. I wanted to last, so I started putting in the effort. It was something I really liked, for the first time. I put my whole self into it. I grew up.

I started cooking my way through a number of fine dining restaurants across London, working hard, all day and all night, until I got to the Michelin-star level, where there was no talking allowed on the line. The chefs didn't even say hello or look one another in the face. This wasn't a band. We weren't friends. It was cutthroat, sink or swim. The one kindness I do remember was on my first day, someone handed me a tasting spoon and said, "If anyone offers you something to taste, eat it, because that's all you'll have to eat." They were right. We just didn't have time to stop. (Because of the memory of that experience, I now make staff food a priority at my bakery, often cooking it myself. And I put all my love into feeding my team.)

After a year and a half of killing myself in ultrafine dining, I walked. I took a head chef job in a supercool bistro in East London. Cooking real food, for people I liked and admired—friends, artists, movie stars, and locals—in a beautiful but unpretentious setting, was a total pleasure. I had the time and space to drink a coffee and have a chat with my team. It felt like being in that band again, and I loved it.

This was also when I realized that I didn't know how to make bread. We would buy bread from a local baker for the restaurant, but whenever we ran out, I'd pick up some famous chef's cookbook and follow whatever token bread recipe had been included. The bread was inevitably terrible. Now, as a baker, I can tell you: don't bother looking for a great bread recipe in a fancy chef's book.

I fell in love then, too, and moved to California with my now ex-wife, Ashley, who is from the Bay Area. When we arrived, I was incredibly lucky to get a job at Ubuntu, in Napa, with Jeremy Fox. Ubuntu was the best restaurant I'd ever worked in, and Jeremy was the most exciting and inspiring chef, a real legend, though he'll hate me for saying so.

In California, there are laws against working people into the ground. I wasn't used to working only a forty-hour week. For the first time in years, I had spare time, and I wanted to learn to make bread. One of the pastry chefs at Ubuntu told

me about a bakery called Della Fattoria, in Petaluma, the town where I lived. They had once baked all the bread for the venerable French Laundry, before Thomas Keller opened Bouchon Bakery.

I got my start as a baker at Della Fattoria, first in my spare time from Ubuntu, and then in a full-time job. It was a great place to learn the craft. You walked into a wooden barn with two roaring wood-fired ovens and immediately felt the intense power of those beasts. It was an exciting place, a high-volume operation. Having been a chef, I fed off adrenaline, and Della Fattoria was a nonstop adrenaline rush. It was constant, from the moment I got there to the moment I finished.

The first task I was assigned was to unload the finished loaves from the oven. This was my introduction to using a peel. I had to learn how to balance multiple loaves on its surface, and how to coordinate with the person next to me, who would be loading in new loaves. It's an intricate dance, and there was a sharp learning curve, during which I dropped many loaves, and occasionally whacked a fellow baker while making the big turn from the oven to the table.

When I got the hang of unloading baked loaves, I started learning how to load the oven. The placement of each loaf has to be just right, because once you slide it off the peel, it's not going anywhere.

At the start of the bake, the oven was at 800°F / 426°C. We started at this insanely high temperature because we were baking off residual heat stored in the bricks and the oven's stone floor, which dropped with each of the fifteen or so bakes we did in a day. What might take forty-five minutes in my modern steam tube deck oven would take just ten minutes in the roaring Della oven at its highest heat. The crust on those first loaves was like a thin, crisp eggshell. As the day went on and we continuously loaded, rotated, and unloaded loaves, the temperature would drop by about 30°F per batch, and the bake times got longer.

Because the oven was so hot to start, there was a real risk of burning the bread on the oven's stone floor, so we'd bring the floor temperature down to about 400°F / 205°C, using cold water. The baker swung a mop across the oven floor in a quick and focused way, until the laser-enabled instant-read thermometer told us it was safe to load in the loaves. You have to work fast, and you have to keep going. It was an efficient but not entirely precise system, and of course, we didn't nail it every time; there would occasionally be loaves whose bottoms turned charcoal black.

But as frustrating as that could be, I saw it all as just more to learn. I became obsessed with learning everything I could about bread and baking. As a student, I'd never been very interested in reading for its own sake, but cooking changed that. I had a ton of cookbooks, and I now devoured every bread book I could find, trying to learn as much as I could,

as fast as possible. I wanted to discover any trick, technique, or idea I could find to improve my baking.

I started going to every bakery, too. On my day off, I took a job at another bakery, Wild Flour, in Freestone, California, where I learned to bake in a very different style: cheese breads, huge sticky buns as big as your head, and a bread with peppers and spring onions. Through the huge windows, I'd watch the dawn arrive. The thick fog layer on the California coast obscured everything until the rising sun burned through, revealing the most idyllic scene of rolling hills, ancient trees, and grazing cows. It was a magical place to work on the days when I wasn't working at Della.

Kathleen Weber, the founder of Della Fattoria, was a brilliant and generous self-taught baker and a true mentor to me. She pushed me in all directions, to learn everything I could, just as she had done. She had the bug and I found it infectious. She had a huge library of cookbooks and baking books that she'd been collecting since the age of twelve. She gave me a copy of Nancy Silverton's Breads from the La Brea Bakery. Nancy is one of the pioneers of American bread baking, a true enthusiast, and an absolutely lovely human. I've had the huge privilege to get to know her over the years, and she is now a dear friend. Kathleen also gave me a copy of Daniel Leader's Bread Alone, which is an amazing, romantic book. He tells the story of going to Paris and meeting the legendary Lionel Poilâne, who reinvigorated the art of sourdough baking in France; it was just such an eye-opening narrative, and it inspired me to become the best baker I could be. Kathleen was also a big fan of The Italian Baker by Carol Field. Every book she told me to read, I loved.

When I'd been at Della for about a year, Kathleen told me about a bakery in San Francisco called Tartine, owned by a baker named Chad Robertson.

I drove an hour to buy a loaf of Chad Robertson's bread, and failed; there were always long queues outside the shop, and on that first visit, they had already sold out. The next week, I got there really early and was able to get a sesame country loaf, which I put in the car and didn't touch until I got back to Della.

As soon as Kathleen and I tasted that Tartine bread, we both knew it was something special. The texture of the loaf was different than anything I'd ever come across. The crust had a light crispness that shattered as you bit it, and then you'd get a wonderful chew. The crumb was so soft but moist, and the flavor—a complex balance of sweet and sour—kept changing and evolving in the mouth. It was an absolute game changer for me.

Kathleen said, "Doesn't this make you green with envy?"

I started showing up at Tartine then, trying to get a job, offering to work for free, and I kept hearing, "Sorry, there's no space."

I kept at it, though at times I felt discouraged. For a while, I thought about giving up and going back to London to start a bakery. No one was doing anything like the kind of bread I'd been making in California. Maybe because the Great Fire of London started in a bakery, Londoners weren't too keen on huge roaring wood-fired ovens. *That was 1666,* I thought. Maybe it was time for London to let go of the fear.

But the truth is, I wasn't good enough. I hadn't learned enough. I wanted to be so much better, so I kept trying my luck at Tartine. I would talk to Chad, we exchanged numbers, he might send me a couple of texts, and then I wouldn't hear from him again for a month or more.

The problem was, none of the bread bakers ever left Tartine, and it's the same thing now at my bakery. If you get a job there, you never want to leave.

And then, after several months of showing up, I got a message from Chad, saying that there was a job coming up, and that he'd like to offer it to me. It was my birthday.

At Tartine, I began my exploration and discovery of living dough. This was aided by the fact that we were working on a relatively small scale. At Della, we made 1,400 loaves a day; when I started at Tartine, it was just 100. Eventually we went to 150, then 200, but even so, that's still such a small amount, and it really gave us time to experiment. We constantly spoke about the dough, the fermentation, the weather, the humidity, the time of year, the flour, and how to make the bread better.

I thrived at Tartine, and within a short space of time, I was head baker. And the world beyond California started to become interested in what we were doing. Beautiful bread, as it turned out, made fantastic Insta-porn. Suddenly, everyone around the world could see what we were doing, and a lot of connections were made very quickly. We started getting invited places.

While traveling with Chad to do various events, I met a lot of incredible chefs and restaurateurs, living legends. We did an event in Copenhagen, and Chad and I had lunch at Noma, René Redzepi's iconic restaurant, named who knows how many times the best restaurant in the world. I wondered if it was going to be all style over substance, but it was fucking *incredible.* I was totally blown away by Noma—I still am, every time.

A year or so later, Chad and I went to Australia for the Melbourne Food & Wine Festival and had lunch at the Noma pop-up in Sydney. After our meal, René asked if we knew any bakers who might want to work with him in Copenhagen.

I was happy living in California but was missing Europe. Chad and I did talk about expanding Tartine into London, but it never came to fruition.

I worked my bollocks off for Tartine. I believed in it, 100 percent. I gave everything and was there for seven good years, and I loved every one of them. If Chad hadn't taken a chance on me, I would not be the baker I am today. But as Tartine started expanding within California, I didn't feel as much a part of it as I had before. There were new investors and new chiefs, and things were going in a different direction.

I reached out to René.

He said that I should come to Copenhagen to open a bakery with him as a partner, and then I could go anywhere I wanted to go—my dream was London and Paris. That was a really exciting prospect. So my family and I packed up our lives in Northern California and moved to Denmark, to a new country, new climate, new culture, and an unknown future that I was being trusted to create.

I took a space in the test kitchen, which was above the original location of Noma. I experimented with baking bread, using flour from local mills. It was an anxious time for me. I wanted to get started, but I didn't yet have a bakery space. It made me feel guilty, and uncomfortable, to be paid a salary without bringing in revenue.

A few days into my existential crisis, one of the Noma staff asked if I would mind helping them. I said *of course,* and was given two huge garbage bags full of twigs, from which I had to pick these tiny little balls, which might have been flower buds or a rare edible fungus or maybe an insect egg—I don't remember. So I spent a whole day picking these little specks off tiny branches as fast as I could. I didn't mind it—anything to help—but I hadn't come to Copenhagen for this.

Fortunately, the next day René suggested that I visit Batting Bakery. The owner and head baker, Lars Batting, as it turns out, loved Tartine. We got on really well, and I was so happy to be shaping bread again, talking about flour, about ovens, about everything to do with baking. And for the next six months, while I wasn't out looking for my space to build the bakery, I worked at Batting.

Batting Bakery is slightly outside the city, which means it often gets overlooked, but Lars is an incredible bread baker, one of the best in Copenhagen, hands down. His bread is amazing. It's a small operation, just six employees or so, and he runs the place with his wife, Anne, who left behind a career in teaching to make all the pastries. Lars gave me a really solid foundation in rye bread technique, for which I am hugely grateful, because it was all completely new to me, coming from California.

After eight months of constantly looking, calling my property agent every morning, and riding my bike like crazy from one end of the city to the other, we still didn't have a space. I was really starting to freak out, but then, finally, we found an available storefront on Gammel Kongevej. It was pretty fucked up. There was a sticky coating of grease on everything. I'd been looking for 400 square meters on one floor, and this was 380 square meters on three floors. But I could see that the street was really busy, with a lot of great shops, people, and car and bike traffic. The space wasn't ideal, but I thought, *Okay, I will make this work.*

It took six months to do a super-deep clean, put in a new electrical system, and boost the gas power. There were many, many holes cut into the floors and walls and ceilings. I spent a lot of time standing in that bakery, looking around, asking myself, *How can we do the best with what we have to work with?*

At the heart of the renovation was the beautiful gas-fired deck oven, custom-built on-site, heavily insulated and surrounded by tons of concrete so that it holds a ridiculous amount of mass heat. It's an absolute beast, capable of baking 144 loaves of bread every 40 minutes without an appreciable drop in temperature.

We finally opened for business on a Sunday at the end of September, in 2018. There was a queue down the block, all day long, and we were baking bread like maniacs. It was a huge success, really exhilarating. I went home late that night and went straight to bed. At 4 a.m., I got a phone call.

"Is that Richard? This is the police, and we're with the fire department. Your bakery's on fire."

Aris Albiñana, with whom I'd worked for years at Tartine, had come over from California to help me open the bakery, and was staying in my house. I woke him up, saying, "There's a fire, there's a fucking fire, man, there's a *fire.*"

We got on our bikes and rode at top speed over to the bakery, with no idea what had happened or how bad it might be. I was just out of my mind with panic as we rode. *Is the bakery gone? There are people living in apartments above the bakery; have we* killed *them?*

When we got there, to my enormous relief, I could see that the building was still intact, and there were no visible flames. But inside, it was clear that the heat from the oven's gas burner was causing the wooden floorboards to smolder. It was only because of a lack of sufficient oxygen that the whole thing hadn't already gone up in flames. Someone had screwed up in a major, potentially catastrophic way, in planning and executing the construction of an extremely hot oven, built specifically to hold heat, on wooden floorboards, without insulating the burner.

It could have been so much worse, but it was still an absolute disaster for the bakery. We'd had one incredible day, built up so much goodwill and excitement in the community, and then right away, we were knocked out of the game, for who knew how long. We had a fridge full of proofing bread, and we couldn't bake any of it. The whole place smelled like smoke and fire. It was gutting.

We borrowed a tiny electric oven that could bake sixteen loaves at a time and forged ahead as best we could. We decided not to share with the public what had happened with the oven. Looking back now, I don't know whether that was the right thing to do. But we didn't want to tie the bakery's reputation to disaster.

I felt like a fucking idiot, and a failure. I was this fancy baker from San Francisco, and after the first day, I couldn't keep up with demand, and no one knew the reason why. We baked for ten hours straight every day, and we constantly ran out.

Meanwhile, the deck oven, which weighed ten tons, was sitting idle on a burned-out wooden floor that could have collapsed into the basement at any moment.

To no one's surprise, extracting an oven surrounded by concrete was not exactly a quiet, clean, or easy task, and we had to close the bakery for a few weeks while a small army of workers did the necessary jackhammering. They pulled the oven out, piece by piece, then removed the wooden floor, laid in a new concrete one, rebuilt and properly insulated the oven. Finally, in mid-January, with the smoke and the smell cleared away, we were back in action, the way we should have been from day two, and we really haven't stopped since. As of writing, there are now eight locations of Hart Bageri in Copenhagen, with more on the way.

I'm so proud of what we've achieved; the whole world seems to be looking at Hart Bageri. It's down to an incredible team of people. I love every one of them. And to the trust René Redzepi put in me. Hart wouldn't exist without that.

Postscript: This book talks about my time in London, California, and Copenhagen and the breads I learned to bake in those places, but by the time it comes out, I will be on my next adventure. I am moving to be closer to my wonderful sons, Bodhi, Indy, Jude, and Remy. They live in California, and it was killing me to be so far away from them. I love them like crazy.

I am deeply grateful to all the people who supported me, and the friends I've made in Denmark. I loved my time in Scandinavia.

So new adventure awaits: new ingredients to discover and play with. A new bakery in the pipeline. If you know and like what I've done in Copenhagen, just wait. I'm hungry for more.

Tools for Building Your Home Bakery

Good tools are an investment worth making. If you buy beautiful, quality things, they'll not only serve you well but be a pleasure to use. You'll love them and take good care of them.

I use my most precious things as much as possible. They make me happy. But of course, what you buy is up to you. Just make sure that you get stuff that works; there's nothing more frustrating than having a tool snap in half while you're using it. You won't need every tool for every bread, but here is a list of what's called for in this book, generally in the order that you'd use it in a typical bake.

DIGITAL SCALE

You need to weigh all your ingredients. I'm all about baking by feel, but you really can't wing it with weight, no matter how developed your intuition is. A digital scale is more accurate than a balance scale and has the added advantage of being able to tare (meaning it can be reset to zero, even if you already have ingredients in your bowl on the scale). I work only in metric (grams) because it's much more precise than nonmetric (ounces and pounds).

STARTER CONTAINER: CLEAR GLASS JAR OR HIGH-SIDED PLASTIC CONTAINER

The container to hold your starter should be taller than it is wide, to minimize surface area. An old jam jar, a plastic container with a lid (like a deli quart container), or a glass canning jar will do just fine. For the amount of starter you'll typically need for the recipes in this book, your jar should have a capacity of between 2 to 4 cups / 500ml to 1 liter.

8-CUP / 2-LITER LIQUID MEASURING CUP OR JUG WITH CENTILITER MARKINGS

For ease, I often use a measuring cup (and centiliters) for water. Liquid measuring cups in the US come with both cups and centiliters marked on them. The recipes will tell you the weight of the water needed, and of course, you can weigh water on the scale, just as you weigh flour and other ingredients. But converting the weight to a volume measurement is easy: 1 gram of water is 1 milliliter.

GLASS, CERAMIC, OR PLASTIC MIXING BOWLS

You'll need a couple of bowls of various sizes to help you not only mix doughs and starters but also regulate their temperature: a smaller bowl to put the dough or starter in, and a larger one filled with warm or cool water to act as a water bath. The dough bowl is set inside the water bath to help warm or cool the temperature of the dough. At home, I'd use a 3-quart / 3-liter bowl for my dough and a 5-quart / 5-liter bowl for the water. Glass, ceramic, and plastic are all fine. I never work with stainless steel, after once killing my starter in a stainless bowl. But that might just be me.

BENCH SCRAPER / DOUGH KNIFE

When I was a kid, I imagined being a pirate with a missing hand. I'd have a hook, but also other replacements: a sword, a magnifying glass, a telescope. As a grown man and baker, I feel like my bench scraper is an extension of my arm. It's a simple, thin, rectangular-ish dull blade made for cutting dough and helping you lift it. You'll use this tool endlessly when working with dough: dividing, shaping, and moving it around your work surface. It's also handy for cleaning up your work bench. I've used tons of different types—some fancier, some way more expensive—but by far my favorite is a wood-handled Dexter.

Opposite: (1) digital scale (2) brush (3) measuring cup
(4) bench scraper (5) flexible plastic scraper (6) scissors
(7) loaf pan (8) pizza cutter (9) couche

FLEXIBLE PLASTIC BOWL/DOUGH SCRAPER

This is like a bench scraper but made of thin plastic. It's the best tool for transferring dough from a bowl or container to a work surface. You can also use it to scrape excess dough from your hands after mixing, folding, and shaping, and it's perfect for cutting slits in the Fougasse (page 189) and Sand Dollar (page 143).

DIGITAL INSTANT-READ THERMOMETER

When you start baking, a digital thermometer will really help you with your understanding of fermentation and the variables involved, including dough temperature and the temperature of added ingredients. As you gain experience, your knowledge and intuition will take over and the thermometer will be less essential.

SPRAY BOTTLE

Any clean bottle with a spray mechanism (as opposite) that you can fill with water works for dampening the surfaces of various proofing breads so that they don't form a skin.

STAND MIXER WITH DOUGH HOOK

Even if you're working in small batches, you'll need a stand mixer for mixing enriched breads like brioche, milk buns, and panettone. Doughs that start with a biga also must be mixed in a stand mixer.

COUCHE (LINEN PROOFING CLOTH)

A thick linen towel that's used to help baguettes, ciabatta, the Sand Dollar (page 143), and English Bloomer (page 186) hold their shape while proofing.

PIZZA STONE

Pizza stones hold a great deal of heat, mimicking the conditions in a brick oven, and help create a crisp, evenly baked crust on pizza, baguettes, and ciabatta. Look for the largest stone that will fit your oven.

BAKER'S PEEL

In order to move baguettes, flatbreads, and ciabatta rolls in and out of your oven, where they will cook directly on a pizza stone, you will need a peel, which is a wooden or metal flat surface with a handle. There are many sizes and shapes available; use one that fits into your oven and is large enough to hold a pizza or a baguette.

WOODEN TRANSFER BOARD ("FLIPPER")

This is a lightweight rectangular piece of wood, used as an intermediary, to gently transfer shaped baguettes from the couche (linen proofing cloth) to the baker's peel without damaging their shape. You could use a thick piece of cardboard; in a pinch, I've used a cutting board.

DUTCH OVEN OR OTHER CAST-IRON VESSEL WITH FLAT LID

A Dutch oven becomes an oven inside your oven. Home ovens are designed to let out the steam, but a Dutch oven traps in all the vapors that escape your dough, and that retained moisture allows the bread to grow to its full potential. The bread is baked on the upturned lid of the Dutch oven, and the pot is inverted over the bread to act as a dome. The flat lid surface is safer and better for maintaining the shape of the bread. If you bake the loaf inside the hot pot itself, you're at risk of burning your hands when you drop the dough inside it; it's quite awkward, and a little scary, to drop dough into a hot pot, and in the process you can end up de-gassing the bread or damaging the shape. Better to use the lid.

At home, I use an enameled cast-iron Dutch oven because it's what I already own, so I unscrew and remove the plastic handle on the lid, which would otherwise melt in the oven's high heat. The dough covers the hole made by removing the handle, thus sealing it. However, some older cast-iron Dutch ovens have handles that cannot be removed, or lids that won't sit flat. If that is what you own, then seek out a Dutch oven with a flat lid, either handleless or with a handle that can be removed. Or invest in a piece of specialized cast-iron bakeware called variously (depending on the brand) bread oven, combo cooker, or bread pan/multicooker.

BANNETONS (BREAD PROOFING BASKETS)

Bannetons are what we use to proof many types of loaves so they keep their shape. There are many kinds made of different materials, including cardboard, wood pulp, and plastic (which I don't think is great for dough). I've always used wicker proofing baskets, lined with linen, and I always will. The wicker and linen not only help the dough keep its structure as it proofs but also allow just the right amount of airflow. This is really important for the crust of your bread. If the dough can't breathe as it proofs, the surface will get soggy, and the crust will be leathery when the bread is baked.

It doesn't necessarily matter whether your bannetons are round (boules) or oblong (bâtards). But it makes sense to match the shape of your Dutch oven (see page 27).

It's important to care for the bannetons after every use. Once the baskets have done their job, use a stiff brush (see below) to remove any excess flour, then let the baskets air-dry completely before using again. You don't need to wash them. If you look after them, they'll last for many years.

Note: You *can* get away with using a colander lined with a linen towel, if you're caught in a tight spot, but it's not ideal.

STIFF BRUSH

For brushing excess flour from bannetons (see above). In the bakery, we use all-purpose scrub brushes that I found at a supermarket. No need to get fancy; just choose one with stiff-enough bristles to dislodge stuck-on bits of flour.

BAKER'S LAME AND RAZOR BLADES

These are for scoring the loaves before they go into the oven. Pronounced "lahm," the lame is the handle that holds an old-school single-edge razor blade, which is used to create the slashes in the dough.

Since baking has become so popular, there are now lots of fancy lames on the market. Some are beautiful pieces of wood or cleverly molded plastic, but I find them awkward to hold and often too long. Mine is just a simple, elegant piece of metal, and I love it. To use a metaphor that makes me sound a lot cooler and more dangerous than I am, it's like a samurai sword instead of a machete.

LOAF PAN

I use two sizes. The one I use for pumpernickel-style breads and babka is 12 × 4 × 4-inch / 30 × 10 ×10cm. For all the rye and whole-grain pan loaves, I use 9 × 5 × 3-inch / 24 × 14 × 7.5cm.

ROLLING PIN

You know what this is. My preference is a French pin, but use what you like best. And in this book it's used for the flatbreads.

HALF SHEET OR QUARTER SHEET PAN

You need these sheet pans for Focaccia (page 175), Roman-Style Pizza (page 179), Brunsviger (page 236), and the various buns and rolls. These are typically made from aluminum or other lightweight metal, with a 1-inch / 2.5cm rim. A quarter sheet usually measures 13 × 9 inches / 33 × 23cm, and a half sheet measures 13 × 18 inches / 33 × 46cm.

COOLING RACK

When your bread comes out of the oven, it needs to cool. A cooling rack lets it do that evenly, without getting a soggy bottom. Get a large one that fits inside a half sheet pan.

TABLETOP GRAIN MILL

This is the only tool here that I don't think is strictly necessary, and really, you don't want one of these to make flour because they overheat the grain while milling. You're better off getting flour from a good professional miller. (For more on milling, see Flour, page 32.) That said, you might want one for cracking grains, which is how I use mine, for breads like pumpernickel and rye.

CONCHA CUTTER

This is, obviously, a tool for making conchas (opposite). It resembles a cookie cutter and is used to incise a design in the topping that's been laid over an unbaked concha, thus giving it its signature seashell stripes (*concha* means "shell" in Spanish).

TOOLS FOR BUILDING YOUR HOME BAKERY

Know Your Ingredients

I want to support sustainable and regenerative farming wherever possible. I choose organically grown ingredients. Pesticides and herbicides destroy the rich biodiversity of the environment and the health of the soil. These chemicals also get into our water supply, and into the crops we eat, and so, ultimately, into us.

I choose eggs from free-range chickens. I don't agree that animals should live in cages.

I always use full-fat, organic dairy and pure honey without added sugar. I believe in the goodness of natural foods that haven't been tampered with.

When it comes to ingredients from further afield, like tea, coffee, and chocolate, they don't just come from a box on the shelf, and it's every bit as important to know who makes them, probably more. I want to know that I am supporting, rather than exploiting, marginalized agricultural communities. Fancy packaging and certifications can be deceptive and misleading. It's more important to do research and source ingredients carefully.

It's not always easy to find the good guys, but it's worth doing. I look for companies that are working directly with growers in a supportive and respectful relationship. A lot of these products come to you through a series of faceless brokers who manipulate the price and take all the value and profit, getting richer off someone else's hard work and hardship. It doesn't have to be that way. There are companies, such as Rare Tea Company and La Rifa chocolate in Mexico, that work for a more sustainable future, for the land and the people who live and work on it to thrive.

Our choices matter.

The Essential Ingredients

FLOUR

The most essential ingredient in bread is, of course, flour. Generally speaking, you can make good bread with good standard flours, as long as you're picking the right type of flour for that particular bread; that's what the guide that follows is for. To make truly *great* bread, though, you'll want *great* flour. For more on my journey to learn what that means, see page 40.

Here are a few basics to consider in choosing your flour:

Protein Content

Gluten, the thing that gives wheat flour its specific structure and character, is composed of two proteins: glutenin, which gives dough strength, and gliadin, which gives it extensibility, or the ability to stretch and rise. Generally speaking, the higher the protein content in a flour, the stronger and more extensible the dough will be.

Bread flour (called strong wheat flour in the UK) typically has a 12% to 14% protein content, all-purpose flour (or soft wheat flour) has 9% to 11%, whole wheat flour has 11% to 15%, and pastry flour has 8% to 9%.

That being said, numbers don't always tell the whole story of how a flour performs when mixed with water and salt. Personally, I prefer actually baking, as the best test, over the data on the label. What are we testing for anyway—our preconceived ideas? You should experiment with your flour. Protein content is important, but there are many more factors, such as ambient temperature and humidity, the age of the flour, storage conditions, and baking technique. The best data comes from your own bread experiments. Flours from different places, milled with different methods, older or younger, will behave in slightly different ways, and you can always react accordingly, by tweaking the hydration, temperature, fermentation time, and/or the mix of flours that you're using for any of the recipes in this book.

Milling Method

Milling is an often overlooked and misunderstood art. It's not in any way an easy or simple process, and it takes a shit ton of experience and passion to do it well. The greatest millers are as important to creating great flour as the farmers who grow the wheat, and the terroir it grows in.

There are two primary types of milling: stone-ground and roller-milled. The flour I use is roller-milled, which may surprise you. There is certainly a romantic attachment to stone-ground, but it's a bit like the romance around wood-fired ovens. I love them, but I'm looking for a bit more control. Used with love and skill, technology doesn't have to be ugly.

When flour is stone-ground, the grain is given a single pass, under high pressure, which can overheat the wheat kernel and damage the starch and the protein within. If the kernel is damaged, the oils in the germ are released, and the wheat is more vulnerable to oxidation and rancidity.

Roller milling cleans the kernel efficiently, removing all debris, so there is less bacteria in the process. My flour goes through fourteen gentle passes, splitting the kernel, which protects the germ from damage. Danny, my Italian miller (see page 43), runs the mill using a low pressure, which creates less friction; this keeps it all very cool. Using the mill in this way produces a lower yield of high-quality flour.

The big industrial roller mills often use higher pressure for higher yields, which can also damage the starch and the protein, and doesn't make great flour. As Danny says, "It's not the machine, it's the method." My millers use small batches, and handle their machinery very delicately, to get beautiful results. It has huge advantages for the end product.

Freshness

For the reasons described above in Milling Method, stone-ground flour has a shorter shelf life than roller-milled flour. Ideally, you should use stone-ground flour within a month of milling, or keep it fridge cold, prolonging shelf life. Roller-milled flour, if milled correctly, as described, has a longer shelf life, up to a year.

No matter which type you use, always look for the freshest flour with the latest sell-by date. Storing flour in the refrigerator, tightly sealed, will extend its shelf life, but bring it back to room temperature before mixing it into a dough.

SALT

My advice about salt is to use the best quality you can find and afford, with no additives. At my bakery, we use a very good-quality gray sea salt from France.

WATER

I can obviously be very exacting about flour and salt, but I'm not precious about water. I don't know how much of a difference it makes to use filtered or treated water. Wherever I have baked, all over the world, I have used the water that's available to the building and have never run into problems. In some places where the water is chlorinated, in theory the chlorine could inhibit microbes in the starter, but I haven't experienced it.

YEAST

There's a somewhat deserved prejudice out there against commercial yeast. It's played a big part in the rise of mass-produced, industrial bread with no nutritional value, because it made it possible to speed up the baking process. A bread that takes eight hours to proof using a natural sourdough leaven will take just two hours when leavened with commercial yeast. The problem is that by shortcutting the process of leavening, the bread doesn't have time to truly ferment, and the loss of flavor and texture in the final product is profound. Also, wheat that hasn't been fermented properly isn't great for your digestion and has contributed to the rise of gluten intolerance.

But commercial yeast is not your enemy. Although some purist sourdough bakers think commercial yeast is evil, and although I work predominantly with sourdough, in certain bread recipes I also use commercial yeast. (I prefer instant dry to active dry because it's milled finer and doesn't require blooming in water before mixing. And I prefer instant dry to fresh yeast because I find it a more stable and consistent product.)

I use yeast to make *better* bread, not easier, shittier bread. You should use commercial yeast because you know what you want, and you know what you're doing.

Commercial yeast is a great tool for making certain breads: Baguettes (page 193), Focaccia (page 175), Real Italian Ciabatta (page 176), Roman-Style Pizza (page 179), English Bloomer (page 186), and English Muffins (page 201). It's a must for proofing enriched breads like Brioche (page 232), whose high fat content would otherwise fuck up the fermentation. You can make sourdough baguettes, sourdough brioche, sourdough croissants. They taste good and look good, but I don't think you get quite the same result as you do with commercial yeast, which makes those breads and pastries lighter, with a more tender texture that I prefer. Why not celebrate what yeast can do, and use it correctly and wisely?

Breads made with commercial yeast get stale much more quickly than sourdough and are really only good on the day you make them.

I've worked in a few bakeries that won't allow a single grain of commercial yeast in the door, for fear that it will completely take over the natural fermentation at work in sourdough. It's true: commercial yeast *is* stronger and more active than the naturally occurring yeast in sourdough, and if added directly to it, it would bully its way around the bucket and establish itself as the dominant strain, making for a less-complex flavor in your bread. However, within a few days, with consistent feedings, it would work its way out, and the yeasts would once again diversify.

At my bakery, each morning we mix our sourdoughs before we touch any of the commercial yeast fermentations, such as Poolish (page 76) and Biga (page 76), and we are meticulous with handwashing, especially after working with those doughs that contain commercial yeast.

The Other Ingredients Used in This Book

In Alphabetical Order, with a Few Notes

Beer: I use dark beers and stouts for their flavor and sweetness.

Butter: All the recipes in the Sweet Breads chapter (page 229) use unsalted butter. Salt is added separately for more accuracy.

Buttermilk: You need this for Buttermilk Rye (page 90). Use full-fat buttermilk, or make your own. Using baker's percentages, add 6% lemon juice or white vinegar to 100% whole milk. (This is the equivalent of adding 1 part lemon juice or white vinegar to 16 parts whole milk.)

Cheese: The Cheese Loaf (page 206) suggests using aged Cheddar, Gouda, and smoked Gouda, but you can truly use any cheese you like.

Chocolate: The Chocolate Milk Buns (page 245) have dark, milk, and white chocolate, plus cocoa. As I mentioned earlier, the global chocolate trade is notoriously full of exploitative practices. I think it's important to look for responsibly sourced chocolate.

Eggs: I use free-range eggs. It's not just from an ethical standpoint; they also taste a lot better.

Figs: Use the best-quality, moistest, and best-tasting dried figs you can find.

Flours: Alongside wheat flour, you'll also find recipes that include rye flour, cornmeal, semolina, emmer, ølands, spelt, and rice flour.

→ **Rye flour** is obviously milled from the rye grain, and is hugely important in Scandinavian baking. There is a consistency to Danish rye flour across various brands, making it easy to predict how a rye dough will behave.

Outside Scandinavia, rye is sold under various names and labels—dark rye, light rye, whole-grain rye, pumpernickel flour, rye meal. What I look for is whole-grain rye that is finely milled; in the States, it is typically labeled dark rye flour, and in the UK, whole-grain rye.

→ **Cornmeal** is milled from dried corn, in a coarser form than corn flour. It is the basis of polenta, which I like to cook and mix into a loaf of Polenta Bread (page 151) and an American-style cornbread (see Superiority Burger Vegan Cornbread, page 216). When faced with a choice of cornmeal labeled "coarse" or "fine," I choose "coarse."

→ **Semolina** is sometimes confused with cornmeal because they have a similar look and consistency, but semolina is the milled endosperm of durum wheat kernels, a particularly hard form of wheat with a high protein content. Semolina flour makes dough that is tender but with strong gluten bonds. Fresh pasta makers rely on semolina flour for the way it holds various shapes. It's easy to find both coarse and fine grinds of semolina, and I like to use them in combination in the Semolina City Loaf (page 125).

→ **Emmer and einkorn** are ancient cereal grains, precursors to what we now know as wheat. They are harvested and milled with the hull intact, giving them a higher protein content than conventional wheat but a lower gluten content. Einkorn is slightly richer and heartier than emmer; the flavor of both is nutty and sweet. You won't find a recipe for an einkorn loaf in this book, because at the time of working on the book, I couldn't find any good einkorn flour, but if you *can* find it, use it in place of the emmer in the Local Grain Pan Loaf (page 105). It's delicious.

→ **Ølands** is a Swedish heirloom variety of winter wheat that yields a rich, nutty whole-grain flour, which makes a sweet and tender pan loaf (see page 105). I used it at Hart because it's the local grain.

→ **Spelt** is another ancient variety of wheat, whose flour, like whole wheat, includes the bran, endosperm, and germ. It has a subtly nutty and acidic flavor, as you'll see in the Toasted Spelt Bread (page 154), and it performs beautifully as a pan loaf (see page 105).

→ **Rice flour** is blended with all-purpose flour for coating the proofing baskets and keeping work and bread surfaces from getting sticky. Rice flour can absorb more liquid than wheat flour, keeping the wet dough from sticking to the couche or banneton liner. I blend the two together because rice flour on its own is a little too gritty.

Grains, whole and processed: A number of recipes in the Rye Breads and Pan Loaves chapter (page 79) and the Wheat Loaves Flavored with Other Grains chapter (page 133) call for one or more of the following whole and/or processed grains: quinoa, rye berries, pearl barley, jasmine rice, rolled oats, barley flakes, rye flakes, cracked rye, wheat germ, wheat bran, spelt, masa (see below), and cornmeal (see page 36).

Malt powder, diastatic: Malt is grain that has been soaked, sprouted, and roasted. Malt powder is not a common ingredient you'll find in your local shops, but it's readily available from online baking retailers. Diastatic malt powder is made from malted barley that has been dried at a relatively low temperature, which allows its naturally occurring enzyme to remain active. It's then ground into a powder. The enzyme helps break down starch into sugar, making it more efficient for the yeast to digest the flour. It also lends a deeper color and a slight malty sweetness to your loaf.

Malt powder, nondiastatic/dark: Nondiastatic/dark malt powder gives rye breads their distinctive color and contributes to their dark, coffee-like flavor. Its sprouted barley has been dried and roasted at a higher temperature than is used for diastatic malt powder (see above), leaving it without its active enzyme, so it has no effect on fermentation.

Malt syrup: You might also need to look online for this dark brown, sticky syrup extracted from malted barley, with a deep, rich, malty flavor. If you're stuck, you could use honey, but the result will taste somewhat sweeter.

Masa: This is a dough made from corn kernels that have been nixtamalized (soaked in an alkaline solution to remove the outermost hull of the corn kernel and ground). Masa is the base dough for corn tortillas and tamales, and when I can get fresh masa, I use it for my Sand Dollar (page 143). In the US, fresh masa is almost always obtained by going to a tortilla factory. Failing that, however, the next best thing is to make a masa using masa harina, a dried and finely ground nixtamalized corn flour that is widely available in North American grocery stores, but small producers of masa harina using heirloom corn are becoming more popular.

Milk powder: I use this in relatively modest quantities for a number of the recipes in the Sweet Breads chapter (page 229). Milk powder adds a richness and sweetness to the dough without additional liquid, and it helps keep the bread tender.

Miso: At Hart Bageri, we were super lucky to have a rye bread miso made for us by the Noma fermentation lab. Before we found our space, I spent my days baking at the Noma test kitchen, and the team there gave me tastes of everything they had in their dry stores and larder. The thing that really stood out for me was a miso made from rye bread, which seemed like a perfect ingredient to add *to* rye bread.

Obviously, that's not an ingredient you can get your hands on. Barley miso is just as good (well, almost) for using in the Rye Breads and Pan Loaves chapter (page 79). It's not a traditional ingredient in bread, but it adds such a depth of flavor and savoriness.

I don't suggest you go to the trouble of making your own miso, unless you're a fermentation maniac. If you *are* a maniac, grab a copy of *The Noma Guide to Fermentation* and fill your boots.

Oils: A few of the recipes call for neutral oil (like grapeseed, sunflower, or vegetable oil), both as an ingredient and for coating pans or proofing containers. For the olive oil in Perfect Sandwich Bread (page 172), Focaccia (page 175), and Roman-Style Pizza (page 179), use the best-tasting olive oil you can find.

Potatoes: Starchy, floury, or fluffy varieties, such as Russet or a Maris Piper potato, are best for the Mashed Potato Buns (page 211). The skin is mashed into the mixture and baked into the buns.

Raisins: These are used in Hot Cross Buns (page 263), Classic Panettone (page 284), and of course, Cinnamon Raisin Bread (page 259). Make sure to thoroughly rinse and dry them before use; you'll be amazed how much wax, dust, and debris are on them.

Seeds: A handful of my breads—notably those in the Rye Breads and Pan Loaves chapter (page 79), along with a few City Loaves (pages 113–127) and the Bagels (page 196)—call for flax, sesame, pumpkin, sunflower, poppy, and/or caraway seeds. As always, try to taste them before buying them, and definitely before using them, as their fats can go rancid in storage. Just make sure they taste good to you.

Spices: Some of the breads in the Sweet Breads chapter (page 229) use ground spices, such as cardamom, cinnamon, cloves, and ginger. If you buy small amounts of fresh spices and use them up quickly, you won't risk them getting stale and losing their vibrant flavors because they're sitting in the cupboard for years.

Sweeteners: In addition to malt syrup (see above), I use pure honey and granulated sugar.

Yogurt: The Pita (page 168) and Naan (page 167) recipes call for yogurt. My favorite is Greek yogurt with as high a milk fat content as possible—ideally 10%.

Choosing Your Flour

When I was planning the bakery in Copenhagen, I was a little nervous that local wheat wouldn't be right for the bread I bake.

Once you get deep into baking, you see the differences in flours like you see between tomatoes: San Marzano tomatoes, grown in the rich volcanic soil surrounding Mount Vesuvius, are different from the Brandywine varieties grown in the warm, dry California breadbasket. These are different again from Danish tomatoes, seeded indoors in dark February, and only transplanted to the relatively cold, rainy outdoors after three months. It's the same for wheat, or any crop. The harvest is affected by the crop's unique environment: sunshine, rain, temperature, the health of the soil, the wind, the insects.

When I first got to Copenhagen, I started using various Danish flours, without a great deal of success. The more rain that falls during the growing season, the softer the wheat berries will be. During harvest time, you don't want any rain or you must mechanically dry the wheat, which can be detrimental to the finished flour. That's not to say that Danish flour isn't excellent or delicious, but damp Denmark wasn't ideal for my dream sourdough loaf.

When you are fermenting a bread dough using only wheat grown in colder, wetter climates, the yeast and bacteria in sourdough can very easily access the nutrients in the flour. They digest everything too quickly, making the fermentation process go too fast, and making the dough very acidic, which in turn weakens the gluten, breaking it down before it finishes fermentation. You can slow the fermentation by keeping the dough cold, shaping it fast, and chilling it overnight, but that robs the dough of the chance to develop all the deep, interesting flavor and texture that I'm going for with my bread.

My process is to ferment the dough warm, and then let it have a long retard (rest) in a cool room at around 50°F / 10°C. I build flavor through long fermentation, and I just couldn't do it using Danish wheat.

I needed to find wheat grown in relatively dry conditions, with a lot of sunshine, which leads to harder wheat and higher-protein flour that withstands longer fermentation. There's a test used to measure the strength, density, and fermentation rate of flour, called the Falling Number (see Baking Terms, page 294); the higher the number, the slower the fermentation rate. The average Falling Number rate for wheat I was using in California was between 400 and 450; for Danish wheat, it's in the high 200s. I wanted a European wheat with a California Falling Number.

I got some help from a British baker, Vanessa Kimbell, who introduced me to Gabriele Bonci, the Roman baker, chef, and pizza legend. Although he doesn't speak English, and I don't speak Italian, we hit it off right away. We communicated as best we could, and relied on his right-hand man, Andre, also an awesome baker, who translated to make up for the gaps in our wild gesticulating and sign language.

Gabriele took me to the mill in the Misa valley, in the Marche region of Italy, to meet the family behind Molino Paolo Mariani, who have been growing and milling wheat there for three generations. A soft sea breeze from the Adriatic flows through the fields, cooling the wheat and naturally helping sweep away pests, keeping it dry and healthy.

We met Danny Mariani, a generous, capable, and likable farmer and miller. He took us to one of the fields, where the year before, he had planted two thousand different varieties of wheat in one acre, as an experiment. His father hadn't been happy about it but the next year, when we turned up just before the harvest, it was gorgeous and rich with diversity, full of butterflies and wildflowers and studded with wild oats and much more. The flour they milled from that mixture of wheat, which they called Mazi, was my dream flour: incredible flavor, a medium protein level, and a high Falling Number.

Because the wheat is not a monocrop—Danny now grows many varieties on the land, and he seeds it with nitrogen-fixing ground cover crops during the fallow months—the soil is rich and self-sustaining.

There's a bakery on the farm, and I experimented with the Mazi flour, baking with Bonci, and we made some beautiful bread. After a few days, we had to drive back to Rome, but I just couldn't stop thinking about that flour. I started to feel like some kind of addict, like, *I need to score*. I called Danny from the car and said, "I need that wheat, man. Please, please, I'd love to buy all you can give me." I didn't even have a bakery yet, but it didn't matter. I was hooked on that flour, and the potential of the bread I could bake with it.

My dream flour arrived a few months later, when I was still testing everything in the temporary bakery I had set up at Noma. I started baking right away, and I realized that it wasn't quite my dream flour anymore. It was from a new season, and every year there are different climatic variables, which means that the wheat is different. The protein content was much higher, and the bread I baked with it was really different from the bread I had made back in Italy, with last season's flour. The crumb was much tighter, and the scores just didn't open. It was too strong, and stayed super tight, giving me a much tougher bread than I wanted.

That's when I realized that I needed to blend something softer into this strong wheat to make it work—to blow it up. I've learned over the years that blending gives you more control. Flour is always changing, but you can make little tweaks—even day to day, one batch of flour to the next—to get the result you're after. It's like how Champagne houses figure out how to make a consistent bottle year after year, even though the grapes are different every season. It's a long journey to get the blends right, but when you're obsessed, you're obsessed.

Vanessa helped me again, this time introducing me to the people who run a French mill called Foricher, just south of Paris. I was happy to find a similar setup to Paolo Mariani's: another family-run operation, with seven generations of millers and good people buying and milling locally farmed wheat. It's in a gentler climate, which makes the wheat a little softer than in the Marche region.

I met the head miller, Arnaud Sorin, who was a real kindred spirit—he was completely crazy about blending wheats. His knowledge was amazing and fascinating.

Foricher also has a bakery attached to the mill, with a couple of old-school French bakers working there. I went in to play around with the various flours. The bakers were under the mistaken impression that I was there to learn from them how to make French bread, using their flour and techniques. However, I had my own ideas and was just there to make my bread.

At Foricher, they create specific flours for specific breads: viennoiserie, puff pastry, baguettes, brioche, sourdough bread—and in their minds, each flour is perfect as it is. I started blending all the types of flours together, trying everything. It made no sense to them; they thought I was off my head.

When it came to baking the bread, I asked for the oven to be a certain temperature, and they just said, "No. It will burn."

I tried to explain that I didn't follow the same strict rules that governed their baking lives, and they gave me the famous French shrug. I'll be honest: I started to doubt myself. I thought, "If this fucks up, I am gonna look like a right idiot."

But my bread came out better than I'd hoped for. I was so relieved. The French bakers acted like they were uninterested, but I am pretty sure they were at least a little bit impressed. It was really great bread, and that's hard to argue with. From there, I was set. I had the flours I needed to make the perfect balance, and connections with some passionate millers.

Knowing where my wheat comes from is important to me. I don't know the farmer of every single one of the ingredients I use, but I'd like to. I want to know the people and their land and the relationships between them. I want to know that their practices are as sustainable as possible, that the ingredients are grown without tons of harmful chemicals and crafted with love.

With good technique, and intuition developed over time, you can make a range of good breads using a combination of regular all-purpose, bread, and whole-grain flours; but you can make really *great* bread with really great flour. And of course, not all great flour is the same—that's the point, isn't it? But once you've developed a good feel for your breads, experiment yourself and see if there are local mills in your area or region. Talk to farmers or bakers in your area, and see if you can connect to the world of small, careful, loving grain farms and millers, and the bakers who work with them. Even if you're in it for the bread, making relationships with passionate craftspeople is one of the most gratifying parts of this life.

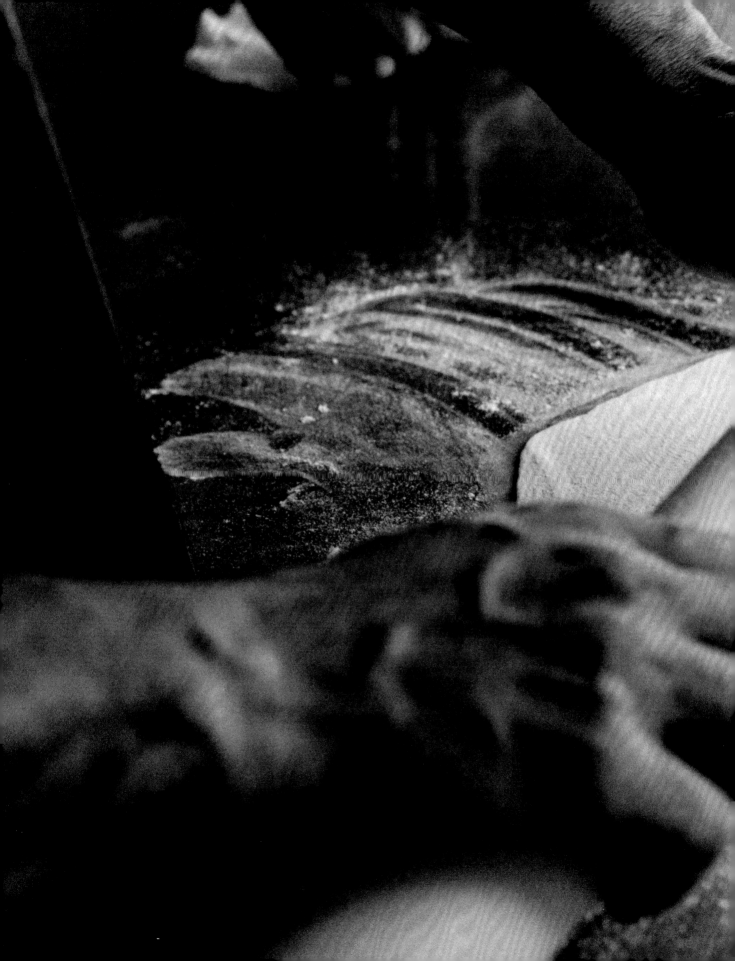

Bread Baking Techniques

This chapter of different concepts and techniques is a good primer to read through and get familiar with before starting to bake. It can then be used as a reference as needed when you're making the recipes. And eventually, all this will become your instinct and you can move on from having to consult these pages.

The way I make bread is constantly evolving along with my techniques. This book is a document of my baking career to date. From the moment I wrote the first draft of the City Loaf (page 113) recipe to the day the publisher sent the manuscript off to be printed, it's changed. I have continued to challenge everything I think I know, everything I do. I'm searching for the perfect loaf.

That said, the core of my approach to baking will always remain the same: I build flavor and texture through long, slow fermentation. I promote maximum wild yeast activity early on, with a warm bulk fermentation, the process in which the dough ferments as one mass, or "bulk." Then I build flavor through a long cool retard stage. I am constantly reading and evaluating the dough, drawing on intuition and experience, and reacting accordingly.

Maybe true perfection is not achievable, but some days, the bread is nearly perfect; and some days it's not. I'm not perfect, myself, by any means. I sometimes make bad dough, and have bad bakes. I burn bread. We all make mistakes. That's a human thing. I'm assessing how I work, and asking if there's a way to be more efficient, faster, cleaner, better. I don't just go through the motions. I'm constantly thinking about it, and in my bakery, we talk about the bread every day, all the time. I trust my team to tell me what they think. If it could be better, or if we could be doing something differently, I want to know. We may agree or disagree, but it's an ongoing conversation, and everyone's informed opinion is valuable. You can't make something better if you can't own up to it being improvable.

Baking great bread takes dedication and work; no one gets it right on the first try. It's almost like learning to play an instrument. You have to form an intimate relationship with the craft, and the only way you improve at it is through practice, repetition, and having a little think after each time about how it went.

If you're already baking bread and you're looking to improve, ask yourself what happened yesterday, and what you could do differently. Or, if yesterday's bread was "perfect" (something that I experience maybe once or twice a year), do everything you can to replicate the conditions that helped make it so.

You're in charge. I can't be in your kitchen with you, but I can explain here, and remind you throughout this book, how to read and adjust to your surroundings, to make the best bread possible.

QR CODES

I've used QR codes throughout my book where a picture or a description just doesn't work. When I started making bread years ago, I used to find it impossible to fathom a process from a series of disjointed images or wordy explanations. When it comes to many bread techniques, like shaping, the technique is a fluid movement and it is much easier for me to show you. Instead of trying to piece it together, you can just watch me do it, over and over.

If you've never used a QR code before, you need a smart-phone. You open the camera and center it on one of the weird symbols that you'll see throughout the text, for instance on page 50, under "Mixing Dough by Hand." Pretty magically, the camera can read this code, and opens up a webpage with a video; you don't have to type anything. Each QR code will take you directly to a video of the technique I'm talking about.

Understanding Baker's Percentage

Baker's percentage is a calculation for (1) writing your own bread recipes, (2) helping you scale an existing recipe up or down, or (3) adjusting a single ingredient within a recipe to improve your bread.

When you look at enough recipes in percentages, you start to understand the effect that every ingredient has and how to alter it to suit what you're looking for.

The core idea of baker's percentage is that the total amount of flour in a recipe is the baseline—the amount of flour is always considered 100%—and the rest of the ingredients are scaled in proportion to that amount.

For instance, if a recipe calls for 1,000g of flour and the hydration percentage (how much water is in the dough) is 75%, that means the water should be 750g. If the hydration percentage is 80%, it would be 800g of water.

I've used 1,000g here to make it easy to do the math, but when the numbers are a bit too tricky for mental arithmetic, there is a formula you can use:

Baker's Percentage Formula
Flour weight × percentage of other ingredient (expressed as a decimal) = *weight of other ingredient*

Example: 1,000g flour × 0.75 = 750g water

THE MAGIC NUMBER

One great use of the baker's percentage is that it allows you to decide how much dough you're looking to make, and then figure out the amount of each ingredient you need. This beautiful calculation is based on what I call "the Magic Number," or the amount of flour you need in a bread recipe to make a certain amount of bread.

The Magic Number Formula
Total weight of dough **divided by** total of all percentages* = *weight of flour*

with the decimal moved two places to the left

It's a bit mind-boggling, so let's start with an example.

1 **First, you need your baker's percentages.**
   100% flour   70% water   20% starter   3% salt

   That's a total of 193%.

2 **Next, the amount of bread you want to make.**
   Say you want to make three 650g loaves, which would equal 1,950g total dough.

3 **Then, apply the Magic Number formula to your choices.**
   1,950g total dough **divided by** 1.93* = 1,010g

   *To reiterate, this is 193%, the total of baker's percentages—100% flour, 70% water, 20% starter, and 3% salt—but with the decimal point moved two places to the left = 1.93.

4 **You now know you need 1,010g flour for your recipe.**

5 **Armed with the flour weight you can find the amount of the other ingredients using the baker's percentage formula.**
   Water = 1,010g flour × 0.70 = 707g
   Starter = 1,010g flour × 0.20 = 202g
   Salt = 1,010g flour × 0.03 = 30g

Scaling

Okay, so this next bit is a tad confusing, because you can use the baker's percentage to scale a recipe up and down—meaning to multiply or divide a recipe depending on how much bread you want to make. (You'd simply calculate all the ingredient amounts starting with the Magic Number above, then multiply or divide everything depending on whether you want to make a double batch, a half batch, or however much you like.)

But in the bakery, there's *another* use of the term *scaling*, meaning to weigh out all your ingredients before you start mixing, using, obviously, a scale.

You really have to pay attention to weighing your ingredients correctly. I only use metric weights, as grams are far more precise than the ounces and pounds used in the US. The weights in this book are given only in metric units because I want you to succeed at breadmaking, and the more precise you are in your weights, the better chance of success you'll have.

Scaling out all your ingredients before you start gives you a visual sense of everything that will go into a recipe, and the chance to organize it neatly before you. You can also then rechill cold ingredients but still have them ready for mixing.

Hydrating

People obsess over hydration, which is simply the amount of water mixed into a dough, in part because wetter doughs tend to give you a more open crumb and lighter bread.

The hydration percentage for your dough will vary, depending on where you are in the world, and what flour you're using. Based on my experience, a 70% hydration dough in Europe generally produces the same result as an 85% hydration dough in California, because of differences between the wheat grown in these locations. When I started baking, I thought it was important to push hydration as far as possible, chasing that open crumb and trying to show off how wet my dough was. But it didn't always give me better bread. Sometimes you can overdo it, and the bread just collapses. There are many factors that go into making great bread, and hydration is just one of them.

Scalding Flour

Scalding flour with boiling water is a technique that allows you to add more water to a dough. The hot water "pre-gelatinizes" the starch in the flour and allows it to hold on to twice the amount of water, kind of like a sponge. That extra moisture then carries through the rest of the process, creating more steam during baking, and lifting and lightening the bread. It also keeps the finished bread moister and softer longer.

Using scalded whole-grain flour in your dough adds great flavor without negatively affecting the texture of the bread.

To make a scald, use a one-to-one ratio (by weight) of boiling water to flour. Pour the water over the flour, mixing it quickly so the starches gelatinize, and let it cool to room temperature before adding it to a dough. You can add anywhere between 20% and 50% scald to any dough, including enriched doughs like brioche. For example, if you have 1,000g flour, you could add between 200g and 500g scald (which is in turn 100g boiling water plus 100g flour, or 250g boiling water plus 250g flour). And you can do this without otherwise reducing the amount of water in the dough.

Mixing Dough by Hand

AUTOLYSE, OR THE INITIAL MIX

 For the initial mix, or autolyse, you simply combine the flour and the water until there's no dry flour remaining. You don't need to beat the dough; just mix it together. Then, use your flexible plastic bowl scraper to get the excess dough from your hands back into the bowl. Scrape down the insides of the bowl, making sure all the dough is together and your bowl looks clean along the sides. Cover your bowl with a clean tea towel to stop the surface of the dough from getting too dry and forming a skin. Let it rest for at least 20 minutes. This is the stage where the gluten starts to develop, which creates a strong dough without you having to put any effort into mixing or kneading.

You get the benefits of autolyse after 20 minutes, but you can leave your dough for up to a couple of hours to give yourself some flexibility. I typically leave my dough for 45 minutes, because that's how long it takes for my starter to come alive.

ADD THE PRE-FERMENT

After your autolyse, add in the freshly fed starter (and/or yeast and/or poolish, depending on what type of dough you're making). Gently use your hands to massage the starter (and/or yeast and/or poolish) into the dough just to incorporate it; no need to beat it in.

SECOND HYDRATION / BASSINAGE

 I use a two-step method for hydrating my sourdough loaves. Most of the water goes into the dough at the autolyse stage, but I always hold back a small amount of water that goes in after the starter is mixed in. This step is called bassinage. (See Three Reasons to Use Bassinage, opposite, for why I do this.)

ADDING SALT

Once you have added all the water, add the salt and keep massaging until it's fully dissolved and absorbed.

Salt acts to slow down fermentation, and in large amounts would even kill it. I've made plenty of salty mistakes in my time, such as not adding any, or adding it twice. Doubling the salt hugely limits fermentation, and no salt at all makes your dough crazy active, fermenting way quicker than usual.

FOLDING

I only ever fold dough that I'm mixing by hand. Due to minimal mixing and no kneading, hand-mixed doughs need to be strengthened. Folding does this by physically helping along the gluten formation.

To fold the dough: Keeping the dough in the bowl, gently lift and pull it toward you, and fold it over itself. At first, it will pull very easily and stay where you leave it. Rotate the bowl a quarter turn and fold it again, then give the bowl another quarter turn and fold it again. After four or five turns and folds, it will be as tight as it needs to be and the dough will resist being folded any more. That's when you know it's time to stop.

I fold the dough twice during the first 1½ hours of fermentation (once after 45 minutes and again at 90 minutes). After that, I like to leave the dough alone to ferment and let all the lovely flavorful gases build up undisturbed. Folding also gives you a good opportunity to check on your dough. As bulk fermentation progresses, you should start to see it come alive, with a few air bubbles.

MIXING PAN LOAVES

Pan loaves require only a minimal amount of mixing. Flours like rye, emmer, and einkorn contain a small amount of gluten, so kneading or heavy mixing is unnecessary. You just need to combine the ingredients and let the dough ferment in the pan.

Mixing Dough by Machine

At the bakery, we use multiple spiral mixers. When you get to mixing half a ton of dough every day, a mixer is the way to go. Also, any dough with a biga should be mixed by machine; bigas are too stiff to be adequately mixed by hand. While there's no one correct method for mixing, I wanted to share my take on it.

→ The flour and water are just mixed and then left to autolyse in the mixer. The starter has been fed and is ready.

→ I add the starter to the mixer and turn on the mixer to speed 1. I mix until the starter is incorporated and the dough starts to feel strong, 3 to 5 minutes. By *strong* I mean that when you pull on the dough, it offers a lot of resistance and doesn't stretch easily; it will be tight.

→ At this point, I start the second hydration, or bassinage, stage of mixing. I turn the mixer to speed 2 and add water until it feels right. I know this sounds odd, but in a professional environment, mixing every day, I know what I'm looking for. I'm constantly reading the flour and adjusting the hydration, paying attention to how the bread came

Three Reasons to Use Bassinage

1 Dough Strength

It's easier to build gluten with a drier dough. Holding some water back helps build a stronger structure in the initial stages. Once you have a strong base, there's less chance of overwhelming the gluten. Think about mayonnaise, where you start with egg yolk and mustard, then stream in the oil slowly. If you go too quickly, you risk breaking the emulsion and ending up with a soupy, oily mess. The same goes for making bread: too much water at once can break the gluten bonds.

2 Changes in Flour

All the recipes in this book have been tested multiple times. Sometimes, even after we've felt that a recipe was perfect, on our final test, we'd end up with a flat, sad-looking loaf. Why? Flour changes from season to season, harvest to harvest, and bag to bag. Bassinage lets you adjust the hydration based on feel.

It's difficult at first to know how much water a dough can take. Each time you mix, note how the dough feels in relation to how it bakes. Over time, you'll build up a memory bank that will help you determine the right point to stop adding water.

3 Temperature Control

Bassinage is useful for controlling the temperature and fermentation of your dough. If your autolyse is too warm, use cold water to bring the dough temperature down. (In a professional environment, with a big quantity of dough, I would use ice; the mass is too big to cool down with just water.) Or conversely, if you need to warm up your dough, use warmer water.

out of the oven that day. The more you make dough, the easier it is to understand what "feels right" means. I find it hard to put into words, but the dough will have the right amount of stretch and integrity. The recipes will get you to a good place, but as you develop experience baking, try to remember what a dough felt like at this stage and connect it to what the final product is like. Keep in mind that a touch more water might give you a little more open of a crumb, but too much and the final bread will collapse. Or you might like a little more density in the loaf, which would call for pulling back the hydration a bit. Just keep noticing, baking, and connecting with your senses as you learn to make the minor adjustments that suit you.

→ When I'm happy with the level of hydration, I add the salt. When the salt has dissolved, I turn on the mixer to speed 2 and mix for another few minutes, until the dough starts to look smooth, shiny, and strong. I stop the mixer and allow the dough to rest for a few minutes. It's easier to judge the hydration of a dough once it's relaxed. If it feels right, I pull it out into buckets for bulk fermentation. If not, I start the mixer again, wait until the dough is smooth and strong, and add in more water until I'm happy with it.

→ With machine mixing, I don't fold the dough at all. It's built up enough gluten strength that it doesn't need it. The older I get, the more I realize you just have to let the dough do its thing.

MIXING ENRICHED DOUGHS

Enriched doughs with high amounts of fat require a machine mix, in a stand mixer with a dough hook. Fat weakens the gluten, which is why it's important to mix a strong dough before adding fat.

For enriched doughs, I chill all my ingredients before mixing, so the dough doesn't overheat. If it gets too hot (above 79°F / 26°C), it will overproof, and the bread won't be as good as it could be. Overproofed bread can deflate in the bake or develop off, alcohol flavors.

To autolyse your dough, mix together the dry ingredients with the eggs, water, and starter until there are no dry bits remaining. At this stage, the yeast, salt, and fat are left out. (Instant dry yeast is fast acting; I hold it back because I want to be able to control the fermentation of the dough.)

After autolyse, I add the salt and yeast and mix on high speed for around 10 minutes, until it's totally strong. The dough will come together as one mass and start to pull away from the sides of the bowl. At this stage, I'm ready to add half the butter. I add half of it, let it mix until fully incorporated, then add the rest of it and repeat. If the recipe has oil, I add it after any butter and only half at a time, making sure it's fully incorporated after each addition.

Controlling Temperature

Wild yeast needs the proper amount of heat and moisture to grow and flourish. In a hot climate, your challenge is to keep everything cool; the opposite is true for a cold climate.

How do you feel right now? If the air is cold and you're wearing a sweater, it is likely your dough will also be cold, and will become colder as it sits. This will slow down fermentation. A dough that ordinarily takes 4 hours to bulk ferment could take 6, 8, or even 10 hours.

On the other hand, if you're hot and sweaty, your dough will be, too. The bulk fermentation will race ahead, and it won't have time to develop precious flavors. It's also hard to control and will likely overproof. During bulk fermentation, the dough can become acidic, and that excess acid breaks down the gluten structure, releasing too much of the stored carbon dioxide gas. As a result, overproofed bread won't rise well in the oven.

The two factors to consider are the temperature of the room and the temperature of your ingredients. The right water temperature can make the difference. If your conditions are cold, use warmer water. If your conditions are hot, use cooler water, or even ice water if you're working with a large quantity of dough. (If you're including the chunks of ice, which I do when it's really hot, just weigh the ice and water together as the water in the recipe.)

In ideal conditions—a nice, moderately warm room, with dough that's kept consistently warm—bulk fermentation takes 4 hours. But conditions aren't always ideal.

In my bakery in Copenhagen, all winter long, we'd let the dough bulk ferment for 6 hours. I let it go those 2 hours longer because as we'd divide the dough for shaping, it would cool down very quickly. I wanted to make sure that there was enough yeast activity in the dough to counteract the cooling, so that fermentation didn't slow down too much.

At the other end of the spectrum, when I was baking on blistering-hot days in California, dividing the dough in a hot room, bulk fermentation was often done within 3 hours. The dough was very warm and active, and once divided, it kept quickly fermenting. We would divide it "young," meaning slightly underfermented, because in a hot room, the dough won't stop fermenting; while the preshaped dough rested, it would continue to ferment on the table. By the time we were ready to final shape it and put it into a proofing basket, it was the way we wanted it.

I share these examples to drive home the fact that there can be huge variations in temperature from place to place, and season to season, and you need to adjust your techniques and handle your dough accordingly. This is why it is crucial, if you want to bake great bread, to pay attention to your environment.

If you're just beginning to bake bread, I recommend that you use a digital thermometer to make sure that your dough and water are within the optimal ranges that I suggest in my recipes.

When you're putting dough into a bulk ferment, take its temperature. In a cold climate, it should be around 88°F / 31°C. In a hot climate, it should be around 80°F / 27°C. You want to keep it at that temperature throughout its whole bulk fermentation. If it's too cold, set the bowl of dough in a larger bowl of hot water to heat it up. I say "hot" and not "warm" because a cold bowl of dough will immediately cool down hot water to warm. (I'm not talking about water boiled on the stovetop; what I mean is hot tap water.) While it's warming up, fold the dough at least once, to evenly distribute the heat.

If the dough is too warm, do the same using cool or ice water. You don't need to be hypervigilant—it's not an exact science—but check it every 45 minutes to 1 hour, and adjust accordingly.

Bulk Fermentation

This is the process in which the dough ferments as one mass, or "bulk." The technique itself is pretty simple: after mixing the dough, take its temperature, adjust it accordingly, and leave the dough mostly alone to do its thing, apart from the times you fold it. The only judgment call is determining when bulk fermentation is done.

I've done it so many thousands of times that it's almost an involuntary reflex, and I struggle to articulate how I know when the fermentation is done. I've asked my colleague and friend Karishma Sanghi to try and put that decision-making process into words.

HOW TO JUDGE WHEN A DOUGH HAS FINISHED BULK FERMENTATION

Everything begins with your starter, so it's important that it's healthy and freshly fed before being mixed into the dough. You can't compromise on the love that you put into maintaining your starter, so don't expect amazing bread from a neglected starter.

Volume

When you first start the fermentation, note the level of the dough in your proofing container. This will help you judge how much it increases in volume. Make a mark on the side of the container using a marker, rubber band, or a piece of masking tape. On average, wheat sourdough loaves multiply one and a half times in volume by the time bulk fermentation is done. If you have a container with volume markings, a 4-liter dough should end at 6 liters.

Bubbliness

Air bubbles are a clear sign that your dough is fermenting. The yeast and bacteria are digesting the sugar in the dough and giving off carbon dioxide gas, creating air pockets. The gluten in the flour creates a complex network of strands, which traps the gases and causes the level of the dough to rise. In bulk fermentation, air bubbles become fairly evenly distributed throughout the dough. You'll see bubbles on the surface of the dough, and when you tug on a piece of it, you should be able to feel bubbles deflating between your fingers. The dough should feel light and full of life, because it is very much alive. (If, after a few hours your dough feels heavy and lifeless, it's possible your starter wasn't yet ready to use.)

How bubbly is bubbly enough? Well, it depends on whether you have mixed the dough by hand or machine:

→ **Hand-mixed dough:** When you've mixed a dough like City Loaf (page 113) by hand, you'll be folding it, which deflates and redistributes the bubbles, so your final dough may have slightly smaller bubbles, and feel a little heavier, than dough mixed by machine.

→ **Machine-mixed dough:** If you've used a mixer, you've built enough gluten strength that you won't need to fold the dough. In this case, the bubbles have been left untouched and will be slightly larger and more visible on the surface, and the dough will feel lighter than hand-mixed dough.

Troubleshooting

→ **Underfermented dough:** You'll know you've underfermented your dough if it feels heavy when you're preshaping. It will be slack on the bench and seem kind of lifeless. You may be able to salvage it by giving it a slightly longer final proofing before you tuck it away for the overnight cool retard in the fridge. After baking, you'll notice large, irregular air pockets, which are a result of too short or underdeveloped bulk fermentation. Remember how the dough felt, and go for a longer, warmer bulk ferment the next time around.

→ **Overfermented dough:** When you go to preshape the dough, and it feels like you're cutting and shaping marshmallow, you know you've let it go too far. In this case, give it a short bench rest, followed by a very quick proof in the basket, and put it into a cool spot in the fridge. The baked loaf may be flatter than normal, since the yeast and bacteria wore themselves out in bulk fermentation, and there won't be much potential left for them to create the gases that make the dough rise in the hot oven.

Preshaping

Preshaping creates some tension in the entire loaf and sets the dough up for final shaping.

To preshape your dough, gently use your flexible plastic scraper to ease the bread out of the bowl or container in which it was bulk fermented and onto your clean, dry work surface. Treat it tenderly. You don't want to be rough with it and de-gas it, bursting all the air bubbles in it and sending them out of the dough.

With wet hands and your bench scraper, quickly and decisively divide the dough, using a digital scale if necessary to make sure that the dough is evenly divided. Get one piece directly in front of you. Don't be afraid to pick it up with your bench scraper and move it to where you need it. Using your hand and bench scraper in unison, work the dough toward you, using your fingers to swiftly tuck the outer edges back under the surface of the loaf, shaping it into a neat round (or oval) with good surface tension. Confident, swift movements are best. There will be some sticking, which is why wet hands are essential. Try not to work the dough too much. You don't want to let out the beautiful gases you've spent all this time creating. It takes a lot of practice, but you'll know when you have it right—it should look like there's a nice, tight skin wrapping the ball of dough, and it should sit up a bit proud.

Final Shaping

The final shaping gives the last bit of tension, to help with the final lift in the oven.

To shape the City Loaf (page 113) and all its variations: Using your bench scraper and wet hands, turn the dough into an oval shape, using just a few moves to get it into more of an oval than a round. Hold one hand over the center of the loaf, take your scraper in the other hand, and scrape evenly across the surface of the table toward the loaf, lifting it up and into the other hand. Put down the scraper and cradle the loaf in both hands. Now fold it inward as if closing a book, and gently place it into the proofing basket, seam side up. If it tries to fall back open, you can gently pinch it together at the top. That's it. It's safe and happy just the way it is. No need for aggressive shaping.

Final Fermentation

COLD RETARD

Cold retard is the process by which fermentation is slowed down by placing the dough into a cold environment; it's a key factor not only in making the most flavorful sourdough loaves but also in creating the best texture, crust, and crumb.

The dough needs to be in an environment that is cold enough to slow fermentation, which will keep the dough from overproofing, but not so cold that it *stops* fermentation, which would result in a one-dimensional bread that is much less complex tasting.

In a professional environment, I always cold retard at a warmer temperature than a home fridge, which is set at or below 41°F / 5°C, a temperature that stops bacterial growth. When fermenting dough, we want that bacterial growth to happen; it is the source of all the complex flavors in the baked bread.

In my bakery, I use a fridge with a temperature range set at 54–59°F / 12–15°C. The best advice I can give to home bakers is to use a cellar or wine fridge, or cover the dough and place it on a balcony, or in the garden, if the outdoor temperature is in this ideal range. Otherwise, you can leave the shaped dough in its baskets on the kitchen counter for 3 hours to proof at room temperature before putting them into the cold fridge.

This is hands down the best method for City Loaf (and all its variations) and a few others in this book. Cold retarding contributes to the bread's overall texture in a few ways:

→ It helps set the outside shell of the loaf, which will result in a crisp and delicious final crust. Having the loaf's structure set before baking is important when working with such a high-hydration dough, whose gluten strength is challenged by all that water.

→ The resultant slow fermentation makes for very fine bubbles on the outside shell of the crust, which reminds me of the crisp crunch of chicharrón.

→ The long, slow fermentation makes these breads capable of staying fresh for many days.

Typically, loaves cold retard overnight, or up to 12 hours (at *most* 15 hours, after which the dough will become overproofed).

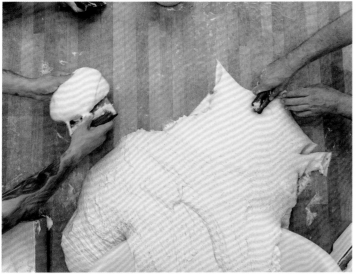

Challenging the Intricate Shaping Technique

At Tartine, we did intricate final shaping with all our loaves. We did so much to them, it was like we were dancing a ballet with a piece of dough. It looked pretty cool, and was mesmerizing to watch, and it took ages to master. It's also one of the skills that most intimidates beginning bakers.

And when we started my bakery, we did it, too. Then one day the dough was too dry. If we'd shaped it the usual way, the loaves would have been too tight and wouldn't have relaxed, with the crumb too tight and the loaf too dense. So instead of shaping, we just folded them in half, like closing an open book, and put them in the proofing baskets. Pick it up, fold it, put it in. And it *worked*. It was kind of a miracle: The bread opened up when we scored it and put it into the oven, and it baked into beautiful loaves. It shaved two hours off our day.

For years, I had thought you needed to build the last bit of strength with a tight final shape. Once scored and baked, your loaf would blow up in the oven, with a beautiful slash, just the way you wanted it. I thought that if you didn't shape, you'd have this slack blob. It turned out that wasn't true at all. I'd never have known if we hadn't made such a lucky mistake.

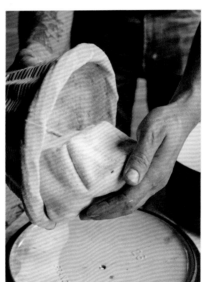

Room temperature—or "ambient"—proofing definitely has a place in great breads: rye breads, baguettes, ciabatta, and Perfect Sandwich Bread (page 172), to name a few.

Unlike the breads that require long, slow fermentation, the best rye breads need a high level of well-fermented sourdough and a quick ambient proof. You get so much flavor from the mature starter, the rye flour, and all the other ingredients. And due to the way it's fermented, lots of tiny air bubbles form in the dough, and stay in the bread after it's been baked.

If you were to put any of my rye dough recipes into a cold ferment, the resulting bread would be overproofed and too sour in flavor, and the tiny air bubbles you create from a quick ambient proof would collapse, giving you a dense, rubbery bread.

I learned this method during my time in Denmark, and it is explained in more detail in the Rye Breads and Pan Loaves chapter (page 79).

Baguettes and the other wheat breads mentioned don't get a long cold fermentation because it would make the texture and the flavor all wrong. I use sourdough and other pre-ferments to enhance their flavor, and I also use commercial yeast to give them a more powerful rise, creating a light texture and a superthin crisp crust. The idea is not to develop the same complex flavors as the City Loaf. I believe baguettes and ciabatta and the other breads should be much sweeter and not look or taste like a typical sourdough loaf. They're just right as they are. Otherwise, why not just make sourdough?

Because of the quick ambient rise and the commercial yeast, these breads get stale very quickly. They're perfect straight from the oven or the day that they're made, and after that, they're good for breadcrumbs.

Scoring

 Sometimes you'll see bread with lots of pretty slashes in the crust, or even whole works of art. This isn't just decorative; it's important to score your bread. As the yeasts expand in the oven, the increasing amount of gas needs somewhere to go, an escape route. If you didn't create a pathway with a score, it would blow up from the sides or the bottom of the loaf. So when you're scoring, you're dictating where the bread will split or grow. This way, you're in charge of its beauty.

Use a lame and a razor blade. Hold the lame delicately between your thumb and first two fingers. Score the dough quickly and decisively, using the corner of the blade. You want to keep it almost flat against the bread, maybe at a 10- to 15-degree angle. You're just slashing the "skin" open a bit, not carving a deep gully. Keeping the depth even on every score is important, too; remember, you're creating pathways for the gases to escape, so the more evenly the scores go across the loaf, the more consistent the crumb and texture of the bread will be. This is something you will learn over time, but if your bread is looking slightly underproofed (relatively lifeless and flat) that day, you should score deep, and if it's looking slightly overproofed (too puffy or marshmallowy), you should score shallow.

 For breads with a lot of grain on top, I use scissors. I cut 6 to 8 little snips (1 inch / 2 to 3cm deep) through the center of the loaf, holding the scissors nearly flat to the surface of the bread, which gives it a mohawk effect.

Baking

IN A DUTCH OVEN

Baking bread in a Dutch oven most closely replicates what a professional bread oven can do for your sourdough and other breads.

A professional bread oven traps the steam inside; or in fact, a good one can inject steam while baking. But many home ovens are designed to let *out* the steam. So baking your bread in a Dutch oven inside your oven traps that steam, which prevents the crust from setting before the crumb has fully expanded and the loaf has risen to its full potential.

As I mentioned earlier, I use an enameled cast-iron Dutch oven with a cast-iron lid, and I unscrew and remove the plastic handle on the lid so it won't be damaged at the high heat I bake at. Then I use the lid as the base for my dough (the dough covers the hole made by removing the handle and seals it), and I invert the Dutch oven itself over the bread and onto the lid to act as a dome.

For the City Loaf (page 113) and all its variations, the first 20 minutes of baking happens under the inverted Dutch oven, while the dough is still wet and pliable. Then it gets uncovered for the last 20 minutes so that the loaf can get beautifully caramelized and crisp.

When you're getting ready to bake, turn your oven on as high as it goes, and put your Dutch oven in it for at least 1 hour, so it's raging hot. After that, set the oven to the bake temperature the recipe specifies.

Being very careful, take out the Dutch oven; use heavy-duty oven gloves or heavy dry towels. Set the lid on a sturdy, heatproof surface. These vessels are designed to hold their heat, so don't panic or rush; you have time.

Take a basket of chilled dough out of the fridge. Gently loosen the edges of the loaf with your fingertips, and then flip the dough straight onto the screaming-hot lid. Score with a lame and carefully cover it with the inverted pot, like a dome.

ON A PIZZA STONE

Place a sheet pan or shallow roasting pan on the floor of the oven. Arrange a rack in the center of the oven and place a pizza stone on the rack. Preheat the oven to 500°F / 260°C. (The stone will absorb the heat readily, so no need to preheat it for a long time.)

Sprinkle a bit of rice flour onto a baker's peel. Place the transfer board alongside the dough you're about to bake. Using one hand, pull the edge of the couche (linen proofing cloth) that you've been resting your dough on, and gently invert the dough onto the board. Slide the dough from the board onto the peel. Use a lame to score the dough. Transfer the dough from the peel to the pizza stone in the oven. Add about 250ml water to the pan on the oven's floor, taking care to avoid exposing your skin directly to the resultant steam, which can burn.

Bake the dough per the recipe.

IN LOAF PANS

Place a sheet pan or shallow roasting pan on the floor of the oven. Arrange a rack in the center of the oven. Preheat the oven to 425°F / 220°C.

Place the loaf in the oven and add about 250ml water to the pan on the oven's floor, taking care to avoid exposing your skin directly to the resultant steam, which can burn.

Bake the loaf per the recipe. Rotate the pan front to back halfway through the baking time. Use an instant-read thermometer to take the internal temperature of the loaf. It should read 203°F / 95°C when it's done. If it's not quite there, give it a few more minutes. Remove the bread from the oven, then turn it out onto a rack to cool for several hours before slicing.

Cooling and Storing

Letting bread cool is actually part of the baking process. The starches need a certain amount of time to set. The amount of time varies from bread to bread. It could be just a few minutes for baguettes and morning buns. The City Loaf (page 113) needs an hour or so.

Rye breads are characterized by a group of complex sugars called pentosans, which absorb water and swell as the dough ferments and bakes. If you were to slice a rye loaf before it cools completely, you'd have an impossibly sticky, gummy bread. The texture will be much nicer—firmer, less sticky, and with well-distributed moisture—once the loaf cools. Be patient; it's worth it.

I recommend you use a cooling rack so that air can circulate around all sides of the bread. I wrap my bread in a tea towel once it's cooled, to keep it fresh. It's not a perfect solution, but it works better than leaving it uncovered. Wrapping it in plastic ruins the crust. Being a baker, I have the luxury of getting fresh bread every day, so I'm going to let my cowriter, Laurie, explain how a home baker stores bread.

HOW LAURIE STORES HER BREAD

I have a small household and couldn't possibly finish all the bread I bake before it gets dried out. I'll keep a loaf for a day or two in a paper bag on the kitchen counter, then slice the remaining bread, put it into a double layer of plastic bags, and keep it in the freezer, thawing it out or toasting it a slice or two at a time. This method works to extend the life of any of the breads in this book.

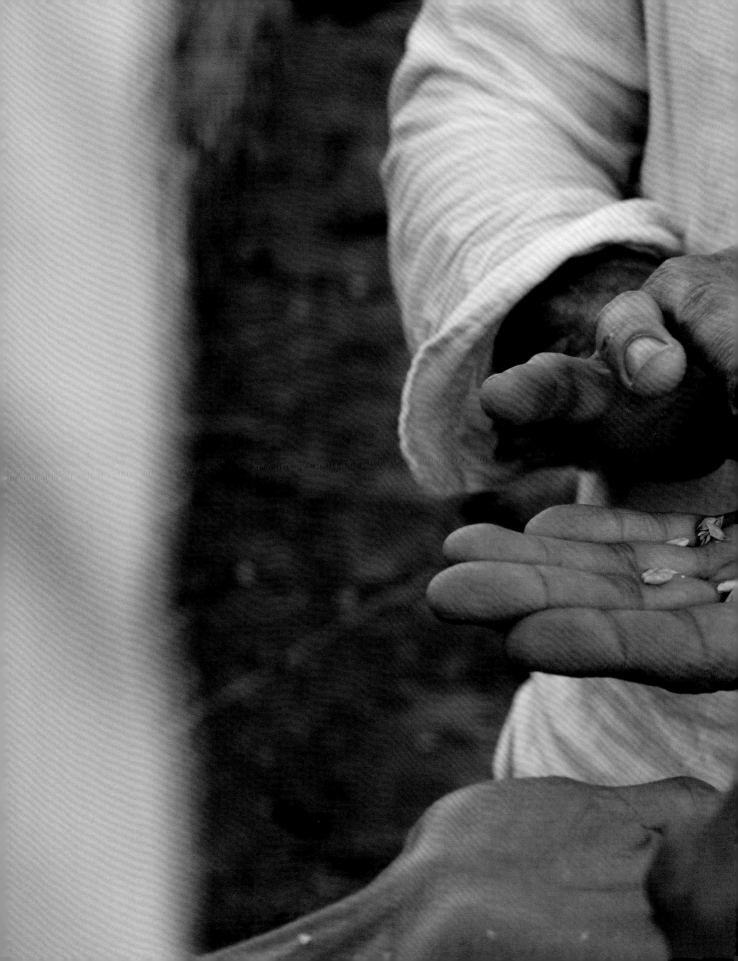

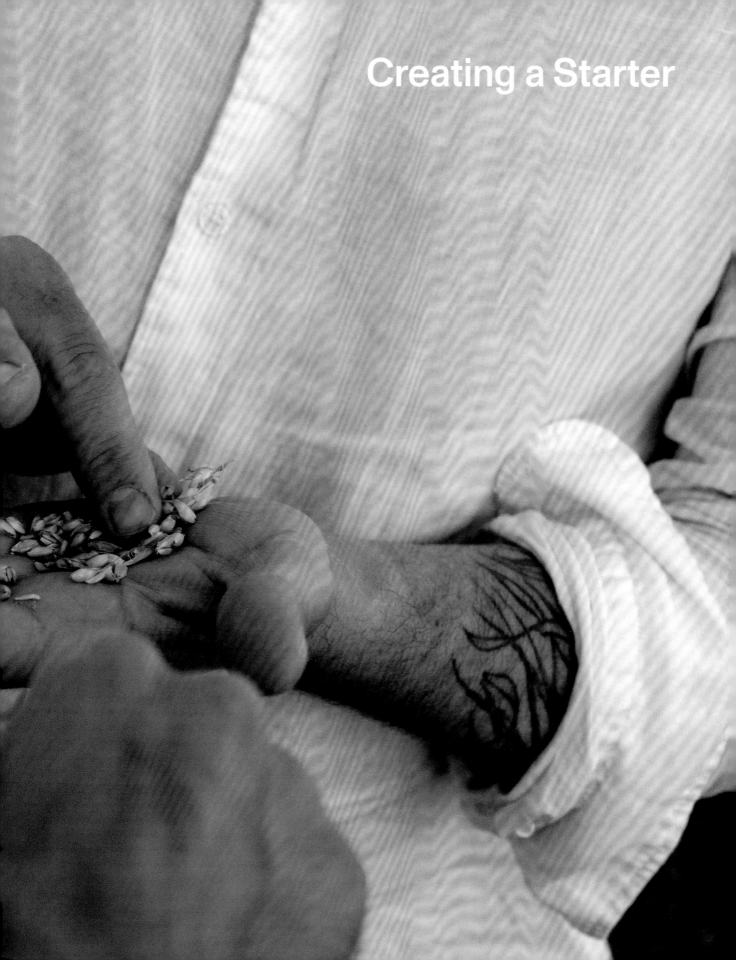

Sourdough starter is at the heart of all my bread. It's the true beginning and the original way of making bread. It's the best way to build flavor; it creates unbeatable texture. Bread made with natural starter lasts for days, whereas bread made only with commercial yeast stales overnight.

It's better for your health, too: the microbes in sourdough predigest certain parts of the wheat, making it easier for our own digestive systems to handle.

Although sourdough isn't as simple as just mixing some yeast into your dough, it's worth every bit of effort to make a starter, then keep it alive. But don't worry, it's actually quite easy, as long as you remember the most important things:

Sourdough Is Alive and Needs to Be Fed

Think of sourdough starter as a farm. The flour and water are the pasture and feed, and the yeast and bacteria in your starter are your herds and flocks. When the animals come to a fresh pasture full of grass, they eat it to survive and grow.

In sourdough, your herd of yeasts and bacteria convert the starches in the flour into sugar, then they feed on the sugar, creating carbon dioxide gas (that raises your bread), ethanol, and lactic acid.

Of course, the farmer doesn't just feed the herds and flocks one time. Once they've eaten all the grass in a pasture, the farmer makes sure the animals have new pasture, so they can survive and grow.

In your starter, you do this by discarding some of your spent sourdough and adding fresh flour and water. This daily feeding is like changing the pasture. Your herd of yeast and bacteria have taken all they can from their current environment, which is to say, the slurry of flour and water that you fed them yesterday.

Some people are uncomfortable with chucking out a portion of their starter every day. Don't think of it as a wasted product. There are a number of things you can make from sourdough discard, like Cracked Rye Bread (page 227), Sourdough Crumpets (page 223), or crackers (see page 224).

More important, you haven't wasted flour and water; you've kept your herd alive.

Keep It Warm

People often ask me, "Can I put my starter in the fridge?" My answer is, "No, not really." People *do* do it, thinking they won't have to feed it every day because the microbial activity slows down. But by putting your sourdough starter in the fridge, and not feeding it, you will deplete the yeast. It needs to be warm to multiply vigorously and do its thing. You want a starter that's packed full of happy, active yeast.

Herds and flocks, or pets, or children, for that matter, all rely on us to keep them fed, watered, and comfortable. If you stick any of them in the fridge and don't feed them, they're going to be pissed off with you. Your sourdough, too, will get sluggish and unhappy if you make it cold and stop feeding it.

Right after you feed your sourdough in a warm environment, the yeasts and bacteria are super happy. They're in a symbiotic relationship, partying hard in a hot tub of love. For the next several hours, they're multiplying, feasting, farting, and burping. Yeast produces the lovely gas that causes the bubbles and air pockets you see in baked bread. Starting when the dough is warm and continuing even as it cools, the bacteria create the lactic acid that gives sourdough its characteristic tangy flavor.

Fridge temperature, typically about 41°F / 5°C, slows the digestive activity down to an almost complete washout of the party. The yeast goes into near dormancy. The bacteria can handle the cold somewhat better than the heat-loving yeasts. Refrigerating your sourdough enables the bacteria to take over while the yeasts are sleeping. The starter gets more and more sour, without developing the crucial gases, throwing off the balance that you need to make good bread.

That said, I do have a technique that I use if I am going away for a week or more, traveling with my sourdough, or unable to bake for a while. The basic principle is to store it very dry, almost in a flour form. The day I'm going away, I feed my sourdough flour only, no water. Turning it into a powder makes the sourdough activity go super slow and keeps it from getting too acidic. I refrigerate it, keeping it cold to slow fermentation even more.

When you're ready to bake again, you'll have to lovingly resurrect it, adding warm water and some fresh flour, keeping it at room temperature, and resuming a regular feeding schedule. Depending on the climate, it will take one to five days for the starter to reach full yeast activity and be ready for baking.

So, in short: if you're baking regularly, just keep your starter on the counter where you won't forget about it, and feed it every day. It is a fermented product, and it's not going to go bad. (Well, if you leave it unfed for weeks and weeks, it *will* go bad, or even mold. But if you're reading this book and you want to make great bread, don't neglect it. And if you do, don't panic—just start again.)

A Conversation

About Why You Don't Need a Hundred-Year-Old Starter, and What You Can and Can't Control

Richard: I'm not precious about that whole "I've got a ten-year starter, a hundred-year starter" thing. I think that's rubbish.

Laurie: Is it? What do you mean by *rubbish*?

Richard: I believe that when it comes to sourdough starter, it's almost like you start a rebirth every day when you feed it and the bacteria and yeast multiply. To say that it's so old, who cares? It's such a tiny amount of the original, and it all moves into a new life. I just think it's a silly idea.

Laurie: Let's say somebody *does* have a starter that they've been regularly maintaining for ten years. Is there any greater strength or complexity to it than one started a month ago?

Richard: No. People get attached to these things, they give them cute names. Maybe it's their grandma's starter or whatever, but, literally, all you have in your jar is fermented flour and water. You could just chuck it out, and start again, and it'll take a few days to come to life, but then once it's there, it doesn't collect new generations of yeast and bacteria along the years, you know, like, baby bacteria, mommy bacteria, daddy bacteria, grandma bacteria all living and loving together in the pot. I understand that people might not like hearing that. They might be sentimental. But it's just fermented flour, and water.

Laurie: Do you taste your starter every day?

Richard: I don't, no. I know a lot of bakers do, but I think it's kind of gross. I smell it, and look at it, and taste the bread. How's the acidity? How's the flavor? What does it feel like when you chew it? How does the crust shatter?

Sourdough starter *can* go off balance. There are times throughout the year when the balance of bacteria to yeast changes, and it throws me off. It throws everyone off, every baker. All of a sudden your bread starts acting weird. It won't rise properly in the oven, or it looks dead in the basket.

The young bakers, at first, blame the flour; I blame the young bakers. After a few days of that, I say, "Sorry, it's not you," and it generally turns out to be the starter. You carry on, you make slight alterations, and it works its way out. It usually happens when the seasons change. I can't really explain it.

Even at this stage in my career, things go wrong, and that's okay. Last time I killed my starter, I blamed the stainless steel bowl it was in, but who knows, really? It's never boring. If it wasn't this way, I might have already moved on to a new career. It's sad when it all goes wrong, but it's exhilarating when it works.

Rye Starter

MAKES 175 GRAMS

I think you should make your first starter with whole rye flour. It's packed full of the enzymes, nutrients, and complex sugars that yeast and bacteria thrive on, and it will begin to ferment faster than any other flour. You can make a starter out of any kind of grain flour, but rye will be the fastest and most reliable, and the results will help you build confidence as a sourdough baker.

Once you've established life in the matrix of an all-rye starter, which should happen within two or three days, you can blend in whole wheat and white flour, converting it into a wheat sourdough starter (see Wheat Starter, page 73). A wheat starter requires twice-daily feedings, versus once-daily required by rye, but wheat flour may be easier to find and less expensive.

As for the ideal container, I recommend a glass jar or transparent (or translucent) plastic container, so that you can see the bubbles and expansion happening. It ought to be taller than it is wide, to keep the surface area at a minimum.

I mix my starter by hand to get a feel for its viscosity, temperature, and texture. You *could* use a wooden spoon, but why not get into an intimate relationship with what you're doing?

One last thing: Antibacterial soaps are the standard in many kitchens, but as the name suggests, they kill bacteria, *all* bacteria, even the good ones. When you wash your hands to use them to mix the starter, I suggest using a simple bar soap that isn't antibacterial.

Actually *this* is the last thing: If you're too impatient to wait on the power of flour and water, just go to your local bakery. Ask really nicely if you can have some sourdough starter. Some bakeries will sell it to you, but I think that's ridiculous. I'm happy to give it to anyone who asks. The more of us baking bread, the better.

BAKER'S %	WEIGHT	INGREDIENT
100%	125g	Rye flour
100%	125g	Warm water (82°F / 28°C)

TIMING

Day 1: Mix starter.

Day 2: Check and mix the starter.

Day 3: Feed the starter, mix and ferment.

Day 4: Discard half the starter, feed, and ferment.

Day 5: Discard half the starter, feed, and ferment.

Day 6: Discard half the starter, feed, and ferment.

EQUIPMENT

Jar or plastic container, flexible plastic dough scraper, digital thermometer, bowl or other vessel for water bath

DAY 1

Mix the flour and water: In a clean jar or plastic container, combine 50g of the flour and 50g of the water and mix it well by hand to form a homogenous dough. It will be quite sticky. Use the dough scraper to scrape any excess from your fingers and back into the mixture.

Take its temperature. If it's below 77°F / 25°C, set the container in a larger container of warm water to bring it up a few degrees. The water should completely surround the starter container in order to insulate it. Don't go crazy with boiling or scalding water, as there is an upper limit (131°F / 55°C) to how warm the starter can be before you start to kill off the yeast and bacteria. Put a lid on the container.

Don't expect much excitement in the first day or so. As long as you're keeping the starter warm enough, you can leave it alone for 24 hours.

DAY 2

Check on your starter: To be honest, it probably won't look all that different. It may have separated a bit, with some liquid at the top, and if that's the case, just mix the liquid back in. Don't worry! That's just evidence that the process has started, but the mixture hasn't entirely fermented yet. It's completely normal, as unappetizing as it may look.

Put your clean fingers into the mixture and stir it around a bit, to add some oxygen. Take its temperature and warm the container in warm water as necessary. Cover the container and let it sit again for 24 hours.

Recipe continues

DAY 3

Feed the starter: By now, you should be seeing some noticeable bubbling and expansion in the mixture. Go ahead and add 25g of the flour and 25g of the water and mix it in by hand. Scrape the excess off your fingers and add it to the mixture.

And if you're still not seeing clear signs of life, don't worry. Just check that it's warm enough and wait another day.

DAY 4

Feed it again: Check again for bubbling and expansion, which should be evident by Day 4. Discard half the mixture and mix in the remaining 50g flour and 50g water.

If by Day 4, there is no evidence of fermentation in your mixture, despite your having refreshed it and kept it warm, it's quite likely that your starter is fucked. And definitely so if you see red or orange streaks of mold or other visible growths. You should chuck it out, buy some fresh flour, and start over.

DAY 5 AND BEYOND—MAINTENANCE

At this point, you should have a nicely fermented starter, with real, clear signs of active life: bubbles and a steady rise in volume over the course of several hours, after which it will likely deflate a bit as the gas bubbles break through the surface. You are now ready to use this starter to make bread.

From here, you will maintain a daily feeding schedule by discarding about 90% of it and refreshing it with flour and water, equal parts by weight. For a rye starter, you can do this once a day. For wheat, I recommend feeding it twice a day, which is what we do at my bakery, because it keeps the starter active and happy, and it fits best with our production schedule. Some bakers feed their wheat starter three times per day; some do it just once. I believe deeply in feeding your starter every day; it needs healthy, happy yeast to make great bread. Some people try to feed it less frequently or put it in the fridge, the idea being that the cold temperature slows down the whole process, allowing you to feed it less frequently. While that's true, the fact is that the yeasts are also not multiplying happily. I don't recommend it, but if you do do this, you'll need to bring it back to room temperature and give it a good feeding for a few days before it will make good bread for you.

KEEPING YOUR STARTER FED WHILE NOT BAKING (OR: HOW MUCH STARTER DO YOU NEED ON HAND?)

For days when you're not baking, you really don't need to keep more than 100g of starter on hand. Every day, discard all but 10g of your starter and feed it 45g flour and 45g water. That way, it's fed and healthy, and you're not wasting too much flour keeping your starter happy and alive. For rye starter, you can do this once per day, and for wheat starter, do it twice a day, roughly 12 hours apart.

PLANNING AHEAD FOR THE BAKE

The recipes in this book call for varying amounts of starter. Before you go to bake, plan ahead to know how much starter you'll need, and adjust your feeding amounts accordingly. For example, for the pan loaves, you'll need 250g of 12-hour starter, so the day before you make your dough, you would discard 90% of your existing starter, leaving 10g, and feed it 125g flour and 125g water, which would give you enough for the recipe and leave you with starter to carry over for the next feeding.

Everything (Else) You Need to Know About Your Starter

How can you tell that it's healthy?

A healthy starter shows clear signs of active life: bubbles and a steady rise in volume over the course of several hours, after which it will deflate a bit, as the gas bubbles break through the surface. This should happen consistently, after every time you feed it.

How can you tell that it's going sideways, and what can you do to turn it around?

If you fail to see the signs of life described above, it's not healthy. You can try to save it by discarding all but a tiny bit of it—less than a teaspoon—and then give it a few days of feedings, discarding more than you normally would. If your starter develops visible mold spores or red streaks, chuck it entirely and start again.

What do you do if you've missed a feeding (or two or three)?

First, know that any bread you bake with starter that you've ignored for a few days isn't going to be amazing. Give it a few days of good regular feedings before you bake with it.

If you have put it in the fridge for a few days, how do you get it back to its thriving room temperature state?

It's the same as if you've missed a few feedings: don't expect to bake good bread with it until you've brought it back to room temperature and revived it with a few days' worth of regular feedings. Once it's bubbling and showing a rise and fall in volume, you can bake with it again. But as mentioned, I don't really suggest chilling the starter as a way of feeding it less frequently (see page 65).

Wheat Starter

MAKES 240 GRAMS

Once you have established good fermentation with your rye starter, you can convert it to a wheat flour starter, if you like. You will have to feed a wheat starter twice a day, versus once a day for rye. Rye tends to prefer to live in a slightly more acetic environment, whereas wheat starters are better when they're in a more lactic environment.

There's no magic to the conversion from rye to wheat. It's all about keeping your yeast and bacteria fed and happy, and they'll thrive, as long as you're regularly feeding them and keeping them warm.

BAKER'S %	WEIGHT	INGREDIENT
100%	100g	Whole wheat flour
100%	100g	Warm water (82°F / 28°C)
40%	40g	Rye Starter (page 69)

Feed the starter: In a clean jar or plastic container, combine the whole wheat flour, water, and rye starter and mix it well by hand to form a homogenous dough. It will be quite sticky. Use the dough scraper to scrape any excess from your fingers and back into the mixture.

Take its temperature. If it's below 77°F / 25°C, set the container in a larger container of warm or hot water to bring it up a few degrees. Put a lid on the container.

After 12 hours, you can make bread with this converted starter, or discard a portion of it and feed the rest as per Maintenance (page 70), but do so twice daily. Wheat starter is best and healthiest when fed every 12 hours.

12-Hour Starter Versus Freshly Fed Starter

You'll notice that, in each recipe that uses sourdough starter, I'll specify whether to use a 12-hour starter or a freshly fed starter.

12-hour starter: Let's assume that if you're baking from this book, you're regularly feeding a sourdough starter. A 12-hour starter is simply one that was last fed 12 hours ago, so the yeasts are spent and the remaining starter is pungent and will add a depth of flavor to a bread that's quickly leavened with commercial yeast.

Freshly fed starter: This is just like it sounds—a starter that has been recently fed, usually less than an hour before being mixed into an autolysed dough. Freshly fed starter is used in doughs that are mixed, fermented, and shaped, but then get a long, cold overnight retard, before being baked the next day. Because it has less acidity, freshly fed starter is suited well to a long fermentation; all the acid notes will come out later in the retard stage. If you were to use a 12-hour starter and treat it this way, your final bread would end up way too acidic, which would overpower every other nuance in the final loaf.

Other Pre-ferments: Biga and Poolish

The term *pre-ferment* refers to any mixture of flour and water that has been fermented separately from the bread dough, before being mixed with it. Sourdough starter is a pre-ferment that relies on naturally occurring yeasts and bacteria; biga and poolish, on the other hand, are pre-ferments that rely on a tiny amount of commercial yeast.

I use biga and poolish for a number of breads, sometimes in combination with sourdough. Biga is a relatively dry mixture of flour, water, and yeast, and poolish is a wetter mixture of the same three things. French bakers prefer to use poolish in their traditional baguettes and other breads, while Italian bakers favor biga for ciabatta, pizza dough, and similar breads. I'm neither Italian nor French, so I use them both.

You may have baked breads before using a straight dough method, in which commercial yeast is mixed directly with all the flour, water, and salt that make up the final dough, causing it to rise quickly, dramatically, and predictably. Pre-ferments like biga and poolish will also make your bread dough rise, but they work more slowly, and with different and way more interesting results.

By the time you mix a biga or poolish into the dough, the power of the yeast within those pre-ferments has been almost completely spent in the process of pre-fermentation. The yeast has efficiently broken down some of the proteins in the flour, which makes for a thin, crisp crust, a soft, yielding crumb, and a sweet, creamy, and slightly nutty flavor overall.

Poolish

Poolish is a pre-ferment made of equal parts flour and water, with a tiny amount of commercial yeast. I use instant (fast-acting) dry yeast because it's more consistent than fresh yeast, but feel free to use whatever yeast you like.

Poolish has a creamy, sweet yeasty smell, and it's essential for breads with a thin, crisp crust and a light crumb like Baguettes (page 193) and Perfect Sandwich Bread (page 172).

White flour is the standard, but you can make a poolish with any type of grain flour.

BAKER'S %	WEIGHT	INGREDIENT
100%	100g	All-purpose flour
100%	100g	Water
1%	1g	Instant dry yeast

TIMING

If you're using hot (104°F / 40°C) water, your poolish will be ready to mix into dough in about 4 hours. You can also go more slowly, using tepid (77°F / 25°C) water for a poolish that will be ready to use in 8 hours, and up to 12 hours before it becomes spent, after which time it will have a volatile alcohol aroma.

The hotter, faster version is what I'd use in a time crunch, but I prefer the tepid version, which has a more complex, creamier flavor.

EQUIPMENT

Jar, plastic container, or mixing bowl; flexible plastic dough scraper; tea towel

In a clean jar, plastic container, or bowl, combine the flour, water, and yeast and mix well by hand. Use the dough scraper to scrape any excess from your fingers and back into the mixture. Cover with a clean tea towel and let it ferment at room temperature for 4 hours if using hot (104°F / 40°C) water or for 8 (and up to 12) hours if using tepid (77°F / 25°C) water, during which time it will expand, with visible bubbles, and become fragrant.

Biga

Biga is a much stiffer pre-ferment than poolish, better mixed in a bowl than a jar. The low ratio of water to flour means that it will feel quite dry and crumbly. As the biga ferments, the texture will soften, and it will feel less shaggy and more like a dough.

Gabriele Bonci taught me how to work with biga when he came from Italy to do his pizza pop-up at Hart Bageri. Breads made with biga have a bigger, more irregular crumb structure, and are less sour than those made with poolish.

Working with biga was a whole new thing for me, and I started wondering how I could use it for other breads.

I decided to use biga (along with poolish and sourdough starter) to build the English Bloomer (page 186), and it's also in the recipes for Real Italian Ciabatta (page 176), Roman-Style Pizza (page 179), English Muffins (page 201), and Bagels (page 196).

BAKER'S %	WEIGHT	INGREDIENT
100%	175g	All-purpose flour
0.35%	6g	Instant dry yeast
30%	52g	Warm water (82°F / 28°C)

TIMING

Mix and ferment for 8 to 12 hours before using.

EQUIPMENT

Mixing bowl (or other container), flexible plastic dough scraper, plate (or lid)

In a mixing bowl, combine the flour and yeast. Add the water and mix it in by hand, rubbing the biga between your fingers to make a wet, breadcrumb-like consistency. There will be many small clumps of flour and water; it will not be a smooth or uniform dough. This is good: if you overmix biga, it tends to ferment too quickly. Use the dough scraper to scrape any excess dough off your fingers and back into the mixture, and scrape down the insides of the bowl, if necessary.

Cover the bowl with a plate and set it aside in a cool spot in your kitchen or basement. The ideal temperature for fermenting biga is 54°F / 12°C. If you're in a very warm place, you can leave it out at room temperature for a couple of hours, then place it in the refrigerator.

Rye Breads
& Pan Loaves

I've put this chapter, on pan loaves and my favorite rye breads, first because this technique is surprisingly easy to master, and the result is pretty spectacular.

The mixing process is very straightforward, and the dough ferments right in the pan for just a few hours before you put it in the oven. Though they may not look like the sexy slashed wheat loaves that have become synonymous with sourdough, these loaves *are* very much sourdough loaves.

Rye was a kind of new starting place for me. After spending years focused mostly on wheat in America, I was excited and intrigued to work on rye bread when I moved to Denmark. I mean *real* rye bread: bread made with rye, not what usually passes for rye bread in the US and UK: wheat bread with a sprinkle of rye flour in it.

Growing up in the UK, and bringing up my own kids in the US, I know the bread most people start out on is sliced white sandwich bread. Even my own kids would pick "Mom's bread" from a plastic bag over a fresh loaf I had just baked, totally breaking my heart. Now that their tastes are maturing, my bread is more popular, but for little children, the lure of sweet, bland softness is a killer winner. And you can easily get hooked. We hold on to a deep nostalgia for the food we grow up with, even when we know, like that bread, it's quite shit, nutritionally speaking.

In Denmark, their addiction is to something very different. They grow up on rye bread and build their emotional connection there. Rye bread is what nearly everyone chooses first. It's what people mean when they say the word *bread*. Unless you are an absolute freak of a child, rye is what you want in your Danish lunch box.

When I worked at Tartine, we made what we called a Danish rye, and while it had lots of great flavor and ingredients, it was a mix of rye and spelt. The starter was made from wheat, and the fermentation method was similar to that of regular sourdough bread. I had never eaten a 100% rye bread that I thought was delicious until I arrived in Copenhagen.

I thought the only reason people would make 100% rye bread was because they didn't have access to the right wheat flour. Of course I was wrong. Eating and learning to bake these breads was like discovering a whole new alphabet.

Bread made with 100% rye flour opens up new worlds of flavor and texture. The good stuff is moist and firm, like a delicious British fruitcake. Biting into a slice, it's particularly toothsome, especially with butter. The denseness of the rye holds up to *slices* of creamy butter, as thick as cheese. Ideally you want to see your teeth marks evenly deep through both bread and butter. They even have a word for it in Danish: *tandsmør,* or "tooth butter."

Then there's the chew. It's not brittle or mealy, but deep, soft, and satisfying. And it's packed full of complex flavors. You get the maltiness of a great pint of ale, dark chocolate notes, a tart tang, toasted seed flavors, nuttiness, and rich umami.

Thinly sliced rye forms the basis of smørrebrød, the much-beloved Danish open-faced sandwich topped with anything from pickled herring and lump fish roe to cheese, raw beef, and egg. I love it as toast with Marmite or marmalade, and it makes a beautiful fried egg sandwich with crispy onions and chilies. I also crumble the bread, toasting it in a pan with butter, then use it to top all kinds of things, such as salad, mashed potatoes, anything that could do with a little crunch. The possibilities are endless.

In order to make rye, I had to learn a completely new way of fermentation for me, which I found super exciting.

You have to think differently about rye. There is no stretchy gluten network in rye flour (although there is some gluten). You're not looking for a light, airy loaf but a uniform density, supported by the pan that it's proofed and baked in. Instead of using long, slow fermentation to build flavor, texture, and structure, as I do with wheat, this is a fast process, no more than a couple of hours. The flavor comes from the rye itself, the starter, and the delicious ingredients added to the dough, like seeds, malt, and miso.

The following recipes are all variations on a common method: mix and ferment a rye starter; combine it with rye flour, water, and other ingredients; let that ferment for a few hours; bake and cool. This last step is crucial. The loaf needs to cool to the very center to set. If you slice it still warm, the bread will be unfinished and gummy. The smell of a freshly baked loaf is irresistible, of course, and I certainly wouldn't blame you for slicing off an outer edge and having a little taste, with a lot of butter.

Super Seed Rye Bread

When I first arrived in Copenhagen, René Redzepi, my business partner who helped me get set up in Denmark, said, "You need to get the Danes to fall in love with your rye bread. Then they will fall in love with you." Super Seed Rye Bread is my love letter to Copenhagen.

This is a complex loaf. The crust, covered with seeds, is super crunchy, and although the bread is dense, the crumb is tender and chewy. Its flavor comes from many sources: rye flour and starter, malt powder and syrup, dark stout, four different seeds, and miso.

I started by testing all the local rye bread. I began to experiment with different types of rye flour, and adding various things to my test loaves, racking my brain for a winning combination. I knew that it needed dark beer for flavor, and a ton of seeds. I don't toast the seeds because that creates too strong a flavor that overpowers the other elements. The seeds on the outside of the bread do get toasted during baking, enhancing the nutty flavors.

Danish rye bread is very dark in color thanks to the dark malt powder. It's bitter on its own, like dark-roast coffee, but it gives the bread an intense depth of flavor. I use miso to add an extra umami boost.

DOUGH

BAKER'S %	WEIGHT	INGREDIENT
100%	188g	Rye flour
100%	188g	12-hour rye starter (see page 69)
50%	94g	Sunflower seeds
25%	47g	Flaxseeds
25%	47g	Ground flaxseeds
15%	28g	Sesame seeds
15%	28g	Pumpkin seeds
5.5%	10g	Salt
2%	4g	Dark malt powder
105%	193g	Hot water (104°F / 40°C)
30%	56g	Dark stout
12%	22g	Malt syrup
5%	9g	Dark barley miso

ADDITIONAL INGREDIENTS

Butter* (enough to coat the inside of the loaf pan)

A handful each of sunflower, flax, sesame, and pumpkin seeds (enough to coat the loaf)

I prefer butter because it sticks well to the sides of the pan, but if you don't eat butter, use another fat of your choice.

TIMING

Mix dough, shape loaf, ferment for 2 to 4 hours, and bake for about 1 hour: 4 to 6 hours total

EQUIPMENT

Loaf pan (5 × 9 inches / 13 × 20cm), flexible plastic dough scraper, bowl or pitcher of warm water (for rinsing), large mixing bowl, digital thermometer, tea towel, sheet pan or shallow roasting pan, cooling rack

Mix the dough: Coat the inside of a loaf pan with butter (or other fat).

Make sure your dough scraper and a bowl of warm water are close at hand.

In a large bowl, combine all the dough ingredients. Use your hands to mix it all together gently to form a thick dough with no dry streaks of flour remaining. The texture will be similar to a wet and sticky Play-Doh. Use the scraper to scrape the dough from your hands back into the bowl. Rinse your hands in the warm water, along with your scraper.

Shape the dough: Wet your hands, loosen the dough from the bowl with your scraper, and, as if you are shaping clay, squidge the dough together into one mass. Use both hands to shape the dough into an oblong that's more or less the shape of the loaf pan but slightly less wide. This dough is easy to manipulate and very forgiving, so don't worry if you need to mess around with it a bit to get it into the shape.

On a wide plate, combine the additional handfuls of sunflower, flax, sesame, and pumpkin seeds and roll the loaf in the seeds so that it is well coated.

Gently set the loaf into the buttered pan and take its temperature, adjusting it as necessary by setting the pan in a bowl of hot, warm, or cool water to bring it to about 82°F / 28°C. (See Controlling Temperature, page 52.)

Ferment the loaf: Let the loaf ferment, covered with a tea towel, for 2 to 4 hours, making sure to keep it warm. When it's ready to bake, it will have risen by 30% and will have 2mm-wide cracks.

Bake the loaf: Place a sheet pan or shallow roasting pan on the floor of the oven. Arrange a rack in the center of the oven.

Preheat the oven to 425°F / 220°C.

Place the loaf in the oven and add about 250ml water to the pan on the oven's floor, taking care to avoid exposing your skin directly to the resultant steam, which can burn.

Bake the loaf for 30 minutes, then rotate the pan front to back and bake for another 30 minutes. The seeds on top will be nicely toasted and fragrant. Use an instant-read thermometer to take the internal temperature of the loaf. It should read 203°F / 95°C. If it's not quite there, give it a few more minutes. Remove the bread from the oven, then turn it out onto a rack to cool for several hours before slicing.

Everyday Rye Bread

MAKES ONE 1-KILOGRAM LOAF

I put this on the menu at Hart Bageri because Super Seed Rye Bread (page 82) is popular but very expensive to make. I wanted to keep it affordable, and the food cost margin was killing us. I needed a rye bread that was delicious, with fewer expensive ingredients. Everyday Rye Bread is a simpler loaf. It's darker, with more malt powder; it uses fewer seeds but is boosted by cooked rye berries.

It's still very much a Danish-style rye bread: rich and complex. Sliced thin, it makes a wonderful base for sandwiches, and as a bonus, it's great for any little (or big) kids who get freaked out by too many seeds.

DOUGH

BAKER'S %	WEIGHT	INGREDIENT
100%	262g	Rye flour
100%	262g	12-hour rye starter (see page 69)
100%	262g	Hot water (104°F / 40°C)
3.75%	10g	Salt
5%	13g	Dark malt powder
25%	70g	Sunflower seeds
25%	70g	Flaxseeds
30%	79g	Cooked rye berries (see Cooked Whole Grains, page 106)

ADDITIONAL INGREDIENT

Butter* (enough to coat the inside of the loaf pan)

A handful of rye flour (for dusting the top of the loaf)

I prefer butter because it sticks well to the sides of the pan, but if you don't eat butter, use another fat of your choice.

TIMING

Cook and cool rye berries, mix dough, shape loaf, ferment for 2 to 4 hours, and bake for about 1 hour: 4 to 6 hours total

EQUIPMENT

Loaf pan (5 × 9 inches / 13 × 20cm), flexible plastic dough scraper, bowl or pitcher of warm water (for rinsing), large mixing bowl, digital thermometer, tea towel, sheet pan or shallow roasting pan, cooling rack

Mix the dough: Coat the inside of a loaf pan with butter (or other fat).

Make sure your dough scraper and a bowl or pitcher of warm water are close at hand.

In a large bowl, combine all the dough ingredients and use your hands to mix it all together gently to form a thick dough with no dry streaks of flour remaining, at which point you can consider the dough sufficiently mixed. The texture will be similar to a rather wet and sticky Play-Doh. Use the plastic scraper to scrape the dough from your hands back into the bowl, and rinse your hands in the bowl of warm water, along with your scraper.

Shape the dough: Wet your hands, loosen the dough from the bowl with your scraper, and, as if you are shaping clay, squidge the dough together into one mass, then use both hands to shape it into an oblong that's more or less the shape of the loaf pan but slightly less wide. This dough is easy to manipulate and very forgiving, so don't worry if you need to mess around with it a bit to get it into the shape.

Gently set the loaf into the buttered pan and take its temperature, adjusting it as necessary by setting the pan in a bowl of hot, warm, or cool water to bring it to about 82°F / 28°C. (See Controlling Temperature, page 52.) Evenly dust the top of the loaf with rye flour.

Ferment the loaf: Let the loaf ferment, covered with a tea towel, for 2 to 4 hours, making sure to keep it warm. When it's ready to bake, it will have risen by 30% and will have 2mm-wide cracks.

Bake the loaf: Place a sheet pan or shallow roasting pan on the floor of the oven. Arrange a rack in the center of the oven. Preheat the oven to 425°F / 220°C.

Place the loaf in the oven and add about 250ml water to the pan on the oven's floor, taking care to avoid exposing your skin directly to the resultant steam, which can burn.

Bake the loaf for 30 minutes, then rotate the pan front to back and bake for another 30 minutes. Use an instant-read thermometer to take the internal temperature of the loaf. It should read 203°F / 95°C. If it's not quite there, give it a few more minutes. Remove the bread from the oven, then turn it out onto a rack to cool for several hours before slicing.

Miso Rye

MAKES ONE 900-GRAM LOAF

The first time I made this bread was in the test bakery I set up at Noma, when I was still looking for a home for Hart Bageri.

The team invited me to taste all their ferments and magical creations. They had a miso made from leftover rye bread, called Ryeso. When I tasted it, I knew it had to go in a rye bread, completing the circle. I love the super-umami flavor of miso. I wondered how much I could cram into the dough without killing the fermentation. It turned out that 35% was the sweet spot.

There is less salt in this recipe than in any other rye loaves because miso is salty. You can make this bread with any miso you like. If you want to exceed 35% miso, go for it, but scale back your salt a bit so that you don't slow the fermentation too much.

DOUGH

BAKER'S %	WEIGHT	INGREDIENT
100%	208g	Rye flour
100%	208g	12-hour rye starter (see page 69)
100%	208g	Hot water (104°F / 40°C)
2%	4g	Salt
5%	10g	Dark malt powder
35%	73g	Miso
50%	104g	Cooked rye berries (see Cooked Whole Grains, page 106)
20%	42g	Flaxseeds
20%	42g	Sunflower seeds

ADDITIONAL INGREDIENT

Butter* (enough to coat the inside of the loaf pan)

A handful of rye flour (for dusting the top of the loaf)

I prefer butter because it sticks well to the sides of the pan, but if you don't eat butter, use another fat of your choice.

TIMING

Cook and cool rye berries, mix dough, shape loaf, ferment for 2 to 4 hours, and bake for about 1 hour: 4 to 6 hours total

EQUIPMENT

Loaf pan (5 × 9 inches / 13 × 20cm), flexible plastic dough scraper, bowl or pitcher of warm water (for rinsing), large mixing bowl, digital thermometer tea towel, sheet pan or shallow roasting pan, cooling rack

Mix the dough: Coat the inside of a loaf pan with butter (or other fat).

Make sure your dough scraper and a bowl or pitcher of warm water are close at hand.

In a large bowl, combine all the dough ingredients and use your hands to mix it all together gently to form a thick dough with no dry streaks of flour remaining, at which point you can consider the dough sufficiently mixed. The texture will be like a wet and sticky Play-Doh. Scrape the dough from your hands back into the bowl, and rinse your hands in the bowl of warm water, along with your scraper.

Shape the dough: Wet your hands, loosen the dough from the bowl with your scraper, and, as if you are shaping clay, squidge the dough together into one mass, then use both hands to shape it into an oblong that's more or less the shape of the loaf pan but slightly less wide. This dough is easy to manipulate and very forgiving, so don't worry if you need to mess around with it a bit to get it into the shape.

Gently set the loaf into the buttered pan and take its temperature, adjusting it as necessary by setting the pan in a bowl of hot, warm, or cool water to bring it to about 82°F / 28°C. (See Controlling Temperature, page 52.)

Ferment the loaf: Let the loaf ferment covered with a tea towel for 2 to 4 hours, making sure to keep it warm. When it's ready to bake, it will have risen by 30% and will have 2mm-wide cracks.

Bake the loaf: Place a sheet pan or shallow roasting pan on the floor of the oven. Arrange a rack in the center of the oven. Preheat the oven to 425°F / 220°C.

Place the loaf in the oven and add about 250ml water to the pan on the oven's floor, taking care to avoid exposing your skin directly to the resultant steam, which can burn.

Bake the loaf for 30 minutes, then rotate the pan front to back and bake for another 30 minutes. Use an instant-read thermometer to take the internal temperature of the loaf. It should read 203°F / 95°C. If it's not quite there, give it a few more minutes. Remove the bread from the oven, then turn it out onto a rack to cool for several hours before slicing.

Naked Rye

MAKES ONE 900-GRAM LOAF

One day I thought, *If everyone in Copenhagen is so crazy about rye bread, I'll make them a pure, stripped-back rye that's just rye, starter, water, and salt.* Rye alone has such a beautiful flavor: deeply earthy, nutty, grassy, and naturally sweet. I wanted to let it sing on its own.

I thought this version would sell really well, but in Denmark, my customers wanted what they knew as rye bread, *Danish* rye bread, with seeds, and that characteristic malt flavor. I still love this bread, regardless. And this book is for everyone, all over the world, so, rye lovers, this is for you.

DOUGH

BAKER'S %	WEIGHT	INGREDIENT
100%	285g	Rye flour
100%	285g	12-hour rye starter (see page 69)
62%	177g	Hot water (104°F / 40°C)
3.5%	10g	Salt
50%	143g	Cooked rye berries (see Cooked Whole Grains, page 106)

ADDITIONAL INGREDIENTS

Butter* (enough to coat the inside of the loaf pan)

A handful of rye flour (for dusting the top of the loaf)

* I prefer butter because it sticks well to the sides of the pan, but if you don't eat butter, use another fat of your choice.

TIMING

Cook and cool rye berries, mix dough, shape loaf, ferment for 2 to 4 hours, and bake for about 1 hour: 4 to 6 hours total

EQUIPMENT

Loaf pan (5 × 9 inches / 13 × 20cm), flexible plastic dough scraper, bowl or pitcher of warm water (for rinsing), large mixing bowl, digital thermometer, tea towel, sheet pan or shallow roasting pan, cooling rack

Mix the dough: Coat the inside of a loaf pan with butter (or other fat). Make sure your dough scraper and a bowl or pitcher of warm water are close at hand.

In a large bowl, combine all the dough ingredients and use your hands to mix it all together gently to form a thick dough with no dry streaks of flour remaining, at which point you can consider the dough sufficiently mixed. The texture will be similar to a rather wet and sticky Play-Doh. Use the plastic scraper to scrape the dough from your hands back into the bowl, and rinse your hands in the bowl of warm water, along with your scraper.

Shape the dough: Wet your hands, loosen the dough from the bowl with your scraper, and, as if you are shaping clay, squidge the dough together into one mass, then use both hands to shape it into an oblong that's more or less the shape of the loaf pan but slightly less wide. This dough is easy to manipulate and very forgiving, so don't worry if you need to mess around with it a bit to get it into the shape.

Gently set the loaf into the buttered pan and take its temperature, adjusting it as necessary by setting the pan in a bowl of hot, warm, or cool water to bring it to about 82°F / 28°C. (See Controlling Temperature, page 52.) Dust the top of the dough with a sprinkle of rye flour held at chest height for an even coating.

Ferment the loaf: Let the loaf ferment, covered with a tea towel, for 2 to 4 hours, making sure to keep it warm. When it's ready to bake, it will have risen by 30% and will have 2mm-wide cracks.

Bake the loaf: Place a sheet pan or shallow roasting pan on the floor of the oven. Arrange a rack in the center of the oven. Preheat the oven to 425°F / 220°C.

Place the loaf in the oven and add about 250ml water to the pan on the oven's floor, taking care to avoid exposing your skin directly to the resultant steam, which can burn.

Bake the loaf for 30 minutes, then rotate the pan front to back and bake for another 30 minutes. Use an instant-read thermometer to take the internal temperature of the loaf. It should read 203°F / 95°C. If it's not quite there, give it a few more minutes. Remove the bread from the oven, then turn it out onto a rack to cool for several hours before slicing.

Buttermilk Rye

MAKES ONE 1-KILOGRAM LOAF

In addition to the earthy rye and the sweet, complex malt, this loaf has a creamy, almost yogurt tartness from toasted oats that have been soaked in buttermilk. The buttermilk hydrates the dough, and that additional fat gives the bread a slightly softer texture.

TOASTED OATS

BAKER'S %	WEIGHT	INGREDIENT
50%	125g	Rolled oats
100%	250g	Buttermilk

DOUGH

BAKER'S %	WEIGHT	INGREDIENT
100%	250g	Rye flour
100%	250g	12-hour rye starter (see page 69)
3%	8g	Salt
10%	25g	Malt syrup

ADDITIONAL INGREDIENTS

Butter (enough to coat the inside of the loaf pan)

100g rolled oats (for coating the loaf)

TIMING

Day 1: Toast and soak oats overnight.

Day 2: Mix dough, shape loaf, ferment for 2 to 4 hours, and bake for about 1 hour: 4 to 6 hours total

EQUIPMENT

Sheet pan or shallow roasting pan, large mixing bowl, loaf pan (5 × 9 inches / 13 × 20cm), flexible plastic dough scraper, bowl or pitcher of warm water (for rinsing), digital thermometer, tea towel, cooling rack

DAY 1

Toast and soak the oats: Preheat the oven to 480°F / 250°C.

Arrange the oats in a single layer on a sheet pan and toast for 5 to 7 minutes, until they are golden brown and have a nutty smell. Keep a close eye on them; they can go from toasted to burned fairly quickly.

Transfer the oats to a large bowl and cover with the buttermilk. Stir well, cover, and let this mixture soak, refrigerated, overnight.

DAY 2

Mix the dough: Remove the oats from the refrigerator and let them come to room temperature.

Coat the inside of a loaf pan with butter.

Make sure your dough scraper and a bowl or pitcher of warm water are close at hand.

Once the oats are at room temperature, add all the dough ingredients. Mix it all gently by hand to form a thick dough with no dry streaks of flour remaining, at which point you can consider the dough sufficiently mixed. The texture will be similar to a wet and sticky Play-Doh. Scrape the dough from your hands back into the bowl, and rinse your hands in the warm water, along with your scraper.

Shape the dough: Wet your hands, loosen the dough from the bowl with your scraper, and, as if you are shaping clay, squidge the dough together into a mass, then shape it into an oblong that's more or less the shape of the loaf pan but slightly less wide. It is easy to manipulate and very forgiving, so don't worry if you need to mess around with it a bit to get it into the shape.

Roll the loaf in the additional oats to cover completely.

Gently set the loaf into the buttered pan and take its temperature, adjusting it as necessary by setting the pan in a bowl of hot, warm, or cool water to bring it to about 82°F / 28°C. (See Controlling Temperature, page 52.)

Ferment the loaf: Let the loaf ferment, covered with a tea towel, for 2 to 4 hours, making sure to keep it warm. When it's ready to bake, it will have risen by 30% and will have 2mm-wide cracks.

Bake the loaf: Place a sheet pan or shallow roasting pan on the floor of the oven. Arrange a rack in the center of the oven. Preheat the oven to 425°F / 220°C.

Place the loaf in the oven and add about 250ml water to the pan on the oven's floor, taking care to avoid exposing your skin directly to the resultant steam, which can burn.

Bake for 30 minutes, then rotate and bake for another 30 minutes. The oats should be toasted and fragrant. Use an instant-read thermometer to take the internal temperature of the loaf. When it's 203°F / 95°C, remove the bread from the oven, then turn it out onto a rack to cool for several hours before slicing.

100% Rye Marble Rye

MAKES ONE 1-KILOGRAM LOAF

For years I have been in love with marble rye, which is basically a wheat dough with a small amount of rye in it. I thought, *Wouldn't it be cool to make a 100% rye marble rye?*

This bread is made with two rye doughs—one made dark with malt powder and syrup, the other left light—marbled and fermented together in one pan.

DARK DOUGH

BAKER'S %	WEIGHT	INGREDIENT
100%	162g	Rye flour
62%	100g	Hot water (104°F / 40°C)
90%	146g	12-hour rye starter (see page 69)
10%	16g	Dark malt powder
10%	16g	Malt syrup
30%	49g	Cooked rye berries (see Cooked Whole Grains, page 106)
3.5%	6g	Salt
3%	5g	Caraway seeds

LIGHT DOUGH

BAKER'S %	WEIGHT	INGREDIENT
100%	162g	Rye flour
62%	100g	Hot water (104°F / 40°C)
90%	145g	12-hour rye starter (see page 69)
50%	81g	Cooked rye berries
3.5%	6g	Salt
3%	5g	Caraway seeds

ADDITIONAL INGREDIENT

Butter* (enough to coat the inside of the loaf pan)

* I prefer butter because it sticks well to the sides of the pan, but if you don't eat butter, use another fat of your choice.

TIMING

Cook and cool rye berries, mix dough, shape loaf, ferment for 2 to 4 hours, and bake for about 1 hour: 4 to 6 hours total

EQUIPMENT

Loaf pan (5 × 9 inches / 13 × 20cm), flexible plastic dough scraper, bowl or pitcher of warm water (for rinsing), two large mixing bowls, digital thermometer, tea towel, sheet pan or shallow roasting pan, cooling rack

Mix the doughs: Coat the inside of a loaf pan with butter (or other fat).

Make sure your dough scraper and a bowl or pitcher of warm water are close at hand.

Work in separate batches, to create two separate doughs, the dark and the light.

In one large bowl, combine all the dark dough ingredients and use your hands to mix it all together gently to form a thick dough with no dry streaks of flour remaining, at which point you can consider the dough sufficiently mixed. The texture will be similar to a rather wet and sticky Play-Doh. Use the plastic scraper to scrape the dough from your hands back into the bowl, and rinse your hands in the bowl of warm water, along with your scraper.

In the other large bowl, repeat the procedure above with the light dough ingredients.

Shape the dough: Use one hand to remove a handful of the dark dough from its bowl and gently press it into one corner of the buttered pan. Do the same with a handful of the light dough, pressing it into another section of the pan. Continue building your loaf, alternating the dark and light doughs in whatever pattern you like.

Take its temperature, adjusting it as necessary by setting it in a bowl of hot, warm, or cool water to bring it to about 82°F / 28°C. (See Controlling Temperature, page 52.)

Ferment the loaf: Let the loaf ferment, covered with a tea towel, for 2 to 4 hours, making sure to keep it warm. When it's ready to bake, it will have risen by 30% and will have 2mm-wide cracks.

Bake the loaf: Place a sheet pan or shallow roasting pan on the floor of the oven. Arrange a rack in the center of the oven. Preheat the oven to 425°F / 220°C.

Place the loaf in the oven and add about 250ml water to the pan on the oven's floor, taking care to avoid exposing your skin directly to the resultant steam, which can burn.

Bake the loaf for 30 minutes, then rotate the pan front to back and bake for another 30 minutes. Use an instant-read thermometer to take the internal temperature of the loaf. It should read 203°F / 95°C. If it's not quite there, give it a few more minutes. Remove the bread from the oven, then turn it out onto a rack to cool for several hours before slicing.

Rye Wrapped in Fig Leaves

MAKES ONE 900-GRAM LOAF

I created this bread in Israel with Henrietta Lovell, my love. We were invited to do an event that turned out to be a true collaboration, with a lovely man and great chef, Ezra Kedem, in his studio/restaurant, called Arcadia, close to Jerusalem.

We paired Ezra's food with my bread and Henrietta's iced oolong tea, blended with fresh garden herbs. (If you know anything about Henrietta, you'll know she is the drinks master, with the most amazing palate. They call her the Tea Lady, but her love and skill extend way beyond tea.)

Arcadia is set on a rural farm, on a beautiful mountainside with spectacular views. The day before the event, I walked around the kitchen garden, totally inspired by what they were growing. I thought that making a rye bread with Ezra's seasonal farm ingredients was the way to bring our worlds together.

He had a few fig trees on the property, and I wondered what it would be like to line the bread pans with the leaves. It looked amazing and added a great flavor, almost a coconut scent. To make it even more figgy, I've added dried figs to this recipe, soaked in tea as a tribute to that day.

TEA-SOAKED FIGS

BAKER'S %	WEIGHT	INGREDIENTS
100%	120g	Dried figs
100%	120g	Freshly brewed black tea

DOUGH

BAKER'S %	WEIGHT	INGREDIENTS
80%	192g	Rye flour
20%	48g	Whole wheat flour
100%	240g	12-hour rye starter (see page 69)
60%	144g	Warm water (82°F / 28°C)
25%	60g	Yogurt
4%	10g	Salt
25%	60g	Coarsely chopped walnuts
60%	145g	Tea-soaked figs (above)

ADDITIONAL INGREDIENT

Fresh fig leaves

TIMING

Soak figs, mix dough, shape loaf, ferment for 2 to 4 hours, and bake for about 1 hour: 4½ to 6½ hours total

EQUIPMENT

Two large mixing bowls, loaf pan (5 × 9 inches / 13 × 20cm), flexible plastic dough scraper, bowl or pitcher of warm water (for rinsing), digital thermometer, tea towel, sheet pan or shallow roasting pan, cooling rack

Soak the figs in tea: Coarsely chop the figs and place them in a bowl. Pour the hot tea over them and let them soak for 30 minutes. Drain the fruit and set it aside. (If you like, you can drink the tea, or make a black tea and fig syrup by adding sugar in a 1-to-1 ratio and reducing it over high heat.)

Mix the dough: Line the loaf pan completely with the fig leaves, overlapping them as necessary so that there are no gaps.

Make sure your dough scraper and a bowl or pitcher of warm water are close at hand.

In a large bowl, combine all the dough ingredients, including the soaked figs, and use your hands to mix it all together gently to form a thick dough with no dry streaks of flour remaining, at which point you can consider the dough sufficiently mixed. The texture will be similar to a rather wet and sticky Play-Doh. Use the plastic scraper to scrape the dough from your hands back into the bowl, and rinse your hands in the bowl of warm water, along with your scraper.

Shape the dough: Wet your hands, loosen the dough from the bowl with your scraper, and, as if you are shaping clay, squidge the dough together into one mass, then use both hands to shape it into an oblong that's more or less the shape of the loaf pan but slightly less wide. This dough is easy to manipulate and very forgiving, so don't worry if you need to mess around with it a bit to get it into the shape.

Gently set the loaf into the fig leaf–lined pan and take its temperature, adjusting it as necessary by setting the pan in a bowl of hot, warm, or cool water to bring it to about 82°F / 28°C. (See Controlling Temperature, page 52.) Pat down any fig leaves that may be jutting out above the level of the dough, enveloping the top surface of the loaf with them.

Ferment the loaf: Let the loaf ferment, covered with a tea towel, for 2 to 4 hours, making sure to keep it warm. When it's ready to bake, it will have risen by 30% and will have 2mm-wide cracks.

Bake the loaf: Place a sheet pan or shallow roasting pan on the floor of the oven. Arrange a rack in the center of the oven. Preheat the oven to 425°F / 220°C.

Place the loaf in the oven and add about 250ml water to the pan on the oven's floor, taking care to avoid exposing your skin directly to the resultant steam, which can burn.

Bake the loaf for 30 minutes, then rotate the pan front to back and bake for another 30 minutes. Use an instant-read thermometer to take the internal temperature of the loaf. It should read 203°F / 95°C. If it's not quite there, give it a few more minutes. Remove the bread from the oven, then turn it out onto a rack to cool for several hours before slicing. Remove the fig leaves before serving; they will have imparted a lovely fig flavor to the bread but are bitter on their own.

Pumpernickel Pan Loaf

MAKES ONE 850-GRAM LOAF

This is a German bread, and I find it fascinating that it uses no flour. It's made with cracked and cooked whole rye berries, and it's nothing like the tasteless cardboard plank breads you come across in supermarkets with German names and pictures on the label of people doing athletic activities and wearing cutting-edge 1970s sporting gear. This recipe was given to me by a friend, Monika Walecka, a fantastic baker I met in San Francisco, who now has a brilliant bakery in Warsaw. She coined the phrase "rye high" for the hit you get from the aroma of the freshly baked loaf. The malt smell is phenomenal. The whole thing turns to a sticky, rich, dark, caramel deliciousness.

This bread, once baked, needs to mature for a week or so in the fridge, where it will then keep for weeks.

It couldn't be easier to assemble, but it does take its time, with an extremely long bake, at low temperature, for 24 hours. I bake it in my oven at home, because I don't have an oven free for that long at the bakery. It fills my home with that amazing "rye high."

If you can't find cracked rye in a store, it's easy to crack your own using a tabletop mill or pulsing it in a heavy-duty blender.

DOUGH

BAKER'S %	WEIGHT	INGREDIENT
100%	375g	Cracked rye
53%	199g	Cooked rye berries (see Cooked Whole Grains, page 106)
60%	225g	Warm water (82°F / 28°C)
2%	8g	12-hour rye starter (see page 69)
2%	8g	Salt
12%	45g	Malt syrup

ADDITIONAL INGREDIENT

Butter* (enough to coat the inside of the loaf pan)

* I prefer butter because it sticks well to the sides of the pan, but if you don't eat butter, use another fat of your choice.

TIMING

Day 1: Cook and cool rye berries, mix and ferment dough for 1 hour, and begin baking.

Days 2 and 3: Finish baking and cool the bread.

Days 3 through 9: Let the bread mature for a week before eating.

EQUIPMENT

Large mixing bowl, loaf pan (5 × 9 inches / 13 × 20cm), parchment paper, flexible plastic dough scraper, two tea towels, sheet pan, foil, cooling rack

DAY 1

Mix and ferment the dough: In a large bowl, combine all the dough ingredients and mix well with your hands. Let the mixture sit at room temperature for 1 hour.

Shape the dough: Butter the inside of the loaf pan and line the bottom and sides with parchment paper. You need enough overhang to cover the top of the dough completely. Use the dough scraper to transfer the mixture to the pan and distribute it evenly. Fold the parchment over the top of the loaf.

Bake the loaf: Preheat the oven to 210°F / 100°C.

Drench two tea towels in water. On a sheet pan, place one of the completely soaked towels. Put the loaf pan on top and cover it with the second soaked towel. Wrap the whole thing in foil. Bake for 24 hours.

DAYS 2 AND 3

Cool the bread: Remove the pan from the oven, take off the foil and the towels, and let the bread cool for an hour or so in the pan. Carefully invert the pan onto a rack to release the bread. Let the whole thing cool completely overnight, or until you're certain the center is no longer warm (otherwise, once wrapped, it might mold).

DAYS 3 THROUGH 9

Mature the bread: Wrap the cool loaf in foil and let it mature in the fridge for a week before slicing and eating. You might think, *No way*, but that is what I have been advised, and what I have always followed. The bread will keep, wrapped, in the fridge for weeks. You can eat it sliced cold, at room temperature, or toasted—whatever your preference.

Multigrain Pan Loaf, Pumpernickel Style

TIMING

Day 1: Cook and cool rye berries, mix and ferment dough for 1 hour, and begin baking.

Days 2 and 3: Finish baking and cool the bread.

Days 3 through 9: Let the bread mature for a week before eating.

EQUIPMENT

Large mixing bowl, loaf pan (5 × 9 inches / 13 × 20cm), parchment paper, flexible plastic dough scraper, two tea towels, sheet pan, foil, cooling rack

MAKES ONE 1-KILOGRAM LOAF

The way my brain works, when I learn a new method, I get all these ideas about how I can use it in new ways, with different grains or flours. This recipe and the next one (Barley Bread, Pumpernickel Style, Test #1) follow the exact same method as the Pumpernickel Pan Loaf in the previous recipe, but using a variety of grains and barley, respectively. The very slow baking tends to impart the grains with a caramelly, malty flavor and a sticky, rich texture.

DAY 1

Mix and ferment the dough: In a large bowl, combine all the dough ingredients and mix well with your hands. Let the mixture sit at room temperature for 1 hour.

Shape the dough: Butter the inside of the loaf pan and line the bottom and sides with parchment paper. You need enough overhang to cover the top of the dough completely. Use the dough scraper to transfer the mixture to the pan and distribute it evenly. Fold the parchment over the top of the loaf.

Bake the loaf: Preheat the oven to 210°F / 100°C.

Drench two tea towels in water. On a sheet pan, place one of the completely soaked towels. Put the loaf pan on top and cover it with the second soaked towel. Wrap the whole thing in foil. Bake for 24 hours.

DOUGH

BAKER'S %	WEIGHT	INGREDIENT
100%	166g	Cracked rye
60%	100g	Quinoa
60%	100g	Rolled oats
75%	125g	Toasted rice (see Note)
80%	133g	Cooked rye berries (see Cooked Whole Grains, page 106)
36%	60g	Malt syrup
6%	10g	Salt
6%	10g	12-hour rye starter (see page 69)
180%	300g	Warm water (82°F / 28°C)

DAYS 2 AND 3

Cool the bread: Remove the pan from the oven, take off the foil and the towels, and let the bread cool for an hour or so in the pan. Carefully invert the pan onto a rack to release the bread. Let the whole thing cool completely overnight, or until you're certain the center is no longer warm (otherwise, once wrapped, it might mold).

ADDITIONAL INGREDIENT

Butter* (enough to coat the inside of the loaf pan)

* *I prefer butter because it sticks well to the sides of the pan, but if you don't eat butter, use another fat of your choice.*

DAYS 3 THROUGH 9

Mature the bread: Wrap the cool loaf in foil and let it mature in the fridge for a week before slicing and eating. You might think, *No way*, but that is what I have been advised, and what I have always followed. The bread will keep, wrapped, in the fridge for weeks. You can eat it sliced cold, at room temperature, or toasted—whatever your preference.

NOTE

To toast rice, heat a heavy-bottomed pan over medium-high heat for a few minutes, then add the rice and stir constantly. Monitoring the heat so that the rice doesn't burn, continue to stir until the rice is just turning golden brown and smells toasty and nutty. Immediately remove from the heat. Spread the rice out on a plate to cool.

Barley Bread, Pumpernickel Style, Test #1

MAKES ONE 860-GRAM LOAF

Quite a few years ago, sitting in a London airport, I had a pint of London Pride. To this day, it is still my favorite draft beer. As I sat there, about to go off on my journey, I was struck by this incredible barley aftertaste. It blew me away then, and it still does, every time I take a sip. It got me thinking how I could re-create this intense barley flavor in a bread.

Adding straight barley flour to my sourdough bread is similar to adding straight concrete. It makes it so hard and heavy. There are three barley bread recipes in this book; I'm still trying to find that London Pride taste. I don't think I'm there yet, but these are delicious, and the seeking is what I'm all about.

The texture of this bread is the same as the previous two loaves, with a lot of chew from the grains, and this specific bread has a lot of great malt flavor from the long, slow bake.

DOUGH

BAKER'S %	WEIGHT	INGREDIENT
100%	375g	Cracked pearl barley
53%	199g	Cooked pearl barley (see Cooked Whole Grains, page 106)
60%	225g	Warm water (82°F / 28°C)
2%	8g	12-hour rye starter (see page 69)
2%	8g	Salt
12%	45g	Malt syrup

ADDITIONAL INGREDIENT

Butter* (enough to coat the inside of the loaf pan)

I prefer butter because it sticks well to the sides of the pan, but if you don't eat butter, use another fat of your choice.

TIMING

Day 1: Cook and cool pearl barley, mix and ferment dough for 1 hour, and begin baking.

Days 2 and 3: Finish baking and cool the bread.

Days 3 through 9: Let the bread mature for a week before eating.

EQUIPMENT

Large mixing bowl, loaf pan (5 × 9 inches / 13 × 20cm), parchment paper, flexible plastic dough scraper, two tea towels, sheet pan, foil, cooling rack

DAY 1

Mix and ferment the dough: In a large bowl, combine all the dough ingredients and mix well with your hands. Let the mixture sit at room temperature for 1 hour.

Shape the dough: Butter the inside of the loaf pan and line the bottom and sides with parchment paper. You need enough overhang to cover the top of the dough completely. Use the dough scraper to transfer the mixture to the pan and distribute it evenly. Fold the parchment over the top of the loaf.

Bake the loaf: Preheat the oven to 210°F / 100°C.

Drench two tea towels in water. On a sheet pan, place one of the completely soaked towels. Put the loaf pan on top and cover it with the second soaked towel. Wrap the whole thing in foil. Bake for 24 hours.

DAYS 2 AND 3

Cool the bread: Remove the pan from the oven, take off the foil and the towels, and let the bread cool for an hour or so in the pan. Carefully invert the pan onto a rack to release the bread. Let the whole thing cool completely overnight, or until you're certain the center is no longer warm (otherwise, once wrapped, it might mold).

DAYS 3 THROUGH 9

Mature the bread: Wrap the cool loaf in foil, and let it mature in the fridge for a week before slicing and eating. You might think, *No way*, but that is what I have been advised, and what I have always followed. The bread will keep, wrapped, in the fridge for weeks. You can eat it sliced cold, at room temperature, or toasted—whatever your preference.

Ballymaloe Brown Yeast Bread

MAKES ONE 900-GRAM LOAF

Some years ago, I taught a bread class with Chad Robertson at Ballymaloe, a cooking school built in the middle of a very beautiful farm in County Cork, Ireland.

We were there for three days, in which time we fell completely in love with the school founder, Darina Allen, and all of her team. She is an incredible woman who has lost none of her joy, energy, or enthusiasm over many decades. I think it's actually grown with the years. Doing something you really love and are truly proud of seems like pretty good rocket fuel.

Recently I returned to Ballymaloe for a wonderful party that lasted three days. I ate this bread every day and was blown away, each time, by how delicious it is. I asked Darina for the recipe to include in this book, and I was truly grateful that she agreed to share it, although she was quick to tell me it wasn't hers. It's based on a loaf created by Doris Grant, a British nutritionist, in the 1940s. The recipe was developed during World War II to help people eat well on their slim wartime rations.

It's a really quick bread to make. From mixing to putting it in the oven, it takes less than an hour, and from start to finish is 2 hours. I don't normally make breads using only yeast, but for this bread, I think it makes the sweetness of the whole wheat shine. It is surprisingly moist for a straight yeast bread, due to the high hydration; it's a great recipe to have if you're in a pinch and would like to have fresh bread.

DOUGH

BAKER'S %	WEIGHT	INGREDIENT
90%	405g	Whole wheat flour
10%	45g	Bread flour
3%	14g	Salt
2%	9g	Malt syrup
95%	425g	Hot water (104°F / 40°C)
1.5%	7g	Instant dry yeast

ADDITIONAL INGREDIENT

Butter* (enough to coat the inside of the loaf pan)

I prefer butter because it sticks well to the sides of the pan, but if you don't eat butter, use another fat of your choice.

TIMING

Mix dough, proof for 30 minutes, and bake for 1 hour: 2 hours total

EQUIPMENT

Mixing bowl, loaf pan (5 × 9 inches / 13 × 20cm), tea towel, digital thermometer, cooling rack

Mix the dough: In a mixing bowl, mix all the dough ingredients together by hand. The dough will be loose and too wet to knead.

Proof the dough: Preheat the oven to 450°F / 230°C.

Brush the sides and bottom of the loaf pan with butter. Scoop the dough into the pan. Put the pan in a warm place, covered with a tea towel, to prevent a skin from forming, and let rise until the dough comes to the top of the pan, about 30 minutes.

Bake the loaf: Bake the loaf for 20 minutes, then reduce the temperature to 400°F / 205°C and bake for 40 more minutes, or until it is nicely browned and has an internal temperature of 203°F / 95°C. Remove the bread from the oven, then turn it out on a rack to cool.

Local Grain Pan Loaf

Mix dough, shape loaf, ferment for 2 to 4 hours, and bake for about 1 hour: 4 to 6 hours total

EQUIPMENT

Loaf pan (5 × 9 inches / 13 × 20cm), flexible plastic dough scraper, bowl or pitcher of warm water (for rinsing), large mixing bowl, digital thermometer, tea towel, sheet pan or shallow roasting pan, cooling rack

MAKES ONE 900-GRAM LOAF

The idea here is that you can make bread using your local wheat, spelt, ancient grain, or whatever interests you, with a high amount of sourdough and a quick fermentation. This method really allows whatever grain you use to shine. I have given many variations, just to show how versatile this formula and method are.

I love making this with ølands flour. It's very unlikely you will find ølands flour, which is from Denmark and Sweden, unless you live in Scandinavia, but it really is just a suggestion to use whatever locally milled flour you can easily find. There are so many interesting varieties of wheat being milled in small batches by dedicated farmers and millers, and the base recipe here is your chance to experiment with them.

As I said earlier in the book (page 40), the local wheat in Denmark wasn't ideal for making my dream sourdough loaf, but it is totally suited for this style of bread, and it's amazingly delicious. The same is true of many other grains, including, hopefully, your favorite local one.

For any of the variations on this recipe, feel free to add a small handful of seeds, nuts, or dried fruit of your choice for added flavor, though you may wish to let the loaves be naked so as to let the flavor of the grains come through.

Mix the dough: Coat the inside of a loaf pan with butter (or other fat).

Make sure your dough scraper and a bowl or pitcher of warm water are close at hand.

In a large bowl, combine all the dough ingredients and use your hands to mix it all together gently to form a thick dough with no dry streaks of flour remaining, at which point you can consider the dough sufficiently mixed. The texture will be similar to a rather wet and sticky Play-Doh. Use the plastic scraper to scrape the dough from your hands back into the bowl, and rinse your hands in the bowl of warm water, along with your scraper.

Shape the dough: Wet your hands, loosen the dough from the bowl with your scraper, and squidge the dough together into one mass. Scoop it straight into the prepared pan.

Take the dough's temperature, adjusting it by setting the pan in a bowl of hot, warm, or cool water as necessary to bring it to about 82°F / 28°C. (See Controlling Temperature, page 52.)

Ferment the loaf: Let the loaf ferment, covered with a tea towel, for 2 to 4 hours, making sure to keep it warm. When it's ready to bake, it will have expanded to about double its original volume and be close to the top of the pan.

Bake the loaf: Place a sheet pan or shallow roasting pan on the floor of the oven. Arrange a rack in the center of the oven. Preheat the oven to 425°F / 220°C.

Place the loaf in the oven and add about 250ml water to the pan on the oven's floor, taking care to avoid exposing your skin directly to the resultant steam, which can burn.

Bake the loaf for 30 minutes, then rotate the pan front to back and bake for another 20 minutes. Use an instant-read thermometer to take the internal temperature of the loaf. It should read 203°F / 95°C. If it's not quite there, give it a few more minutes. Remove the bread from the oven, then turn it out onto a rack to cool for 1 hour before slicing.

DOUGH

BAKER'S %	WEIGHT	INGREDIENT
100%	330g	Emmer, ølands, spelt, or other flour of your choice
100%	330g	12-hour adjusted starter (see Adjusting the Starter, on page 106)
70%	231g	Warm water (86°F / 30°C)
3%	10g	Salt

ADDITIONAL INGREDIENT

Butter* (enough to coat the inside of the loaf pan)

I prefer butter because it sticks well to the sides of the pan, but if you don't eat butter, use another fat of your choice.

Cooked Whole Grains

I love adding whole grains—as in the whole berries—to bread dough to add a bit of texture and a different expression of the grain that we often bake as flour. In California, I experimented with using sprouted rye grains in various rye breads, but I could never get the rye berry to soften up enough to make it a pleasant eating experience. Eating a too-hard berry in an otherwise tender loaf is similar to chomping down on an unpopped kernel of popcorn. Add to that high bread baking temperatures, which make irrelevant the health benefits of eating sprouted grains anyway.

In Copenhagen, I decided to start cooking grains, including rye berries, before adding them to dough.

This is the method for cooking whole grains to be added to any of the pan loaves or breads, and the principle, no matter which grain you use, is the same: Bring the grains to a boil in plenty of unsalted water, then cook them at a simmer until they are very tender. The timing will likely vary, depending on the grain.

You may be tempted to salt the water, as you might if you were making a grain salad or soup. For bread baking, however, it's best to cook these grains in unsalted water to avoid having an oversalted dough, which will slow down fermentation.

INGREDIENTS

Whole grains, such as rye berries, pearl barley, wheat berries, or farro

In a medium pot, cover the grains by a few inches with water and bring to a boil. Reduce the heat to a simmer and let them cook, uncovered, until very tender. Begin to check for doneness at about 30 minutes; they will be somewhat tender. Keep cooking until they are soft, likely about 40 minutes. Drain the grains and spread them on a plate or sheet pan to cool. Store unused cooked grains in the refrigerator for up to 4 days.

Generally speaking, 100 grams of dry grain absorb their weight in water to become approximately 200 grams of cooked grain.

Adjusting the Starter

For emmer, ølands, and spelt loaves, I recommend using a rye starter (see page 69), fed with whatever flour you'll use for the loaf. So, for example, the evening before you want to make an emmer pan loaf, feed your rye starter with emmer flour, so that you'll have the required amount of starter for the recipe. If you don't have an active rye starter but would like to make one of these loaves anyway, you can, of course, always use a wheat starter.

City Loaf & Variations

Everyone has their own vision of an ideal sourdough loaf. Some people think that its flavor ought to be markedly sour. Some think a very successful loaf should have huge holes in the crumb. For others, an intricate pattern of blown-out scores is the ultimate mark.

My ideal sourdough loaf shows a complete range of color: white flour on the outside of the loaf from the proofing basket, and crust that's intermittently golden, reddish orange, and increasingly deeper brown, skirting the edge of black. The thin, shatteringly crisp surface, heavily dotted with tiny bubbles, reminds me of chicharrón. The top of the loaf is rough and rugged, not intricately scored; it's *slashed.*

The inside has an irregular crumb structure, which will differ from day to day (and that's okay). I'm not necessarily looking for huge holes, but when you hold up a slice, you'll see an intricate system of caverns, with various-sized holes, where starches have gelatinized into a sheen. Squint a little and you may even see some fractal patterns.

My ideal sourdough loaf, the one that I strive to make every day, has complex flavor built through a slow fermentation. I promote heavy yeast activity early on, throughout the warm bulk fermentation, and then promote acetic acid development through a long chilling period, called retarding. As a result, when you eat the bread, it keeps giving. The more you chew, the more the flavor builds and grows, with some sweetness, a slightly sour flavor, and caramelization in the crust: a whole array of nuanced flavors that you didn't know were possible in a loaf of bread. That's what I call my City Loaf.

Once you have the original City Loaf down, the variations that follow are reworkings on the recipe, showing different ingredients and flavors, but based on the same foundation.

City Loaf Master Recipe

MAKES TWO 950-GRAM LOAVES

My sourdough City Loaf is the full expression of everything I've learned in all my time as a baker.

For years, I'd been making a bread called Country Loaf, which is a fairly common name for a slightly wheaty sourdough bread. I started calling my bread City Loaf when I moved to Copenhagen, seeing as I was in a city. You can call your bread anything you like. It's as simple as that. When you make something that's popular, whatever you call it sticks.

Start off with all your equipment at hand, and keep a bowl of warm water nearby to easily rinse off your hands and dough scraper.

STARTER

BAKER'S %	WEIGHT	INGREDIENT
100%	104g	Hot water (104°F / 40°C)*
100%	104g	Whole wheat flour
40%	42g	12-hour wheat or rye starter (your choice; see pages 73 and 69)

DOUGH

BAKER'S %	WEIGHT	INGREDIENT
50%	500g	Bread flour
50%	500g	All-purpose flour
75%	750g	Hot water (104°F / 40°C)*
20%	200g	Freshly fed starter (above)
2.5%	25g	Salt

ADDITIONAL INGREDIENTS

A handful each of all-purpose and rice flour (for coating baskets and tops of loaves)

As of this writing, I am baking in Copenhagen, and the specifics of this recipe reflect those climatic conditions. The temperatures listed here are for bakers working in temperate climates. If you're in a very hot place, the water should be cooler (86°F / 30°C), to avoid speeding up fermentation too much. Otherwise the temperature of the hot water (104°F / 40°C) is perfect because once you've added all your other ingredients, the temperature of the dough will be around where you want it, 86°F / 30°C.

TIMING

Day 1 (morning): Feed starter, autolyse and mix dough, ferment, preshape, and final shape: a total of 8 hours (most of which is allowing the dough to bulk ferment and proof), plus an overnight cold retard of up to 12 hours

Day 2 (morning): Preheat oven, transfer dough to Dutch oven, score, and bake: a total of 2½ to 3 hours

EQUIPMENT

Medium and large mixing bowls, digital thermometer, flexible plastic dough scraper, bowl or pitcher of warm water (for rinsing), two tea towels, bench scraper, two bannetons (proofing baskets), cast-iron or enameled Dutch oven (with a flat, handleless lid), lame or scissors, cooling rack

DAY 1

Feed the starter: In a medium bowl, use your hands to mix the water, flour, and 12-hour starter for a minute or so. You'll notice that you're making 250g freshly fed starter, but the dough calls for only 200g. The extra 50g are held back as starter for tomorrow's bread.

Take the starter's temperature. At this point, it should be about 86°–95°F / 30°–35°C. Don't worry if it isn't in this range; simply place the bowl into a larger bowl of warm or cold water, if necessary, depending on which direction you need it to go. (See Controlling Temperature, page 52.)

Make sure your dough scraper and a bowl of warm water are close at hand.

Scrape the excess mixture off your fingers back into the bowl, then rinse your hands in the bowl of warm water. Now, use your plastic scraper to push the starter mix together, getting everything off the insides of the bowl and into one cohesive body. Cover the bowl with a tea towel and leave the freshly fed starter in a warm, draft-free place.

Set a timer for 45 minutes.

Recipe continues

Autolyse the dough: In a large bowl, combine both flours and 650g of the hot water (you'll add the remaining 100g water in the next step), and use your hands to mix them until there is no dry flour remaining. That's all. You don't need to beat the dough; just mix it together. Use the plastic scraper to scrape the dough from your hands back into the bowl, and rinse your hands in the bowl of warm water, along with your scraper. Use the damp scraper to scrape down the insides of the bowl, making sure all the dough is together and your bowl looks clean. Then, cover the bowl with a tea towel.

This dough mixture will need to rest for at least 20 minutes, and up to 45 minutes, before you combine it with the freshly fed starter. This stage of the process is called autolyse (see page 50).

Mix the dough: After the timer for the starter has gone off and you've given the dough at least 20 minutes to autolyse after mixing, scrape 200g of the freshly fed starter into the bowl with the resting dough. Reserve the remaining 50g starter for the next day's bread.

While holding the bowl still with one hand, use your other hand to gently massage the starter into the dough. Now add 50g of the remaining water, which will make the dough slippery and easier to mix. Keep massaging. Once the water is fully absorbed, the mixture will stop being slippery and will have a sticky consistency.

Add the salt and remaining 50g hot water and continue to mix until the water has been absorbed and the salt is dissolved into the dough. The dough should feel soft and pull and stretch easily.

Take the dough's temperature. In a cold climate, it should be around 88°F / 31°C. In a hot climate, it should be around 80°F / 27°C. You want to aim to keep it at that temperature throughout its whole bulk fermentation (which starts in the next step). If it's too cold, set the bowl in a larger bowl of hot water to warm it up. If it's too warm, do the same, using cool or ice water. You don't need to be hypervigilant—it's not an exact science—but check it every 45 minutes to 1 hour during bulk fermentation and adjust accordingly.

Bulk ferment the dough: Wash your hands, scrape down the insides of the bowl, and cover the dough with a tea towel. Set a timer for 45 minutes.

This is the beginning of bulk fermentation, which will take about 4 hours total, including a few folds. Letting the dough rest for 45 minutes before you fold will make it much stronger. The gluten bonds, which started to form the second you added water to the flour, will continue to develop as the dough rests.

The first fold: Once the timer goes off, it's time to fold the dough. Keeping the dough in the bowl, gently pull it toward you and fold it over itself. At first, it will pull very easily and stay where you leave it. Rotate the bowl a quarter turn and repeat the fold. Repeat this process, giving the bowl a quarter turn each time. After four or five folds, the dough will be as tight as it needs to be, and the dough will resist being folded any more. That's when you know it's time to stop.

You do this folding for two reasons: to help the gluten do its thing and to stay connected to your dough. How's it going? Check its temperature and, again, adjust accordingly with a bowl of warm or cool water if necessary, to bring it into that 86°–95°F / 30°–35°C range. Cover it back up with the towel and set a timer once again for 45 minutes, for the second rest.

The second fold: Once the timer goes off, repeat the gentle folds as before and read your dough again. You should see evidence of a few air bubbles below the surface. If you don't, don't worry. It's only just the beginning of the fermentation.

Check the dough's temperature and adjust accordingly. You're about to leave the dough alone for 2½ hours, so it's important to make sure that it's nice and comfortable while it rests, so that it will properly ferment. Remember, we're going for maximum yeast activity, which happens in that ideal temperature range.

Continue bulk fermentation: Now set the timer for 2½ hours.

Do your thing while the dough does its thing, which is to say, the final stretch of bulk fermentation. After this long rest, you should start to see more and larger bubbles under the surface, more of the bounciness as described above, and less moisture on the surface.

 Divide and preshape: By now, the dough has had 4 hours of bulk fermentation, and if it has been kept at a nice consistent temperature and the room is comfortably warm, it will be well fermented. If you discern that it's not quite there yet—not too bouncy, no visible bubbling, kind of slack— give it another 30 to 60 minutes.

You might be used to flouring the work surface before putting your dough onto it, but trust me, you don't need to for this style of bread. You actually want the bottom of the dough to stick to the surface, which will help create tension.

Gently use your plastic scraper to ease the bread out of the bowl and onto your work surface. Treat it tenderly. You don't want to de-gas it.

Wet your hands to keep them from sticking to the top of the dough. Use your bench scraper to quickly and firmly divide the dough in two. Get one piece directly in front of you. Don't be afraid to pick it up with your bench scraper and move it to where you need it. Using your hand and bench scraper in unison, work the dough toward you, using your fingers to swiftly tuck the outer edges of the ball under the surface of the loaf, shaping it into a neat round with good surface tension. Confident, swift movements are best. There will be some sticking, which is why wet hands are essential. Try not to work the dough too much. You don't want to let out the beautiful gases you've spent all this time creating. It takes a lot of practice, but you'll know when you have it right—it will come together and have a nice tight surface. Repeat with the other piece of dough.

Another rest: Leave your two preshaped loaves to rest, uncovered, on the work surface for 45 minutes to 1 hour. After this rest they will have lost some of that tension that came from the preshaping and will look more relaxed than when you left them.

 Final shape: Sprinkle a combination of all-purpose and rice flour into the bannetons and sprinkle a very light dusting of all-purpose flour over the tops of the loaves. Using your bench scraper, shimmy the dough into an oval shape, using just a few moves to get it into more of an oval than a round. Hold one hand over the center of the loaf, take your scraper in the other hand, and scrape evenly across the surface of the table toward the loaf, lifting it up and into the other hand. Put down the scraper and cradle the loaf in both hands. Now fold it inward and gently place it into the basket. If it tries to fall back open, you can gently pinch it together at the top. That's it. It's safe and happy just the way it is. No need for aggressive shaping.

Cold retard: Lightly flour the loaves again, using a combination of all-purpose and rice flour, to keep the towel from sticking, then cover the baskets loosely with a towel, and let the loaves sit overnight, or up to 12 hours (at *most* 15 hours), to develop flavor. The ideal temperature is 54°–59°F / 12°–15°C, so if you have a cool cellar or a wine fridge, place them in there. Or if it's that temperature range outside your windowsill and you don't have a rat, bear, or raccoon problem, place them outside, covered with a tea towel. Otherwise, leave them on the counter in your kitchen for 2 hours, then transfer to the refrigerator.

DAY 2

Preheat the oven and Dutch oven: The following day, preheat the oven to 500°F / 260°C for at least 1 hour, with your Dutch oven (see page 27) inside to get radiant fucking hot. This vessel will be an oven inside the oven.

Once the Dutch oven is preheated, take it out, but be careful: it's radiant fucking hot. Use heavy-duty oven mitts or a few layers of dry tea towels when handling it. Place it on a sturdy, heatproof surface. Take the lid off and lay it down carefully, upside down. These vessels are designed to hold their heat, so don't panic or rush; you have time.

Take one basket of chilled dough out of the fridge. Gently loosen the edges of the loaf with your fingertips and flip the dough straight onto the screaming-hot lid.

Score the loaf: Cut scores into the top of the loaf, using either your lame or scissors. Carefully invert the Dutch oven pot over the dough, to cover it like a dome.

Bake the loaf: Set the inverted Dutch oven back inside your oven, reduce the temperature to 450°F / 230°C, and set a timer for 20 minutes. As your bread bakes, water will escape from the dough. Baking the bread in the closed environment of your Dutch oven ensures that those water vapors are trapped, steaming the bread in the process and allowing the loaf to rise fully.

After 20 minutes, that steam will have done its job. Remove the inverted pot, so the loaf is directly exposed to the oven's heat. Set the timer for 20 more minutes and let the loaf finish baking. Since you'll be baking a second loaf, leave the inverted pot in the oven so it stays hot for the next round.

I prefer to bake my bread pretty dark; I love the taste of a nice caramelized crust, but you're in charge here, so you decide when to pull it out.

If you can wait, you should let the loaf cool on a cooling rack before cutting it open. The inside structure of a bread that's screaming hot from the oven will be gummy and not properly set. Give it at least an hour.

Once you have pulled the first loaf from the oven, repeat these steps with the second loaf, transferring it from basket to pan lid, scoring it, covering it with the inverted pot, and baking for 20 minutes covered and 20 minutes uncovered.

Sesame City Loaf

MAKES TWO 950-GRAM LOAVES

This bread always reminds me of the first bread I ever bought from Tartine: the game changer. It's really just a simple sourdough with well-toasted sesame seeds in the dough, and it's rolled in untoasted sesame (because the seeds on the outside of the loaf will toast during the bake). I love this bread very much, and generally it's the one I bring home from the bakery.

STARTER

BAKER'S %	WEIGHT	INGREDIENT
100%	104g	Hot water (104°F / 40°C)
100%	104g	Whole wheat flour
40%	42g	12-hour wheat or rye starter (your choice; see pages 73 and 69)

DOUGH

BAKER'S %	WEIGHT	INGREDIENT
50%	500g	Bread flour
50%	500g	All-purpose flour
75%	750g	Hot water (104°F / 40°C)
20%	200g	Freshly fed starter (above)
3%	30g	Sesame seeds, toasted
2.5%	25g	Salt

ADDITIONAL INGREDIENTS

A handful each of all-purpose and rice flour (for coating baskets)

A small handful of untoasted sesame seeds (for coating the shaped loaves)

TIMING

Day 1 (morning): Feed starter, autolyse and mix dough, ferment, preshape, and final shape: a total of 8 hours (most of which is allowing the dough to bulk ferment and proof), plus an overnight cold retard of up to 12 hours

Day 2 (morning): Preheat oven, transfer dough to Dutch oven, score, and bake: a total of 2½ to 3 hours

EQUIPMENT

Medium and large mixing bowls, digital thermometer, flexible plastic dough scraper, bowl or pitcher of warm water (for rinsing), two tea towels, bench scraper, two bannetons (proofing baskets), cast-iron or enameled Dutch oven (with a flat, handleless lid), lame, cooling rack

DAYS 1 AND 2

 Follow all the steps of the City Loaf Master Recipe (page 113), with the following additions:

After autolyse, when you mix the dough, add the toasted sesame seeds. When you do the final shaping, scatter the untoasted sesame seeds onto a plate and rock the top half of the pre-shaped loaves in the seeds to coat them before transferring them to baskets for proofing.

Marble Rye City Loaf

MAKES TWO 1-KILOGRAM LOAVES

Don't be confused by the word *rye* in this loaf. It isn't the Danish hard-core style from the previous chapter. This is truly wheat bread sprinkled with rye. I first ate marble rye when I moved to the States, in 2007. The local bakery in Petaluma used to sell it as a sliced sandwich loaf. I thought it was so delicious. The addition of caraway seeds and the beautiful color of the dark and light doughs mixed together make a truly great bread.

Years later, when I was traveling to New York with Tartine to do pop-ups, we were asked if we could design a loaf for the classic Jewish smoked fish purveyor Russ & Daughters. I started working on this marble rye for them, but it wasn't feasible to teach it to the team in New York—a little too far away from San Francisco—so it never went ahead, but this is still my favorite bread of all time. The color and flavor are amazing, though it's worth noting that the color comes from dark malt powder, not the rye flour itself, which is rather light gray/green. Every time I make it I'm in awe of how great this bread is. I don't make it very often, because it's a bit like listening to my favorite album: I don't want to wear it out.

STARTER

BAKER'S %	WEIGHT	INGREDIENT
100%	104g	Hot water (104°F / 40°C)
100%	104g	Whole wheat flour
40%	42g	12-hour wheat or rye starter (your choice; see pages 73 and 69)

CITY LOAF DOUGH

BAKER'S %	WEIGHT	INGREDIENT
50%	250g	Bread flour
50%	250g	All-purpose flour
75%	375g	Hot water (104°F / 40°C)
20%	100g	Freshly fed starter (above)
2.5%	13g	Salt

DARK RYE DOUGH

BAKER'S %	WEIGHT	INGREDIENT
35%	175g	Bread flour
35%	175g	All-purpose flour
20%	100g	Whole wheat flour
10%	50g	Rye flour
10%	5g	Malt syrup
10%	5g	Dark malt powder
70%	375g	Hot water (104°F / 40°C)
20%	100g	Freshly fed starter (opposite)
3%	15g	Salt
3%	15g	Caraway seeds

ADDITIONAL INGREDIENTS

A handful each of all-purpose and rice flour (for coating baskets and tops of loaves)

TIMING

Day 1 (morning): Feed starter, autolyse and mix doughs, ferment, preshape, and final shape: a total of 8 hours (most of which is inactive), plus an overnight cold retard of up to 12 hours

Day 2 (morning): Preheat oven, transfer dough to Dutch oven, score, and bake: a total of 2½ to 3 hours

EQUIPMENT

Medium and large mixing bowls, digital thermometer, flexible plastic dough scraper, bowl or pitcher of warm water (for rinsing), two tea towels, bench scraper, two bannetons (proofing baskets), cast-iron or enameled Dutch oven (with a flat, handleless lid), lame, cooling rack

DAY 1

Feed the starter: Follow the instructions of the City Loaf Master Recipe (page 113). Set a timer for 45 minutes.

Autolyse both doughs: Bear in mind that the two doughs will be split and combined with each other to make two marbled loaves. It doesn't change how you'll do things, but just so you're not confused at some point, thinking, *That's not enough dough.*

Follow the instructions of the City Loaf Master Recipe (page 114) to make the City Loaf dough.

In a separate bowl, to autolyse the dark rye dough, combine all four flours, the malt syrup, malt powder, and 300g of the hot water and mix well by hand until there is no dry flour remaining.

Cover both bowls with tea towels and let them rest until the starter is ready.

Mix the respective doughs with starter and salt: When the starter is ready, add 100g of it to each batch of autolysed dough and mix starter and dough together by hand. (Save the remaining 50g starter for tomorrow's bread.)

To each batch of dough, add the remaining 75g water and mix by hand. Add the salt to each batch of dough and mix until it is well incorporated.

To the dark rye dough, add the caraway seeds and mix until they are distributed.

Fold together the two doughs: Scrape both doughs into a bowl, using the plastic scraper. Gently pull each dough toward you and fold them over each other a few times, to start the marbling effect.

Take the temperature of this dough. It should be 86°–95°F / 30–35°C. If it's outside that range, adjust accordingly by setting it in a larger bowl of hot or cold water. (See Controlling Temperature, page 52.) Set a timer for 45 minutes and cover the dough with a tea towel.

Bulk ferment, preshape, rest, final shape, and cold retard: Follow the instructions of the City Loaf Master Recipe (page 114).

DAY 2

Preheat, score, and bake: Follow the instructions of the City Loaf Master Recipe (page 115).

Half Whole Wheat City Loaf

A handful each of all-purpose and rice flour (for coating baskets and tops of loaves)

TIMING

Day 1 (morning): Feed starter, autolyse and mix dough, ferment, preshape, and final shape: a total of 8 hours (most of which is allowing the dough to bulk ferment and proof), plus an overnight cold retard of up to 12 hours

Day 2 (morning): Preheat oven, transfer dough to Dutch oven, score, and bake: a total of 2½ to 3 hours

EQUIPMENT

Medium and large mixing bowls, digital thermometer, flexible plastic dough scraper, bowl or pitcher of warm water (for rinsing), two tea towels, bench scraper, two bannetons (proofing baskets), cast-iron or enameled Dutch oven (with a flat, handleless lid), lame, cooling rack

DAYS 1 AND 2

Follow all the steps of the City Loaf Master Recipe (page 113).

MAKES TWO 900-GRAM LOAVES

This is about as whole wheat as it gets for me for this style of bread; 50% is really my limit. I find that once the whole wheat percentage gets any higher, the bread gets too sour, and the texture gets too heavy. Also, the crust gets a little tough.

This bread has a lower percentage of starter than the City Loaf (page 113) to stop it from fermenting too fast (the extra fiber in the bran and germ gives the yeast and bacteria more food). You want to slow the fermentation to protect the beautiful, sweet characteristics of the whole wheat.

STARTER

BAKER'S %	WEIGHT	INGREDIENT
100%	104g	Hot water (104°F / 40°C)
100%	104g	Whole wheat flour
40%	42g	12-hour wheat or rye starter (your choice; see pages 73 and 69)

DOUGH

BAKER'S %	WEIGHT	INGREDIENT
50%	500g	Whole wheat flour
50%	500g	Bread flour
70%	700g	Hot water (104°F / 40°C)
12%	120g	Freshly fed starter (above)
3%	30g	Salt

Toasted Bread Bread

MAKES TWO 900-GRAM LOAVES

This bread is a shout-out to my friend Douglas McMaster, chef and owner of Silo, an amazing zero-waste restaurant in Hackney, London. Think about that for a second: zero waste. No waste. No bin.

Nothing comes in that can't be used up or taken back. Doug also has a wonderful book, *Silo: The Zero-Waste Blueprint*. It's more philosophy than cookbook, and it changed me, for the better. After reading it, I bought a copy for all of my staff. I started making changes to the way I run my bakery. It's just small things, but a lot of small things add up. We stopped using bin liners. The rubbish collectors don't care if our garbage is tidied away in neat little bags. At the end of the day, we just wash out our bins. Imagine if every food business in the world did this; how many bin bags that would save. What an impact it could have. We also stopped using single-use plastic wrap. I'm a long way from Doug and Silo, but I want to be better, and make better choices for our planet. Thank you, Doug; you are a visionary, leading the way.

You're not reading this book to figure out new ways of getting rid of your rubbish, so here's a recipe. It's a great one that uses stale bread. Toasting and grinding old bread, and adding it to a dough, creates amazing flavor—imagine fresh bread with an already-toasted aroma.

BREAD MASH

BAKER'S %	WEIGHT	INGREDIENT
100%	160g	Old bread
200%*	280g	Boiling water

* The boiling water's percentage is 200%, because once the bread is toasted, it will weigh 140g (having lost about 20g during toasting).

STARTER

BAKER'S %	WEIGHT	INGREDIENT
100%	104g	Hot water (104°F / 40°C)
100%	104g	Whole wheat flour
40%	42g	12-hour wheat or rye starter (your choice; see pages 73 and 69)

DOUGH

BAKER'S %	WEIGHT	INGREDIENT
50%	384g	Bread flour
40%	307g	All-purpose flour
10%	77g	Rye flour
70%	537g	Hot water (104°F / 40°C)
20%	154g	Freshly fed starter (above)
2.5%	19g	Salt
42%	322g	Bread mash (above)

ADDITIONAL INGREDIENTS

A handful each of all-purpose and rice flour (for coating baskets and tops of loaves)

TIMING

Day 1 (morning): Make and cool bread mash, feed starter, autolyse and mix dough, ferment, preshape, and final shape: a total of 8 hours (most of which is allowing the dough to bulk ferment and proof), plus an overnight cold retard of up to 12 hours

Day 2 (morning): Preheat oven, transfer dough to Dutch oven, score, and bake: a total of 2½ to 3 hours

EQUIPMENT

Serrated knife, sheet pan, medium and large mixing bowls, wooden spoon, digital thermometer, bowl or pitcher of warm water (for rinsing), flexible plastic dough scraper, bench scraper, two tea towels, two bannetons (proofing baskets), cast-iron or enameled Dutch oven (with a flat, handleless lid), lame, cooling rack

DAY 1

Make the bread mash: Preheat the oven to 355°F / 180°C.

Cut the leftover bread into thin slices or 1-inch / 2.5cm cubes and arrange it in a single layer on a sheet pan. Toast for 5 to 10 minutes, until it is deeply and evenly browned.

Crush the toasted bread into a bowl. Pour the boiling water over the bread. Use a wooden spoon to mash it into a homogenous mixture. Let the bread mash cool to room temperature.

Feed the starter: Follow the instructions of the City Loaf Master Recipe (page 113). Set a timer for 45 minutes.

Autolyse the dough: Follow the instructions of the City Loaf Master Recipe (page 114), combining all three flours and using 460g of the hot water. Cover the dough and wait until the timer for the starter has gone off.

Mix the dough, starter, and bread mash: Add the freshly fed starter to the dough and use your hands to mix it well. Add the remaining 77g hot water and the salt and continue to mix the dough by hand until the water has been absorbed and the salt is dissolved.

Add half the bread mash and continue to mix by hand until it is evenly distributed. Add the remaining bread mash and continue to mix.

Bulk ferment, preshape, rest, final shape, and cold retard: Follow the instructions of the City Loaf Master Recipe (page 114).

DAY 2

Preheat, score, and bake: Follow the instructions of the City Loaf Master Recipe (page 115).

Semolina City Loaf

MAKES TWO 900-GRAM LOAVES

Semolina flour is the milled endosperm of the durum grain, a particularly hard form of wheat with a high protein content. For such a hard grain, it makes a surprisingly tender and delicious bread. Semolina has amazing color that makes a fantastic yellow dough. We've added an option to coat the loaf in pumpkin seeds, which adds a beautiful texture and flavor, but the bread is great either way.

STARTER

BAKER'S %	WEIGHT	INGREDIENT
40%	32g	12-hour wheat or rye starter (your choice; see pages 73 and 69)
50%	40g	Coarse semolina
50%	40g	Fine semolina
100%	80g	Hot water (104°F / 40°C)

DOUGH

BAKER'S %	WEIGHT	INGREDIENT
40%	383g	Bread flour
30%	287g	Coarse semolina
30%	287g	Fine semolina
65%	622g	Hot water (104°F / 40°C)
20%	191g	Freshly fed starter (above)
3%	29g	Salt

ADDITIONAL INGREDIENTS

A handful each of all-purpose and rice flour (for coating baskets)

2 handfuls of untoasted pumpkin seeds (to coat loaves; optional)

TIMING

Day 1 (morning): Feed starter, autolyse and mix dough, ferment, preshape, and final shape: a total of 9 to 10 hours (most of which is allowing the dough to bulk ferment and proof), plus an overnight cold retard of up to 12 hours

Day 2 (morning): Preheat oven, transfer dough to Dutch oven, score, and bake: a total of 2½ to 3 hours

EQUIPMENT

Medium and large mixing bowls, digital thermometer, flexible plastic dough scraper, bowl or pitcher of warm water (for rinsing), tea towels, bench scraper, two bannetons (proofing baskets), cast-iron or enameled Dutch oven (with a flat, handleless lid), lame, cooling rack

DAY 1

Feed the starter, autolyse and mix the dough, bulk ferment, preshape, and proof: Follow the instructions of the City Loaf Master Recipe (page 113). I have noticed that this bread tends to bulk ferment for a bit longer than the master recipe, up to an additional 2 hours.

Final shape: Follow the instructions of the City Loaf Master Recipe (page 115). If you want to use pumpkin seeds, scatter them onto a plate and rock the preshaped loaf in the seeds to coat the top half before transferring it to the basket for proofing. Repeat with the second loaf.

Cold retard: Follow the instructions of the City Loaf Master Recipe (page 115).

DAY 2

Preheat, score, and bake: Follow the instructions of the City Loaf Master Recipe (page 115).

Honey-Roasted Walnut Whole Wheat City Loaf

MAKES TWO 900-GRAM LOAVES

This was one of the last breads I added to the book. When I was talking to my team about what was missing, the conversation turned to doing some sort of nut bread.

My first response, as with nearly all breads with added ingredients, was "NO WAY. Good bread is good bread. How about we just put nut butter on it?"

Then the idea of adding honey-roasted walnuts came up, and it was "ABSOLUTELY no way. Are you crazy?"

Then Karishma made it. It was great. Here it is.

HONEY-ROASTED WALNUTS

BAKER'S %	WEIGHT	INGREDIENT
100%	240g	Walnuts
50%	120g	Honey
10%	24g	Olive oil
2%	4g	Salt

STARTER

BAKER'S %	WEIGHT	INGREDIENT
100%	104g	Hot water (104°F / 40°C)
100%	104g	Whole wheat flour
40%	42g	12-hour wheat or rye starter (your choice; see pages 73 and 69)

DOUGH

BAKER'S %	WEIGHT	INGREDIENT
50%	414g	All-purpose flour
20%	166g	Bread flour
30%	248g	Whole wheat flour
70%	580g	Hot water (104°F / 40°C)
15%	124g	Freshly fed starter (above)
2.5%	20g	Salt
30%	248g	Honey-roasted walnuts (above)

ADDITIONAL INGREDIENTS

A handful each of all-purpose and rice flour (for coating baskets and tops of loaves)

TIMING

Day 1 (morning): Caramelize walnuts and let cool, feed starter, autolyse and mix dough, ferment, preshape, and final shape: a total of 9 hours (most of which is allowing the dough to bulk ferment and proof), plus an overnight cold retard of up to 12 hours

Day 2 (morning): Preheat oven, transfer dough to Dutch oven, score, and bake: a total of 2½ to 3 hours

EQUIPMENT

Mixing bowls, silicone spatula, two sheet pans, parchment paper or silicone baking mats, digital thermometer, flexible plastic dough scraper, bowl or pitcher of warm water, tea towels, bench scraper, two bannetons (proofing baskets), cast-iron or enameled Dutch oven (with a flat, handleless lid), lame, cooling rack

DAY 1

Honey-roast the walnuts: Preheat the oven to 355°F / 180°C.

In a mixing bowl, toss the walnuts with the honey, olive oil, and salt, using the spatula, until they are evenly coated. Spread the nuts into an even layer on a parchment paper– or silicone mat–lined sheet pan.

Line another sheet pan with parchment paper or a silicone mat to have at the ready to immediately transfer the nuts to once they are done roasting. Roast the walnuts for 10 to 15 minutes, stirring them with a silicone spatula every 5 minutes to ensure even caramelization. Keep a close eye on the nuts: when the honey has bubbled up and then dropped back down, turning to a deep golden brown, you'll know that the nuts are well caramelized; take them out of the oven immediately. They can go from perfectly cooked to burned very quickly (take it from us), so pay close attention.

As soon as you've taken the walnuts out of the oven, transfer them to the other lined sheet pan and spread them out in an even layer. This needs to be done while they're hot or else you'll end up with a clump of nuts stuck to the pan.

Let the nuts cool completely to room temperature before adding them to the dough. If they have clumped up, break them apart with your hands into individual walnut-sized pieces.

Feed the starter: Follow the instructions of the City Loaf Master Recipe (page 113). Set a timer for 45 minutes.

Autolyse the dough: Follow the instructions of the City Loaf Master Recipe (page 114), using 414g of the hot water. Cover the dough and wait until the timer for the starter has gone off.

Combine the starter, dough, and walnuts: Follow the instructions of the City Loaf Master Recipe (page 114), using your hands to combine the freshly fed starter and the autolysed dough. Mix in the remaining 166g hot water and the salt and continue to mix until the water has been absorbed and the salt is dissolved.

Now add the walnuts and continue to mix by hand until they are well distributed. You may notice that the cooked walnuts lend a slight purplish hue to the dough; don't worry! This is normal and will disappear when you bake the bread.

Take the dough's temperature and adjust if needed by setting the bowl in a larger bowl of hot, warm, or cool water to get the dough to 86°–95°F / 30°–35°C. (See Controlling Temperature, page 52.)

Bulk ferment, preshape, rest, final shape, and cold retard: Follow the instructions of the City Loaf Master Recipe (page 114).

DAY 2

Preheat, score, and bake: Follow the instructions of the City Loaf Master Recipe (page 115).

A Day in My Life

As a Baker in Copenhagen

3 a.m. The alarm is going off. I jump up quickly, turning it off, being as quiet as possible. Henrietta is sleeping beside me. Three a.m. is a ridiculous time to wake up, and this is my vocation, not hers, so I really don't want to disturb her. I move around in the dark, feeling my familiar way.

I lean against the shower wall, not moving, waiting for the water to wake me.

Getting dressed, I start thinking about my dough from yesterday's mix, sleeping in the cool room at the bakery. *Will I have a good bake? Will I have the best bread I've ever made? Did I push the dough too hard? Maybe it will be terrible.* I like to walk a fine line between amazing and disaster. Pushing the boundaries of hydration and fermentation. I'm generally filled with a mixture of hope, worry, and excitement.

I kiss my sleeping love goodbye. She smiles and stretches out into the warm space I've left. I leave for the cold street.

3:20 a.m. I'm on my bike. It's a twenty-minute ride to the bakery, but it takes me thirty minutes at this time of the morning. I'm slow, and my body refuses to go any faster. I look at all the apartments with their lights still on, wondering why people are still awake. I pass four beautiful lakes, looking at the city in their reflection: headlights, traffic lights, neons. On the cycle path, I navigate a silent meeting of ducks. I'm always searching for a glimpse of the moon. Seeing her, I'm reminded that I'm a tiny speck in the universe, and maybe, even if my bread's not that great, everything will be okay.

3:50 a.m. I get to the bakery. I'm the first one there. As I open the door, I feel the heat of the oven, which is a beast, and holds a ton of mass heat. I switch on the lights; it's lovely to see the bakery calm. Usually it's such a chaotic buzz. I make coffee, put my favorite music on, usually Nick Cave and the Bad Seeds. Okay, I'm awake, I'm happy to be here now, and there is really no time to waste.

First job: I set the mixers to autolyse the doughs. They'll be ready for my bakers, who come in at 6 a.m., to start the bread production for tomorrow.

Just after **4 a.m.,** I start the bake. I check the fridge and hope my sleeping dough looks right. It has a good volume, still looks full of life and ready to blow up. Caught at the perfect moment. (I mean, of course I'm going to write about a good day.)

My oven is a gas-fired steam tube oven, made by Bassanina. It's a beast and I love it. Built on-site with a ton of concrete and insulation, it holds thirty-six loaves per deck, and there are four decks.

I place the baskets on the loader before tipping them out to be scored, loaded, and baked. I bake at 480°F / 250°C, and the oven holds so much mass heat, the temperature doesn't drop. I bake on rotation, using plenty of steam. It's the fastest, most fun way I know to bake.

This is what I mean by rotation: I load the first deck with bread, then set a timer for 7 minutes. In that time, I do some small jobs. Once the timer goes off, I load deck two, and once it's loaded I do the same again, setting the timer and carrying on with my small jobs. I continue with this same method until all four decks are loaded.

By the time I've loaded deck four, deck one is ready to be unloaded, swept clean, and reloaded.

This system keeps the oven continuously full, with enough time to get the loaves out of each deck. You only have to set the timer for the first bake, and after that, you're on perfect rotation. As soon as one deck is clear and reloaded, you start on the next one. It's a beautiful system.

I continuously load and unload the oven. There's no set time. I do it on instinct. I pull the bread from the oven once it looks just right, listening to the amazing crackle as it cools on the rack beside me.

5:15 a.m. I feed the starters, so they're ready for the mixer to mix the doughs at 6 a.m.

5:45 a.m. My bread team straggles in, makes coffee, complains about the cold, the rain, or how hot it is, if it's summer. They usually complain about my taste in music and change it. I don't mind; I'm happy to keep Nick for myself. They say it's depressing, but to me it is glorious. I think his lyrics are genius. It makes me feel. I'm not afraid to feel.

6 a.m. One of the team starts to cut morning buns, up to eight hundred pieces, to be baked on the deck.

Whoever is mixing for tomorrow gets to work on the dough. We have the luxury of having four mixers in various sizes, and we make between six and ten different doughs in a day. The standards are City Loaf (page 113), Morning Buns (page 189), Baguettes (page 193), Perfect Sandwich Bread, or BFKAC (Bread Formerly Known as Ciabatta; page 172), Super Seed Rye Bread (page 82), and Everyday Rye Bread (page 85). All that and a special, if the mixer is feeling creative. I encourage my bakers to create. I truly love seeing new breads.

8 a.m. The bread's baked. I clean the oven room. The dough is mixed. The mixing room is cleaned.

The person mixing has begun to scale ingredients for the following day. We drink lots of tea. I make it in my favorite battered metal teapot with a carved maple wood handle, a present from my lady, Henrietta. In summer we drink it iced, cold infused overnight. We snack on bread and bits of broken pastry. We listen to great music and talk a lot of nonsense. We don't take ourselves too seriously.

We're a family. I know everyone says that, and some places are worse than dysfunctional. But I think of my bakery as my house. I'm responsible for making it a good place to be. We support one another; we have a good time. The most important thing is the bread, but the only way to achieve that standard is with a happy team. And that's at the heart of everything. Excellence and fun can coexist. Even at high production of the best stuff, it's not only possible with, but dependent on, a warm and trusting workplace.

8:15 a.m. We preshape baguettes and BFKAC. We shape the rye into prebuttered pans. We brush out the flour from used baskets, ready to be hung up to dry.

We start the final shape of the baguettes and BFKAC. Once they're out, I bake the rye.

It should all line up like clockwork. We've figured out how to be superefficient with our time, although we're always coming up with new tweaks, and then wondering why it took us so long to figure that out.

10 a.m. The morning bun dough is ready to be folded and put in the cool room to chill for the night.

Anytime between **10 a.m. and 11:30 a.m.** the City Loaf dough is ready to divide.

When the dough is ready, we all come to the shaping table. Two bakers divide, and one or two preshape. We have anywhere between three hundred and five hundred loaves to hand cut and preshape. We generally play pumping music

at this stage. Nothing else matters now—we're all focused on speed, and getting through the dough before it gets too big and overproofs. Almost always, one of us will say, "Why did we make so much bread?" Although we all know it's because we sell it.

I love our shaping table. It's a big communal table, and we all face one another and talk nonsense and laugh nonstop. No matter how hard our job is—and I promise you, being a professional baker is really hard, such a physically demanding job—we laugh our arses off. The bread, fun, jokes, and laughter make it so worthwhile. It's always amazing to be there.

It takes around an hour to divide and preshape the dough. We first rest it on the table, and once that fills up, we load it onto numerous racks. We line the dough up in a beautiful honeycomb pattern. Everyone asks why I do it like that. Really, it's to do with fitting as much bread on the table as we can, and because it looks pretty.

Once we finish, the dough rests until it's ready for final shaping. Depending on the dough, the weather, and the time of year, it could be ready straightaway, or it could take one or two or more hours. It needs to relax, but it also needs to be in the right place in its fermentation before it goes into the baskets.

It takes years of experience to know what, how, why, and when. But it does come, like almost everything, with practice.

When the dough is ready, we start the final shape. One person is constantly gathering and flouring three straight lines in baskets. The others are picking up the dough, folding it in half like closing a book, and gently placing it in the basket. It's a constant motion. We work fast, until the loaves are all snug in their baskets.

The shaped dough sits out until it's ready to go in the cool room for the night.

Bakers, front of house, and the pastry team eat lunch together. In between the chaos, someone has made food for everyone. It's an international crew, so we often try someone's comfort food from somewhere in the world. Then, all that's left is to clean everything down and feed the starters for the next day. We often hang around with a beer or two before cycling home.

My ride back is faster than the morning ride. I'm still buzzing from the day. My love meets me by the water for a swim. Even on the coldest days, when the water is almost freezing, the ground icy, a brief dip in the Baltic Sea is like switching a computer off and on. A total reset. I never want to get in, but never regret it. In the brief Danish summer, it's pure heaven.

Wheat Loaves Flavored
with Other Grains

THE GOOD COOK
Breads

When I finished working on the breads for *Tartine Book No. 3,* a book full of heirloom grain loaves, my brain just wouldn't stop. It was still ticking away with new ideas. I love experimenting and dreaming up different ways to build flavor using different grains, and I can't switch it off, even if I want to.

Often, I'd be driving home from San Francisco to Sonoma County and I'd have to pull over so I could jot ideas down. Some days I'd have to pull over fast, because the ideas would just flow and I'd be scared that if I didn't get them down, by the third or fourth idea, I would've forgotten the first one.

A lot of the breads in this section spin off from ideas I had back in those days and kept building on. Each bread features cooked grains added to a wheat dough, with the intention of enhancing the flavor of each individual grain, from the deep corn flavor shining through in the Sand Dollar (page 143), to the hearty barley in Barley Bread Tests #2 and #3 (pages 136 and 152), and a whole range in between.

I think they are all pretty cool, and I'm happy to share them. Hopefully you can take them and go on and experiment even further.

Barley Bread, Test #2

MAKES TWO 1-KILOGRAM LOAVES

This is my second attempt to re-create the London Pride barley flavor I love (see page 101 for Barley Bread, Pumpernickel Style, Test #1).

I started experimenting with a toasted barley soak. I toasted the pearl barley to intensify the flavor, and then soaked it in a load of hot water to soften it. Now I had this beautifully infused barley water and the softened grains, which both had incredible flavor, to add to the dough. In contrast to Barley Test #1, which is a dense, chewy loaf, this bread will resemble City Loaf in style and texture, with an added earthy barley flavor.

TOASTED BARLEY

BAKER'S %	WEIGHT	INGREDIENT
7.5%	75g	Pearl barley
100%	1kg	Water

STARTER

BAKER'S %	WEIGHT	INGREDIENT
100%	104g	Hot water (104°F / 40°C)
100%	104g	Whole wheat flour
40%	42g	12-hour wheat or rye starter (your choice; see pages 73 and 69)

DOUGH

BAKER'S %	WEIGHT	INGREDIENT
50%	500g	Bread flour
50%	500g	All-purpose flour
65%	650g	Barley soaking liquid (above)
20%	200g	Freshly fed starter (above)
25%	250g	Drained soaked barley (above)
3%	30g	Salt

ADDITIONAL INGREDIENTS

A handful each of all-purpose and rice flour (for coating baskets and tops of loaves)

TIMING

Day 1 (evening): Toast and soak pearl barley

Day 2 (morning into afternoon): Drain barley and reserve liquid, feed starter, and mix dough, ferment, preshape, and final shape: a total of 8 hours (most of which is allowing the dough to bulk ferment and proof), plus an overnight cold retard of up to 12 hours

Day 3 (morning): Preheat oven, transfer dough to Dutch oven, score, and bake: a total of 2½ to 3½ hours

EQUIPMENT

Sheet pan, various sizes of mixing bowls, sieve or colander, digital thermometer, flexible plastic dough scraper, bowl or pitcher of warm water (for rinsing), tea towels, bench scraper, two bannetons (proofing baskets), Dutch oven (with a flat, handleless lid), lame, cooling rack

DAY 1

Toast and soak the barley: Preheat the oven to 390°F / 200°C.

Arrange the barley grains in a single layer on a sheet pan and toast for 8 to 10 minutes, until they are golden brown and have a nutty, toasty smell. Keep a close eye on them; they can go from toasted to burned fairly quickly.

Transfer the toasted barley grains to a large heatproof bowl. Bring the 1kg water to a boil, then pour it over the barley. Stir well, and once the mixture has cooled to room temperature, cover the bowl and let soak for 8 hours or overnight. (If you're in a very hot and humid environment, and you know there's a risk of the barley spoiling at room temperature, refrigerate it; otherwise, it's fine to leave it out overnight.)

DAY 2

Drain and reserve the barley and liquid: Place a sieve or colander over a bowl and drain the soaked barley, pressing out as much liquid as possible into the bowl below. Weigh or measure the soaking liquid and supplement with tap water as needed for a total of 650g. Reserve this liquid for hydrating the bread dough. Set the barley aside for stirring into the dough.

Feed the starter: Follow the instructions of the City Loaf Master Recipe (page 113). Set a timer for 45 minutes.

Autolyse the dough: Make sure your dough scraper and a bowl or pitcher of warm water are close at hand.

In a large bowl, combine both flours and 500g of the reserved barley soaking liquid and mix by hand until there is no dry flour remaining. Use the flexible scraper to scrape the dough from your hands back into the bowl and rinse your hands in the bowl of warm water, along with your scraper. Use the damp scraper to scrape down the insides of the bowl.

Take the dough's temperature, which should be 86°–95°F / 30°–35°C. Because the water has come from the barley soak and is probably cooler than the warm tap water you'd use to mix the City Loaf Master Recipe, you will likely need to warm up the dough by setting the bowl in a larger bowl of hot water. Cover the bowl with a tea towel.

Mix the dough, starter, drained barley, remaining soaking liquid, and salt: When the starter is ready, use the flexible scraper to scrape the starter into the bowl with the resting dough. While holding the bowl still with one hand, use your other hand to gently massage the starter into the dough.

Now add about a quarter of the drained barley and about a quarter of the remaining 150g soaking liquid, which will make the dough somewhat slippery and stringy. Keep massaging. Once the barley and water are well incorporated, add another quarter of both the barley and the liquid, and keep massaging and mixing, adding the remaining barley and liquid in two more batches. The mixture will stop being slippery and will have a sticky consistency.

Add the salt and continue to mix until the salt is well incorporated. The dough should feel soft and pull and stretch easily.

Take the dough's temperature, adjusting it by setting the pan in a bowl of hot, warm, or cool water as necessary to bring it to about 82°F / 28°C. (See Controlling Temperature, page 52.)

Wash your hands, scrape down the insides of the bowl, and cover the dough with a tea towel.

Bulk ferment, preshape, rest, final shape, and cold retard: Follow the instructions of the City Loaf Master Recipe (page 114).

DAY 3

Preheat, score, and bake: Follow the instructions of the City Loaf Master Recipe (page 115).

Toasted Wheat Bran and Germ Bread

(Whole Wheat as F***)

MAKES TWO 1-KILOGRAM LOAVES

This bread came about because someone I used to bake with, before Tartine, used to tease me, saying I made only white bread. I thought, *You know what, I'm going to create a whole wheat sourdough bread, using only white flour, but I will add more bran and germ in the mix than you would get if you used just a whole wheat flour.*

There is some truth to the teasing. I love the texture you can get from a white sourdough loaf. It's almost impossible to get that texture with 100% whole wheat flour, but you can add the goodness back in.

The bran and germ are coarse and can be tough on gluten, so I thought that if I soaked them in plenty of water overnight, they would soften. Then I could both use the soaking liquid in the dough and add the softened bran and germ to my white flour dough. This worked really well. Lightly toasting the bran and germ brings out amazing flavors and aromas.

I think it's a fantastic bread. Maybe it's a nod to my old chef days, when you'd constantly pull everything apart and put it back together. (Anyway, if you read this book, Cory/Buddy, this one is for you.)

TOASTED WHEAT BRAN AND GERM

BAKER'S %	WEIGHT	INGREDIENT
3.75%	38g	Wheat bran
3.75%	38g	Wheat germ
100%	1kg	Water

STARTER

BAKER'S %	WEIGHT	INGREDIENT
100%	104g	Hot water (104°F / 40°C)
100%	104g	Whole wheat flour
40%	42g	12-hour wheat or rye starter (your choice; see pages 73 and 69)

DOUGH

BAKER'S %	WEIGHT	INGREDIENT
50%	500g	Bread flour
50%	500g	All-purpose flour
65%	650g	Bran and germ soaking liquid (above)
20%	200g	Freshly fed starter (above)
25%	250g	Drained soaked bran and germ (above)
3%	30g	Salt

ADDITIONAL INGREDIENTS

A handful each of all-purpose and rice flour (for coating baskets and tops of loaves)

TIMING

Day 1 (evening): Toast and soak bran and germ

Day 2 (morning): Drain bran and germ and reserve liquid, feed starter, autolyse and mix dough, ferment, preshape, and final shape: a total of 8 hours (most of which is allowing the dough to bulk ferment and proof), plus an overnight cold retard of up to 12 hours

Day 3 (morning): Preheat oven, transfer dough to Dutch oven, score, and bake: a total of about 3 hours

EQUIPMENT

Sheet pan, mixing bowls, wooden spoon or spatula, sieve or colander, digital thermometer, flexible plastic dough scraper, bowl or pitcher of warm water (for rinsing), two tea towels, bench scraper, two bannetons (proofing baskets), cast-iron or enameled Dutch oven (with a flat, handleless lid), lame, cooling rack

Recipe continues

DAY 1

Toast and soak the wheat bran and germ: Preheat the oven to 350°F / 175°C.

Arrange the bran and germ in a single layer on a sheet pan and toast for 5 to 7 minutes, until they are golden brown and have a nutty, toasty smell. Keep a close eye on them; they can go from toasted to burned fairly quickly.

Transfer the toasted bran and germ to a large heatproof bowl. Bring the 1kg water to a boil, then pour it over the bran and germ. Stir well, and once the mixture has cooled to room temperature, cover the bowl and let this mixture soak for 8 hours or overnight. (If you're in a very hot and humid environment, and you know there's a risk of the mixture spoiling at room temperature, refrigerate it; otherwise, it's fine to leave it out overnight.)

DAY 2

Drain the bran and germ and reserve the soaking liquid: Place a sieve or colander over a bowl and drain the soaked bran and germ, pressing out as much liquid as possible into the bowl below. Weigh or measure the soaking liquid and supplement with tap water as needed for a total of 650g. Reserve this liquid for hydrating the bread dough. Set the soaked bran and germ aside for stirring into the dough.

Feed the starter: Follow the instructions of the City Loaf Master Recipe (page 113). Set a timer for 45 minutes.

Autolyse the dough: Make sure your dough scraper and a bowl or pitcher of warm water are close at hand.

In a large bowl, combine the flours and 500g of the reserved soaking liquid and mix by hand until there is no dry flour remaining. Use the flexible scraper to scrape the dough from your hands back into the bowl and rinse your hands in the bowl of warm water, along with your scraper. Use the damp scraper to scrape down the insides of the bowl.

Take the dough's temperature, which should be 86°–95°F / 30°–35°C. Because the water has come from the bran and germ soak and is probably cooler than the warm tap water you'd use to mix the City Loaf Master Recipe, you will likely need to warm up the dough by setting the bowl in a larger bowl of hot water. Cover the bowl with a tea towel.

Mix the dough, starter, drained bran and germ mixture, remaining soaking liquid, and salt: When the starter is ready, use the flexible scraper to scrape the starter into the bowl with the resting dough. While holding the bowl still with one hand, use your other hand to gently massage the starter into the dough.

Now add about a quarter of the drained bran and germ mixture and about a quarter of the remaining 150g soaking liquid, which will make the dough somewhat slippery and stringy. Keep massaging. Once the bran and germ mixture and the water are well incorporated, add another quarter of each and keep massaging and mixing, adding the remaining mixture and water in two more batches. The mixture will stop being slippery and will have a sticky consistency.

Add the salt and continue to mix until the salt is well incorporated. The dough should feel soft and pull and stretch easily.

Take the dough's temperature, adjusting it by setting the pan in a bowl of hot, warm, or cool water as necessary to bring it to about 82°F / 28°C. (See Controlling Temperature, page 52.)

Wash your hands, scrape down the insides of the bowl, and cover the dough with a tea towel.

Bulk ferment, preshape, rest, final shape, and cold retard: Follow the instructions of the City Loaf Master Recipe (page 114).

DAY 3

Preheat, score, and bake: Follow the instructions of the City Loaf Master Recipe (page 115).

Sand Dollar

MAKES TWO 600-GRAM LOAVES

A few years back, I did a bit of consulting work for the legendary Contramar restaurant in Mexico City. I totally fell in love with the city and the country. I wanted to make a bread that tasted Mexican, that had the flavors everyone was used to eating, and that went with all the fantastic food served at Contramar.

I started playing around with masa, which is basically a dough made from corn kernels that have undergone a process called nixtamalization. Masa is used to make corn tortillas, a daily staple of Mexico since forever.

I started to add the straight masa into a dough as I was mixing. Man, it turned out great. The flavor of the masa, that floral aroma of fresh-made tortillas, just shines through, and the texture of the crumb is super moist and creamy; it's fantastic. I was so happy, and loved the idea of making a bread we could call uniquely Mexican.

At first, I made big, round loaves, but after a while, I started making shaped loaves that you could pull apart and dip into the food.

The round breads had five small cuts in the center, topped with a mixture of colored corn: blue, purple, red, and yellow. Once pulled into shape and baked, they reminded me of the beautiful sand dollars I collect with my boys along the Pacific coast.

STARTER

BAKER'S %	WEIGHT	INGREDIENT
100%	52g	Hot water (104°F / 40°C)
100%	52g	Whole wheat flour
40%	21g	12-hour wheat or rye starter (your choice; see pages 73 and 69)

MASA

BAKER'S %	WEIGHT	INGREDIENT
100%	142g	Masa harina
75%	107g	Water

DOUGH

BAKER'S %	WEIGHT	INGREDIENT
50%	250g	Bread flour
50%	250g	All-purpose flour
65%	325g	Hot water (104°F / 40°C)
20%	100g	Freshly fed starter (above)
50%	250g	Masa (above)
3%	15g	Salt

ADDITIONAL INGREDIENTS

A handful of rice flour (for the couche)

A handful of cornmeal or polenta (for garnish)

TIMING

Day 1 (morning): Feed starter, make masa, autolyse and mix dough, ferment, preshape, and final shape—a total of 8 hours (most of which is allowing the dough to bulk ferment and proof), plus an overnight cold retard of up to 12 hours

Day 2 (morning): Preheat oven, transfer dough to pizza stone, score, and bake: a total of about 3 hours

EQUIPMENT

Two mixing bowls, digital thermometer, tea towels, flexible plastic dough scraper, bowl or pitcher of warm water (for rinsing), bench scraper, one couche (linen proofing cloth), sheet pans, pizza stone, baker's peel, transfer board, cooling rack

DAY 1

Feed the starter: Follow the instructions of the City Loaf Master Recipe (page 113). Set a timer for 45 minutes.

Mix the masa: In a bowl, using your hands, combine the masa harina and water and mix well for 2 minutes, to form a soft dough. Cover the bowl with a tea towel and set aside.

Autolyse the dough: Follow the instructions of the City Loaf Master Recipe (page 114), using 250g of the water. Cover the dough and set aside until the timer for the starter has gone off.

Mix the dough, starter, masa, and salt: When the starter is ready, and you've given the dough at least 20 minutes to rest after mixing, scrape the starter into the bowl with the resting dough. While holding the bowl still with one hand, use your other hand to gently massage the starter into the dough.

Recipe continues

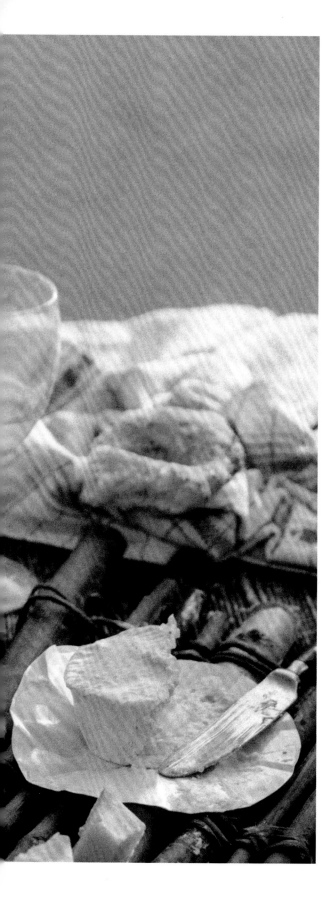

Now add about a quarter of the masa and a quarter of the remaining 75g water, which will make the dough somewhat slippery and stringy. Keep massaging. Once the masa and water are well incorporated, add another quarter of both and keep massaging and mixing, adding the remaining masa and water in two more batches. The mixture will stop being slippery and will have a sticky consistency.

Add the salt and, if necessary to keep the dough pliable, an additional splash of hot water. Keep working the dough with the same gentle touch. The dough should feel soft and pull and stretch easily.

Take the dough's temperature, adjusting it by setting the pan in a bowl of hot, warm, or cool water as necessary to bring it to about 82°F / 28°C. (See Controlling Temperature, page 52.)

Wash your hands, scrape down the insides of the bowl, and cover the dough with a tea towel.

Bulk ferment, preshape, and rest: Follow the instructions of the City Loaf Master Recipe (page 114).

 Final shape: Shape the loaves into rounds. Set a couche on a cutting board or sheet pan and sprinkle it liberally with rice flour. Scatter the handful of cornmeal onto a plate. Dip the shaped loaves in the cornmeal to coat one half, and gently transfer them, cornmeal side up, onto the couche, which will let the dough relax more as it cold retards.

Sprinkle the tops of the loaves with any remaining cornmeal. Arrange the couche around the loaves to support their structure.

Cold retard: Gently but completely cover the loaves with tea towels and refrigerate overnight, up to 12 hours, and no more than 15 hours.

DAY 2

Preheat, score, and bake: Place a sheet pan or shallow roasting pan on the floor of the oven. Arrange a rack in the center of the oven and place a pizza stone on the rack. Preheat the oven to 500°F / 260°C.

Sprinkle a bit of rice flour onto a baker's peel. Place the transfer board alongside one loaf and use the couche to gently invert it onto the board, and then from the board to the peel. Use the flexible dough scraper to make five evenly spaced cuts in the dough, radiating out from the center (like a sand dollar).

Transfer the dough from the peel to the pizza stone. Add about 250ml water to the pan on the oven's floor, taking care to avoid exposing your skin directly to the resultant steam, which can burn. Repeat with the remaining sand dollar.

Bake for 30 to 35 minutes, until the crust is golden brown. Remove the sand dollars and let them cool on a rack.

Oat Bread

MAKES THREE 810-GRAM LOAVES

People have been chucking leftover porridge in bread forever, literally forever. I think with *Tartine Book No. 3* we might have made it cool again. Whatever. I hate the name *porridge bread* anyway, because it sounds so stodgy, but putting cooked oats in a bread dough is fantastic. They're so comforting and taste so good, and they have a lot of natural fat, which makes the dough silky and rich, similar to an enriched dough.

(Also, I kind of buggered up the method in *Tartine Book No. 3*. I think we said to add the oats on the third fold, but folding porridge into a dough that's halfway proofed just doesn't work. Way too much time has passed. WHOOPS. Sorry. I've fixed it this time around.)

OAT PORRIDGE

BAKER'S %	WEIGHT	INGREDIENT
100%	128g	Rolled oats
250%	320g	Water

STARTER

BAKER'S %	WEIGHT	INGREDIENT
100%	104g	Hot water (104°F / 40°C)
100%	104g	Whole wheat flour
40%	42g	12-hour wheat or rye starter (your choice; see pages 73 and 69)

DOUGH

BAKER'S %	WEIGHT	INGREDIENT
40%	359g	Bread flour
40%	359g	All-purpose flour
20%	179g	Whole wheat flour
50%	448g	Hot water (104°F / 40°C)
20%	179g	Freshly fed starter (above)
3%	27g	Salt
50%	448g	Oat porridge (above)

ADDITIONAL INGREDIENTS

A handful each of all-purpose and rice flour (for coating baskets)

A handful of raw rolled oats (for dipping the loaves)

TIMING

Day 1 (morning): Make the oat porridge and let it cool, feed starter, autolyse and mix dough, ferment, preshape, and final shape: a total of 9 hours (mostly bulk ferment and proof), plus an overnight cold retard of up to 12 hours

Day 2 (morning): Preheat oven, transfer dough to Dutch oven, score, and bake: a total of about 4 hours

EQUIPMENT

Small saucepan with lid, wooden spoon, sheet pan, two mixing bowls, digital thermometer, flexible plastic dough scraper, bowl or pitcher of warm water (for rinsing), tea towels, bench scraper, three bannetons (proofing baskets), cast-iron or enameled Dutch oven (with a flat, handleless lid), lame, cooling rack

DAY 1

Make and cool the oat porridge: In a saucepan, combine the oats and water and bring to a boil. Stir well with the wooden spoon, reduce to a simmer, and cover the pan. Let the oats cook until they are very tender and on the cusp of disintegration, 10 to 15 minutes. They should have absorbed most of the water. Transfer to a sheet pan and spread the mixture out so that it cools quickly.

Feed the starter: Follow the instructions of the City Loaf Master Recipe (page 113). Set a timer for 45 minutes.

Autolyse the dough: Follow the instructions of the City Loaf Master Recipe (page 114), using all the water. Cover the dough and set aside until the timer for the starter has gone off.

Mix the dough, starter, oat porridge, and salt: When the starter is ready, scrape it into the bowl with the resting dough. While holding the bowl still with one hand, use your other hand to gently massage the starter into the dough.

Now add a quarter of the oats, which will make the dough slippery and stringy. Keep massaging. Once the oats are well incorporated, add another quarter and keep massaging and mixing, adding the remaining oats in two more batches. The end mixture will have a sticky consistency.

Add the salt and keep working the dough with a gentle touch until it has been incorporated. The dough should feel soft and pull and stretch easily.

Take the dough's temperature, adjusting it by setting the pan in a bowl of hot, warm, or cool water as necessary to bring it to about 82°F / 28°C. (See Controlling Temperature, page 52.)

Wash your hands, scrape down the insides of the bowl, and cover the dough with a tea towel.

Bulk ferment, preshape, rest, final shape, and cold retard: Follow the instructions of the City Loaf Master Recipe (page 114), with the following addition:

When you do the final shaping, scatter the handful of oats onto a plate. Rock the top half of the shaped loaves in the oats to coat, and gently transfer them, oat side down, to the baskets for proofing.

DAY 2

Preheat, score, and bake: Follow the instructions of the City Loaf Master Recipe (page 115).

Rice Bread

MAKES TWO 1-KILOGRAM LOAVES

Henrietta, my love, missed traveling during COVID lockdown, so I cooked her dishes from the places she used to travel to. One morning, I had a ton of congee, a Chinese rice porridge, left over, so I chucked it in my wheat dough. It was awesome. In this recipe, the rice visually disappears during bulk fermentation and baking, but it adds the sweetness of fresh-cooked rice and a super-moist texture.

RICE PORRIDGE

BAKER'S %	WEIGHT	INGREDIENT
100%	128g	White rice (any type), rinsed
200%	256g	Water

STARTER

BAKER'S %	WEIGHT	INGREDIENT
100%	75g	Hot water (104°F / 40°C)
100%	75g	Whole wheat flour
40%	30g	12-hour wheat or rye starter (your choice; see pages 73 and 69)

DOUGH

BAKER'S %	WEIGHT	INGREDIENT
40%	385g	Bread flour
40%	385g	All-purpose flour
20%	192g	Whole wheat flour
50%	480g	Hot water (104°F / 40°C)
15%	144g	Freshly fed starter (above)
45%	450g	Rice porridge (above)
3%	29g	Salt

ADDITIONAL INGREDIENTS

A handful each of all-purpose and rice flour (for coating baskets and tops of loaves)

TIMING

Day 1 (morning): Make the rice porridge and let it cool, feed starter, autolyse and mix dough, ferment, preshape, and final shape: a total of 9 hours (most of which is allowing the dough to bulk ferment and proof), plus an overnight cold retard of up to 12 hours

Day 2 (morning): Preheat oven, transfer dough to Dutch oven, score, and bake: a total of about 4 hours

EQUIPMENT

Small saucepan with lid, wooden spoon, sheet pan, two mixing bowls, digital thermometer, flexible plastic dough scraper, bowl or pitcher of warm water (for rinsing), tea towels, bench scraper, two bannetons (proofing baskets), cast-iron or enameled Dutch oven (with a flat, handleless lid), lame, cooling rack

DAY 1

Make and cool the rice porridge: In a saucepan, combine the rice and water and bring to a boil. Stir it well, reduce the heat to a simmer, and cover the pan. Let it cook until very tender and on the cusp of disintegration, approximately 20 minutes. It should have absorbed most of the water. Transfer it to a sheet pan and spread it out so that it cools quickly.

Feed the starter: Follow the instructions of the City Loaf Master Recipe (page 113). Set a timer for 45 minutes.

Autolyse the dough: Follow the instructions of the City Loaf Master Recipe (page 114), using all the water. Cover the dough and set aside until the timer for the starter has gone off.

Mix the dough, starter, rice porridge, and salt: When the starter is ready, scrape it into the bowl with the resting dough. While holding the bowl still with one hand, use your other hand to gently massage the starter into the dough.

Now add about a quarter of the rice porridge, which will make the dough slippery and stringy. Keep massaging. Once the rice is well incorporated, add another quarter and keep massaging and mixing, adding the remaining rice in two more batches. The mixture will have a sticky consistency.

Add the salt and keep working the dough with the same gentle touch until it has been incorporated. The dough should feel soft and pull and stretch easily.

Take the dough's temperature, adjusting it by setting the pan in a bowl of hot, warm, or cool water as necessary to bring it to about 82°F / 28°C. (See Controlling Temperature, page 52.)

Wash your hands, scrape down the insides of the bowl, and cover the dough with a tea towel.

Bulk ferment, preshape, rest, final shape, and cold retard: Follow the instructions of the City Loaf Master Recipe (page 114).

DAY 2

Preheat, score, and bake: Follow the instructions of the City Loaf Master Recipe (page 115).

Polenta Bread

MAKES TWO 1-KILOGRAM LOAVES

Polenta works so well in wheat bread, making the crumb creamier. I love finding little chunks that haven't broken down in the mix. The crust, dipped in cornmeal after shaping, has a great crunch.

POLENTA

BAKER'S %	WEIGHT	INGREDIENT
400%	300g	Water
100%	75g	Finely ground cornmeal

STARTER

BAKER'S %	WEIGHT	INGREDIENT
100%	100g	Hot water (104°F / 40°C)
100%	100g	Whole wheat flour
40%	40g	12-hour wheat or rye starter (your choice; see pages 73 and 69)

DOUGH

BAKER'S %	WEIGHT	INGREDIENT
40%	375g	Bread flour
40%	375g	All-purpose flour
20%	188g	Whole wheat flour
50%	470g	Hot water (104°F / 40°C)
20%	188g	Freshly fed starter (above)
40%	375g	Polenta (above)
3%	28g	Salt

ADDITIONAL INGREDIENTS

A handful each of all-purpose and rice flour (for coating baskets)

A handful of finely ground cornmeal (for coating the crust)

TIMING

Day 1 (morning): Make and cool polenta, feed starter, autolyse and mix dough, ferment, preshape, and final shape: a total of 9 hours (mostly bulk ferment and proof), plus cold retard of up to 12 hours

Day 2 (morning): Preheat oven, transfer dough to Dutch oven, score, and bake: a total of about 4 hours

EQUIPMENT

Small saucepan with lid, whisk, sheet pan, two mixing bowls, digital thermometer, flexible plastic dough scraper, bowl or pitcher of warm water (for rinsing), tea towels, bench scraper, two bannetons (proofing baskets), cast-iron or enameled Dutch oven (with a flat, handleless lid), lame, cooling rack

DAY 1

Make and cool the polenta: In a saucepan, bring the water to a boil. Add the cornmeal. Whisk continuously until the mixture thickens, just a minute or two. Turn off the heat, cover, and let it sit on the stove for 30 minutes. Transfer the mixture to a sheet pan and spread it out so that it cools quickly.

Feed the starter: Follow the instructions of the City Loaf Master Recipe (page 113). Set a timer for 45 minutes.

Autolyse the dough: Follow the instructions in the City Loaf Master Recipe (page 114), using 400g of the hot water. Cover the dough and set aside until the timer for the starter has gone off.

Mix the dough, starter, polenta, and salt: When the starter is ready, scrape it into the bowl with the resting dough and massage them together by hand.

Now add about a quarter of the polenta and a quarter of the reserved 70g hot water, which will make the dough slippery and stringy. Keep massaging. Once the polenta and water are well incorporated, add another quarter of each and keep massaging and mixing, adding the remaining polenta and water in two more batches. The mixture will have a sticky consistency.

Add the salt and, if necessary to keep the dough pliable, a splash or more of hot water. Keep working the dough with the same gentle touch. It should feel soft and pull and stretch easily.

Take the dough's temperature, adjusting it by setting the pan in a bowl of hot, warm, or cool water as necessary to bring it to about 82°F / 28°C. (See Controlling Temperature, page 52.)

Wash your hands, scrape down the insides of the bowl, and cover the dough with a tea towel.

Bulk ferment, preshape, rest, final shape, and cold retard: Follow the instructions of the City Loaf Master Recipe (page 114) with the following addition:

For final shaping, scatter the handful of cornmeal onto a plate. Rock the top half of the shaped loaves in the cornmeal to coat, and gently transfer them, cornmeal side down, to the baskets for proofing.

DAY 2

Preheat, score, and bake: Follow the instructions of the City Loaf Master Recipe (page 115).

Barley Bread,
Test #3

MAKES THREE 800-GRAM LOAVES

This is another attempt at that London Pride taste, with barley porridge for moisture, sheen, and aroma. I love it, but it still doesn't give me *that* barley aftertaste I'm going for. My copy-editor, Heather, suggests adding reduced London Pride to the dough. I'm keen to try it. If you have other ideas, let me know.

TOASTED BARLEY PORRIDGE

BAKER'S %	WEIGHT	INGREDIENT
100%	90g	Barley flakes or rolled barley
400%	359g	Water

STARTER

BAKER'S %	WEIGHT	INGREDIENT
100%	104g	Hot water (104°F / 40°C)
100%	104g	Whole wheat flour
40%	42g	12-hour wheat or rye starter (your choice; see pages 73 and 69)

DOUGH

BAKER'S %	WEIGHT	INGREDIENT
40%	359g	Bread flour
40%	359g	All-purpose flour
20%	179g	Whole wheat flour
50%	448g	Hot water (104°F / 40°C)
20%	179g	Freshly fed starter (above)
50%	448g	Toasted barley porridge (above)
3%	27g	Salt

ADDITIONAL INGREDIENTS

A handful each of all-purpose and rice flour (for coating baskets)

A handful of barley flakes (for coating loaves)

TIMING

Day 1 (morning): Cook porridge and let cool, feed starter, autolyse and mix dough, ferment, preshape, and final shape: total of 9 hours (mostly bulk ferment and proof), plus overnight cold retard of up to 12 hours

Day 2 (morning): Preheat oven, transfer dough to Dutch oven, score, and bake: a total of about 4 hours

EQUIPMENT

Sheet pan, small saucepan, wooden spoon, mixing bowls, digital thermometer, flexible plastic dough scraper, bowl or pitcher of warm water (for rinsing), tea towels, bench scraper, three bannetons (proofing baskets), cast-iron or enameled Dutch oven (with a flat, handleless lid), lame, cooling rack

DAY 1

Make the barley porridge: Preheat the oven to 480°F / 250°C.

Toast the barley flakes on a sheet pan for 5 to 7 minutes, until golden brown. Keep watch; they can easily burn.

Combine the flakes and water in a saucepan and bring to a boil. Stir well, then reduce to a simmer. Cook until all the water is absorbed. Remove from the heat and spread on a sheet pan to cool quickly.

Feed the starter: Follow the instructions of the City Loaf Master Recipe (page 113). Set a timer for 45 minutes.

Autolyse the dough: Follow the instructions of the City Loaf Master Recipe (page 114), using all the water. Cover the dough and set aside until the timer for the starter has gone off.

Mix the dough, starter, porridge, and salt: When the starter is ready, scrape it into the bowl with the resting dough and massage them together by hand.

Add a quarter of the porridge, which will make the dough slippery and stringy. Keep massaging. Once it is well mixed, add another quarter, and keep massaging and mixing, adding the remaining porridge in two more batches.

Add the salt. Work the dough with a gentle touch to incorporate it, until the dough feels soft and pulls easily.

Take the dough's temperature, adjusting it by setting the pan in a bowl of hot, warm, or cool water as necessary to bring it to about 82°F / 28°C. (See Controlling Temperature, page 52.)

Wash your hands, scrape down the insides of the bowl, and cover it with a tea towel.

Bulk ferment, preshape, rest, final shape, and cold retard: Follow the instructions of the City Loaf Master Recipe (page 114) with the following addition:

For the final shaping, scatter barley flakes onto a plate. Rock the top half of the loaves in the flakes to coat, then gently transfer, barley side down, to baskets for proofing.

DAY 2

Preheat, score, and bake: Follow the instructions of the City Loaf Master Recipe (page 115).

Toasted Spelt Bread

Day 1 (morning): Cook spelt porridge and let it cool, feed starter, autolyse and mix dough, ferment, preshape, and final shape: a total of 9 hours (mostly bulk ferment and proof), plus an overnight cold retard of up to 12 hours

Day 2 (morning): Preheat oven, transfer dough to Dutch oven, score, and bake: a total of 2½ to 3 hours

EQUIPMENT

Sheet pan, small saucepan, whisk or wooden spoon, mixing bowls, digital thermometer, flexible plastic dough scraper, bowl or pitcher of warm water (for rinsing), tea towels, bench scraper, two bannetons (proofing baskets), cast-iron or enameled Dutch oven (with a flat, handleless lid), lame, cooling rack

DAY 1

Make the spelt porridge: Preheat the oven to 355°F / 180°C.

Arrange the spelt flour in an even layer on a sheet pan and toast, keeping an eye on it, for 8 to 10 minutes, just until it's light golden and smells toasty, even popcorn-like. It may not seem to have changed color, but compare it with untoasted spelt flour to confirm.

Let the flour cool to room temperature.

In a saucepan, bring the water to a boil. Add the toasted spelt flour and the flakes. Reduce the heat to low, stir the mixture well with the whisk or wooden spoon, and let it cook for 3 minutes.

Transfer the porridge to a shallow bowl and let it cool to room temperature. It can be cooked a day ahead and stored in the refrigerator overnight. Let it return to room temperature before mixing into the dough.

Feed the starter: Follow the instructions of the City Loaf Master Recipe (page 113). Set a timer for 45 minutes.

Autolyse the dough: Follow the instructions of the City Loaf Master Recipe (page 114), using 395g of the water. Cover the dough and set aside until the timer for the starter has gone off.

Mix the dough, starter, salt, and spelt porridge: When the starter is ready, and you've given the dough at least 20 minutes to rest after mixing, scrape the starter into the bowl with the resting dough and mix them together with your hands. Add the remaining 79g water and continue to mix until incorporated, then add the salt and mix until it is dissolved into the dough.

Add half the porridge and mix with your hands until it's incorporated, then add the rest. Make sure it's evenly distributed throughout the dough.

Take the dough's temperature, adjusting it by setting the pan in a bowl of hot, warm, or cool water as necessary to bring it to about 82°F / 28°C. (See Controlling Temperature, page 52.)

MAKES TWO 900-GRAM LOAVES

I don't have a cool story for spelt, but it's a really delicious grain, high in fiber, protein, and nutrients. Spelt flour is more extensible than wheat flour, with less strength, so I again make a porridge with it and mix it into the dough.

Toasting flour is a great technique for adding flavor to your bread. It brings a nutty complexity and sweetness from the caramelized sugars. However, toasting the flour damages the gluten, so it's better to toast flour for a porridge that you then add to your dough.

SPELT PORRIDGE

BAKER'S %	WEIGHT	INGREDIENT
100%	56g	Spelt flour
500%	280g	Water
100%	56g	Spelt flakes

STARTER

BAKER'S %	WEIGHT	INGREDIENT
100%	75g	Hot water (104°F / 40°C)
100%	75g	Whole wheat flour
40%	30g	12-hour wheat or rye starter (your choice; see pages 73 and 69)

DOUGH

BAKER'S %	WEIGHT	INGREDIENT
100%	789g	Bread flour
60%	474g	Hot water (104°F / 40°C)
15%	118g	Freshly fed starter (above)
3%	24g	Salt
50%	395g	Spelt porridge (above)

ADDITIONAL INGREDIENTS

A handful each of all-purpose and rice flour (for coating baskets)

A handful of spelt flakes (for coating loaves)

Wash your hands, scrape down the insides of the bowl, and cover the dough with a tea towel.

Bulk ferment, preshape, and rest: Follow the instructions of the City Loaf Master Recipe (page 114).

Final shape: Follow the instructions of the City Loaf Master Recipe (page 115) with the following addition:

Scatter the handful of spelt flakes onto a plate. Roll the shaped loaves in the flakes to coat before transferring them to the baskets, spelt side down, for proofing. As the flakes toast during baking, they will add to the spelt flavor.

Cold retard: Follow the instructions of the City Loaf Master Recipe (page 115).

DAY 2

Preheat, score, and bake: Follow the instructions of the City Loaf Master Recipe (page 115).

Triple Rye Bread

MAKES TWO 900-GRAM LOAVES

This bread is another Karishma creation, and it's super tasty. I love using porridges and whole grains in my bread to create flavors, and she nailed it here. The reason this recipe isn't in the rye chapter is because we wanted the style and texture of a wheat dough, with all the wonderful floral flavors that rye has to offer. Her recipe does exactly that.

BOILED RYE BERRIES

BAKER'S %	WEIGHT	INGREDIENT
100%	120g	Whole rye berries
600%	720g	Water

TOASTED CRACKED RYE

BAKER'S %	WEIGHT	INGREDIENT
100%	35g	Cracked rye berries
100%	35g	Water

SCALDED RYE

BAKER'S %	WEIGHT	INGREDIENT
100%	105g	Rye flour
100%	105g	Boiling water

STARTER

BAKER'S %	WEIGHT	INGREDIENT
100%	70g	Hot water (104°F / 40°C)
100%	70g	Whole wheat flour
40%	28g	12-hour wheat or rye starter (your choice; see pages 73 and 69)

DOUGH

BAKER'S %	WEIGHT	INGREDIENT
80%	558g	Bread flour
20%	140g	Whole wheat flour
80%	558g	Hot water (104°F / 40°C)
15%	105g	Freshly fed starter (above)
30%	210g	Scalded rye (above)
3%	21g	Salt
20%	140g	Boiled rye berries (above)
10%	70g	Toasted cracked rye (above)

ADDITIONAL INGREDIENTS

A handful each of all-purpose and rice flour (for coating baskets)

A few handfuls of rye flakes (for coating loaves)

TIMING

Day 1 (evening): Cook and cool rye berries, toast and soak cracked rye, and make scalded rye: a total of about 2 hours (much of which is rye berry cooking time)

Day 2 (morning): Feed starter, autolyse and mix dough, ferment, preshape, and final shape: a total of about 8 hours (mostly bulk ferment and proof), plus an overnight cold retard of up to 12 hours

Day 3 (morning): Preheat, transfer dough to Dutch oven, score, and bake: a total of 2 to 3 hours

EQUIPMENT

Saucepan, sieve, sheet pan, mixing bowls of various sizes, spatula or wooden spoon, digital thermometer, flexible plastic dough scraper, bowl or pitcher of warm water (for rinsing), tea towels, bench scraper, two bannetons (proofing baskets), cast-iron or enameled Dutch oven (with a flat, handleless lid), lame, cooling rack

DAY 1

Boil the rye berries: In a saucepan, cook the whole rye berries in the water as directed in Cooked Whole Grains (page 106) until completely tender, 60 to 90 minutes. Drain the berries in the sieve, cover, and refrigerate.

Toast and soak the cracked rye: Preheat the oven to 355°F / 180°C. Arrange the cracked rye in an even layer on a sheet pan and toast for 8 to 10 minutes, just until it's light golden and smells toasty, maybe even popcorn-like.

Transfer to a bowl, cover with the water, and let it soak, refrigerated, overnight.

Recipe continues

Make the scalded rye: Place the rye flour in a heatproof medium bowl, pour the boiling water over the flour, and mix well with a spatula or wooden spoon until all the water has been evenly absorbed into the flour. Let the mixture cool to room temperature, then cover and refrigerate overnight.

DAY 2

Let the rye additions warm up: Remove the rye berries, cracked rye, and scalded rye from the refrigerator and let them come to room temperature for at least 1 hour.

Feed the starter: Follow the instructions of the City Loaf Master Recipe (page 113). Set a timer for 45 minutes.

Autolyse the dough: Follow the instructions of the City Loaf Master Recipe (page 114), using 419g of the hot water. Cover the dough and set aside until the timer for the starter has gone off.

Combine the starter, scalded rye, dough, salt, and rye additions: When the starter is ready and you've given the dough at least 20 minutes to rest after mixing, scrape the starter and scalded rye into the bowl with the dough and mix them together with your hands. Add the remaining 139g hot water, a little at a time, and continue to mix until it is incorporated, then add the salt and mix until it is dissolved into the dough.

Add the boiled rye berries and cracked rye to the dough and continue to mix until they are well incorporated. The dough should feel strong, showing good resistance when you try to pull a piece away from the mass.

Take the dough's temperature, adjusting it by setting the pan in a bowl of hot, warm, or cool water as necessary to bring it to about 82°F / 28°C. (See Controlling Temperature, page 52.)

Wash your hands, scrape down the insides of the bowl, and cover the dough with a tea towel.

Bulk ferment, preshape, and rest: Follow the instructions of the City Loaf Master Recipe (page 114).

Final shape: Follow the instructions of the City Loaf Master Recipe (page 115) with the following addition:

Scatter the handful of rye flakes onto a plate. Roll the shaped loaves in the rye flakes to coat before transferring them to the baskets, rye side down, for proofing. As the flakes toast during baking, they will add to the rye flavor.

Cold retard: Follow the instructions of the City Loaf Master Recipe (page 115).

DAY 3

Preheat, score, and bake: Follow the instructions of the City Loaf Master Recipe (page 115).

158

WHEAT LOAVES FLAVORED WITH OTHER GRAINS

Flatbreads Plus
Focaccia & Ciabatta

Flatbreads are sometimes over-looked as types of bread, but around the world, people view and make them very differently. It's not all about the loaf. As a bread baker, I have learned to make and have played with all kinds of breads and doughs. I am constantly learning; wherever I go, I love to exchange baking knowledge with friends and fellow bakers, all over the world.

In this chapter, there's a Mexican flour tortilla from my old mate Cameron, Indian naan from Karishma, an Italian cracker from way back in my cooking days in the Napa Valley, pizza dough and ciabatta (kindly taught to me by Giuliano) from the mill I work with in Italy, and other bits and bobs.

For argument's sake, ciabatta and focaccia aren't typically considered flatbreads, but I have added them here because the dough, when shaped, is actually pretty flat, and I think this is where they fit best. And speaking of flatbreads, you might notice that in this chapter I don't suggest taking the temperature of the dough during the fermentation. I don't think it's that crucial in these recipes, because they're flat, and also because some of them have the added punch of commercial yeast anyway.

Flour Tortillas

MAKES TWELVE 50-GRAM TORTILLAS

This recipe came from Cameron Wallace, one of the original Tartine bakers, who did a taqueria pop-up out of the side window at the bakery. There were always huge queues down the block. Cameron made some of the best tacos I have ever had. I've added sourdough starter to Cameron's original recipe, which gives a good depth of flavor. The texture is nothing like a typical fluffy store-bought flour tortilla: it's thin and light and puffs up beautifully when baked in a hot pan.

A note about the use of hot water: the other ingredients, which are at room temperature, will moderate the water temperature, leaving it still warm enough to kick-start the 2-hour fermentation.

DOUGH

BAKER'S %	WEIGHT	INGREDIENT
100%	286g	All-purpose flour
2.5%	7g	Baking powder
1.25%	4g	Salt
7%	20g	Fat (lard, butter, or oil)
47%	134g	12-hour wheat starter (see page 73)
55%	157g	Hot water (104°F / 40°C)

ADDITIONAL INGREDIENTS

A handful each of all-purpose flour (for shaping and rolling out the dough)

TIMING

Mix dough, ferment 2 hours, divide and shape, roll out, and cook: a total of 3½ to 4 hours

EQUIPMENT

Medium bowl, whisk, tea towels, bench scraper, cast-iron skillet or griddle, rolling pin

Mix the dough: In a medium bowl, combine the flour, baking powder, and salt and whisk them together. Add the fat, starter, and hot water and use your hands to mix them together and gently knead the dough into a ball.

Ferment the dough: Cover the bowl with a tea towel and let the dough rest at room temperature for 2 hours, until it has relaxed and expanded to about one and a half times its original size.

Divide and shape the dough: Use the bench scraper to divide the dough into 12 portions of 50g each.

Roll each piece into a ball using the dough balling technique: Flour your dominant hand and tap off the excess. Get one portion of dough in front of you and apply light pressure to the top of it as you use your fingers and thumb to form a kind of circular basket around the dough. Roll it in circles; the dough should be a bit sticky on the bottom as you're pressing lightly on it while rolling; that friction and sticking on the work surface will help the dough come together in a ball. As you roll the dough, your fingers should be tucking it underneath itself to help form a ball. Roll until the dough has a nice, taut surface and a round shape. Repeat with the remaining dough pieces.

Roll out and cook the tortillas: Heat the cast-iron skillet or griddle over medium heat. Flour your work surface and fingers and pat out each ball with your fingertips. Use a rolling pin to roll it into a very thin, flat tortilla 7 to 8 inches / 18 to 20cm in diameter. Carefully transfer one to the hot pan and cook for 1 minute, until the edges of the tortilla just start to lift away from the pan. Flip and cook another minute on the other side, in which time it will puff, which means that the inside is steaming and the tortilla is now fully baked. Flip it back to the first side for about 20 seconds, and when you're happy with the color, transfer it to a plate and cover with a tea towel. Repeat with the remaining tortillas. To serve, briefly reheat each tortilla in a hot pan.

Naan

MAKES EIGHT 130-GRAM NAAN

This recipe was developed by Karishma, who was born and raised in Bombay/Mumbai. Making fresh naan is really easy and so worth the effort. Nothing you'll buy in a package will come anywhere close. With the pre-ferments and the yogurt and the sourdough, this is an incredibly sweet and tender version of the classic Indian flatbread.

When it came to taking pictures for the book, I asked Karishma to make some dal to go with the bread. She looked at me like I was crazy or something, and said, "Dal doesn't go with naan." So I asked, "What *does* go with naan?" To which she replied, "Black dal."

I don't know which one of us is the crazy one, but I love her and her dals, whatever color.

POOLISH

BAKER'S %	WEIGHT	INGREDIENT
100%	50g	All-purpose flour
100%	49g	Tepid water (77°F / 25°C)
0.3%	1g	Instant dry yeast

DOUGH

BAKER'S %	WEIGHT	INGREDIENT
100%	500g	All-purpose flour
3%	15g	Salt
1%	5g	Instant dry yeast
20%	100g	Poolish (above)
20%	100g	12-hour wheat starter (see page 73)
30%	150g	Yogurt
10%	50g	Beaten egg
10%	50g	Tepid water (77°F / 25°C)
10%	50g	Neutral oil
5%	25g	Sugar

ADDITIONAL INGREDIENTS

A handful of all-purpose flour (for rolling out the dough)

Melted butter (for brushing)

Finely chopped garlic, cilantro leaves, and black and white sesame seeds (for serving; optional)

TIMING

Day 1: Mix and ferment poolish, a total of about 12 hours

Day 2: Mix dough, bulk ferment, divide, proof, shape, roll out, and cook: a total of about 4 hours

EQUIPMENT

Mixing bowls, flexible plastic dough scraper, tea towel, rolling pin, cast-iron skillet or griddle

DAY 1

Mix the poolish: In a bowl, combine the flour, water, and yeast and mix well by hand. Use the dough scraper to scrape any excess from your fingers back into the mixture. Cover with a tea towel, and let the mixture ferment at room temperature overnight, or up to 12 hours.

DAY 2

Mix the dough: Transfer the poolish to a larger bowl and add all the dough ingredients. Mix the dough well by hand to form a smooth, well-developed, and strong dough. It should show good resistance when you try to pull a piece of it away from the mass.

Bulk ferment the dough: Cover the bowl with a tea towel and let sit in a warm place for about 2 hours to bulk ferment. The dough will roughly triple in volume, and when you pinch a small amount, you should feel bubbles popping between your fingertips.

Divide, proof, and shape the dough: Divide the dough into 8 portions of 130g and let them proof, covered with a tea towel, at room temperature for 1 hour.

Flour your work surface and use a rolling pin to roll each portion out into an oval shape a scant ¼ inch / 5mm thick.

Cook the naan: Heat a cast-iron skillet or griddle until it's very hot but not smoking. Carefully place a naan into the pan and cook until the bubbles on the surface have begun to set, about 2 minutes. Flip the bread and cook another minute, until done. Repeat with the remaining naan.

When each naan comes out of the pan, brush it immediately with melted butter. If desired, top it with garlic, cilantro, and sesame seeds. If you're not serving the naan right away, stack them and cover them with a tea towel to keep warm.

Pita

MAKES EIGHT 110-GRAM PITAS

Yogurt in the dough keeps pita very tender. This recipe is super easy and delicious; once you've made it, you'll never want to buy pita again.

DOUGH

BAKER'S %	WEIGHT	INGREDIENT
100%	500g	All-purpose flour
50%	250g	Tepid water (77°F / 25°C)
10%	50g	12-hour wheat starter (see page 73)
10%	50g	Yogurt
5%	25g	Sugar
2%	10g	Salt
1%	5g	Instant dry yeast

ADDITIONAL INGREDIENTS

A handful of all-purpose flour (for the work surface and rolling pin)

A handful of semolina flour (for the peel)

TIMING

Mix dough, ferment, divide and shape, rest, roll out, and bake: a total of about 4 hours

EQUIPMENT

Medium mixing bowl, flexible plastic dough scraper, tea towel, bench scraper, pizza stone, rolling pin, baking peel

Mix the dough: In a medium bowl, combine all the dough ingredients and use your hands to mix them into a homogenous dough.

Ferment the dough: Scrape the dough together into a ball, cover the bowl with a tea towel, and set aside at room temperature for about 2 hours. The dough will roughly double in size.

Shape and proof the dough: Flour the work surface with the all-purpose flour. Punch the dough down and reshape it into a ball. Use the bench scraper to divide the dough into 8 portions of 110g each and roll each one into a ball on the work surface. Lightly dust each ball with flour and cover the balls with the tea towel. Let rest 30 minutes.

Roll out and bake the dough: Preheat the oven (and pizza stone) to 425°F / 220°C.

With a rolling pin, lightly floured if necessary, roll each ball into a round about ½ inch / 1cm thick.

Lightly flour a baking peel with semolina and transfer the pitas, one or two at a time, to the hot pizza stone. Let bake for 6 to 8 minutes, until puffed up and lightly browned. Remove them from the oven, let cool for a few minutes, then serve.

Carta di Musica

This is a thin, crisp cracker bread I used to make at Ubuntu in Napa, with chef Jeremy Fox, and we would serve it with everything fancy-schmancy from the garden. Once it's finished, either store it in an airtight container or serve it immediately, topped with anything you like: for example, a beautiful dressed salad (Ubuntu style), thinly sliced cheese, a fried egg, whatever you want.

DOUGH

BAKER'S %	WEIGHT	INGREDIENT
50%	200g	Semolina flour
50%	200g	Bread flour
0.5%	2g	Instant dry yeast
10%	40g	12-hour wheat starter (see page 70)
50%	200g	Tepid water (77°F / 25°C)
10%	40g	Olive oil
2%	8g	Salt

ADDITIONAL INGREDIENTS

A handful each of bread flour and semolina flour (for the work surface and baking peel)

TIMING

Mix dough, ferment, divide, shape, proof, roll out, and bake: a total of about 3 hours

EQUIPMENT

Medium mixing bowl, tea towel, bench scraper, pizza stone, rolling pin, baking peel, scissors or knife

Mix the dough: In a medium bowl, combine all the dough ingredients and use your hands to mix them into a homogenous dough. Let rest for 10 minutes, then quickly knead the dough together to form a smooth ball.

Ferment the dough: Cover the bowl with a tea towel and let the dough rest at room temperature for 2 hours, until it has expanded to about one and a half times its original size.

Divide, shape, and proof the dough: Working on a surface that's lightly coated with bread flour, use a bench scraper to divide the dough into 8 portions of 85g each. Roll each piece into a ball, cover the balls with the tea towel, and let rest for 30 minutes.

Roll out and bake the dough: Arrange a rack in the middle of the oven. Place a pizza stone on the rack. Preheat the oven to 480°F / 250°C.

Working on a lightly floured surface, roll out each dough ball into a very thin round about 5 inches / 12.5cm across.

Sprinkle some semolina flour onto a baking peel and place one of the rolled-out rounds onto the peel, then transfer it to the stone in the oven. The bread will puff up and bake in 4 to 5 minutes. Remove the baked bread from the oven and repeat the process with the remaining rolled-out dough. Carefully move the pizza stone to the lower rack of the oven. Leave the oven on, but reduce the oven temperature to 210°F / 100°C.

Separate and finish the breads: Once the baked breads are cool enough to handle, use scissors or a knife to trim away the entire outer ¼ inch / 6mm of each bread, which will allow the two puffed halves of each bread to separate.

Return the trimmed and separated baked breads to the oven, directly on the rack for better airflow, and let them dry for about 10 minutes, until their consistency is cracker-like. Top them however you like and serve. Store in an airtight container and eat them within a few days.

Perfect Sandwich Bread, or BFKAC

(Bread Formerly Known as Ciabatta)

MAKES TWO 750-GRAM LOAVES

You know, more goes into making a really good sandwich than you might think. The bread can often be overlooked. When I have an idea for a new sandwich, I think of what the perfect bread would be to complement the filling. Will the bread hold up to the ingredients? When sinking your teeth into it, will you end up with the filling in your lap?

This bread is an all-rounder. It will hold up to all your fillings, hot or cold, and when you bite into it, the sandwich holds together.

I had been calling this bread ciabatta until a transformative visit to my mill in Italy, Molino Paolo Mariani. There I learned that the real deal is made with a biga, and is nothing like this bread, so it needed its own name. I am still making this bread, because it's so good: supersoft, tender, and chewy; it has an amazing flavor that comes from the whole combination of yeast, sourdough, scalded rye, and olive oil—it's just not ciabatta.

The scalded rye in this bread acts as a starch, which means the dough can take a lot more hydration, making this a superlight, airy bread.

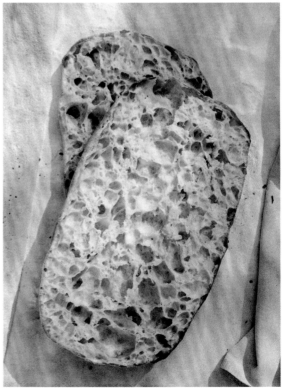

SCALDED RYE

BAKER'S %	WEIGHT	INGREDIENT
100%	55g	Rye flour
125%	70g	Boiling water

POOLISH

BAKER'S %	WEIGHT	INGREDIENT
100%	62g	All-purpose flour
100%	62g	Tepid water (77°F / 25°C)
1%	1g	Instant dry yeast

DOUGH

BAKER'S %	WEIGHT	INGREDIENT
100%	500g	Bread flour
85%	425g	Tepid water (77°F / 25°C)
25%	125g	Poolish (above)
25%	125g	12-hour wheat starter (see page 73)
25%	125g	Scalded rye (above)
3%	15g	Salt
0.6%	3g	Instant dry yeast
20%	100g	Olive oil

ADDITIONAL INGREDIENTS

A handful or two of rice flour (for dusting the work surface, couche, loaves, transfer board, and peel)

TIMING

Day 1 (evening): Scald rye flour and mix poolish: a total of about 30 minutes, plus overnight fermentation

Day 2 (morning): Mix dough, bulk ferment, preshape, proof, final shape, and bake: a total of about 4 hours

EQUIPMENT

Mixing bowls, spatula or wooden spoon, flexible plastic dough scraper, tea towel, bench scraper, sheet pan or shallow roasting pan, pizza stone, couche (linen proofing cloth), baker's peel, wooden transfer board, cooling rack

DAY 1

Make the scalded rye: Place the rye flour in a heatproof medium bowl, pour the boiling water over the flour, and mix well with a spatula or wooden spoon, until all the water has been evenly absorbed into the flour. Let the mixture cool to room temperature, then cover and refrigerate overnight.

Mix the poolish: In a bowl, combine the flour, water, and yeast and mix well by hand. Use the dough scraper to scrape any excess from your fingers back into the mixture. Cover with a tea towel and let the mixture ferment overnight at room temperature, during which time it will expand, with visible bubbles, and become fragrant.

DAY 2

Mix the dough, part 1: In a bowl, combine the flour and 255g of the water. Add the poolish, starter, and scalded rye and mix well with your hands until all the ingredients are well combined. Scrape the mixture into a mass using the dough scraper. Cover the bowl with a tea towel and let the dough rest for 30 minutes.

Mix the dough, part 2: Use your hands to massage in the remaining 170g water, a quarter at a time, mixing between the additions until the dough has completely absorbed the water. With the last addition of water, add the salt and yeast and continue to massage until they have been fully incorporated.

Continue to massage the dough until you have a cohesive mass, which should be strong, though it will also be quite wet. Drizzle in the oil, a small amount at a time, and continue to massage it until the oil is completely absorbed.

Bulk ferment the dough: Scrape the dough together into a mass, cover the bowl with the tea towel, and bulk ferment for 2 hours, until it has doubled in size.

Preshape and proof the dough: Using a wet hand and the flexible scraper, transfer the dough to a clean work surface. Use the bench scraper to divide the dough into two equal portions. Preshape each into an oblong shape and let rest for 30 minutes.

 Final shape and bake: Place a sheet pan or shallow roasting pan on the floor of the oven. Arrange a rack in the middle of the oven. Place a pizza stone on the rack. Preheat to 450°F / 230°C.

Dust the couche with rice flour and gently transfer the loaves to the couche. Gently shape both pieces into flat loaves measuring about 12 × 6 inches / 30 × 15cm. Dust the tops of the loaves with rice flour and let them proof for 30 minutes.

Unless you have a huge pizza stone, you will need to bake the loaves one at a time. Dust a baking peel and a transfer board with rice flour. Gently pull the edges of the couche to flip one loaf onto the transfer board. Invert the loaf onto the peel and transfer it from the peel to the pizza stone.

Add about 250ml water to the pan on the oven's floor, taking care to avoid exposing your skin directly to the resultant steam, which can burn. Bake the loaf for 20 to 25 minutes, until it has developed a golden brown crust. Remove it from the oven and let it cool on a rack, until cool enough to handle.

Repeat with the remaining loaf.

Focaccia

Mixing bowls, wooden spoon, flexible plastic dough scraper, tea towel, half sheet pan (13 × 18 inches / 33 × 23cm), parchment paper, blender, cooling rack

MAKES ONE 1.3-KILOGRAM LOAF

My focaccia became next level when Luca Pedersoli, at Hart, taught me to emulsify oil and water to top the dough. It creates pockets of moisture that enhance the texture and flavor.

SCALDED WHEAT

BAKER'S %	WEIGHT	INGREDIENT
100%	63g	Bread flour
100%	63g	Boiling water

POOLISH

BAKER'S %	WEIGHT	INGREDIENT
100%	63g	All-purpose flour
100%	63g	Tepid water (77°F / 25°C)
1%	1g	Instant dry yeast

DOUGH

BAKER'S %	WEIGHT	INGREDIENT
100%	500g	Bread flour
65%	325g	Tepid water (77°F / 25°C)
25%	125g	Poolish (above)
25%	125g	12-hour wheat starter (see page 73)
25%	125g	Scalded wheat (above)
3%	15g	Salt
0.6%	3g	Instant dry yeast
20%	100g	Olive oil

ADDITIONAL INGREDIENTS

Neutral oil (enough to oil the pan for baking)

63g olive oil and 62g tepid water (77°F / 25°C)

Coarse sea salt, fresh rosemary leaves, and whole garlic cloves, blanched until softened, about 3 minutes (for garnishing the dough)

TIMING

Day 1 (evening): Scald wheat flour and mix poolish and ferment: a total of about 30 minutes, plus overnight fermentation

Day 2 (morning): Mix dough, proof, and bake: a total of about 5 hours

DAY 1

Make the scalded wheat: Place the flour in a mixing bowl, pour the boiling water over the flour, and mix well with a wooden spoon until the water has been evenly absorbed. Let it cool to room temperature, then cover and refrigerate overnight.

Mix the poolish: In a bowl, combine the flour, water, and yeast. Mix well by hand. Scrape any excess from your fingers back into the mixture. Cover with a tea towel and let it ferment overnight at room temperature, during which time it will expand, with visible bubbles, and become fragrant.

DAY 2

Mix the dough, part 1: In a bowl, combine the flour and 200g of the water. Add the poolish, starter, and scalded wheat and mix well with your hands. Scrape the mixture into a mass using the flexible scraper. Cover with a tea towel and let it rest for 30 minutes.

Mix the dough, part 2: Use your hands to mix in the remaining 125g water, a quarter at a time, until the dough has completely absorbed the water. With the last addition of water, add the salt and yeast and continue to mix until fully incorporated.

Massage the dough until you have a cohesive mass, which should be strong and quite wet. Drizzle in the olive oil, a small amount at a time, and massage until completely absorbed.

Proof the dough: Drizzle a little neutral oil onto a sheet pan, coating it lightly, then line with parchment. Use the flexible scraper to transfer the dough from bowl to pan. Use clean, well-oiled hands to press the dough out to the shape of the pan. Proof in a warm place for 4 hours. It will relax, double in size, and be very bubbly.

Bake the loaf: Preheat the oven to 450°F / 230°C.

Combine the additional olive oil and water in the blender and mix until emulsified, 1 to 2 minutes. Immediately drizzle the dough evenly with the mixture. Dimple the dough with your fingertips so that the oil pools and settles in irregular ways. Scatter the sea salt, rosemary, and garlic over the dough.

Bake for 25 to 30 minutes, until the crust is golden brown. Remove from the oven and transfer the bread, still on the parchment, to a cooling rack.

Real Italian Ciabatta

MAKES TEN 100-GRAM ROLLS

For the longest time, I made a bread in my bakery and called it ciabatta (see Perfect Sandwich Bread, page 172), but it wasn't the real deal. This is. I learned it in Italy, from head baker Giuliano Pediconi at Molino Paolo Mariani.

Just before baking, the dough is incredibly light, like marshmallow. After baking, the crust is super thin and crisp, with an amazing holey crumb.

BIGA

BAKER'S %	WEIGHT	INGREDIENT
100%	559g	Bread flour
45%	251g	Tepid water (77°F / 25°C)
1%	6g	Instant dry yeast

DOUGH

BAKER'S %	WEIGHT	INGREDIENT
—	816g	Biga (above)
1%	6g	Diastatic malt powder
2%	11g	Salt
30%	168g	Tepid water (77°F / 25°C)

ADDITIONAL INGREDIENTS

Neutral oil (enough to oil the bulk fermenting / proofing container)

A handful of all-purpose flour (for the work surface and dough)

A handful of rice flour (for the peel)

TIMING

Day 1 (afternoon or evening): Mix biga: less than 5 minutes, plus overnight fermentation

Day 2 (morning): Mix dough, bulk ferment, divide, shape, proof, and bake: a total of about 3 hours

EQUIPMENT

Mixing bowls, stand mixer fitted with the dough hook, wide, shallow container, marker and/or masking tape, tea towel, bench scraper, wooden board or sheet pan, pizza stone, baker's peel, cooling rack

DAY 1

Mix the biga: In a bowl, combine the flour, water, and yeast and rub the ingredients together with your fingertips until the mixture clumps together and looks like wet breadcrumbs. It shouldn't be a smooth or uniform dough. If you overmix biga, it ferments too quickly.

Cover the bowl with a plate and leave it in a cool environment, ideally 53°–57°F / 12°–14°C, for 12 hours or overnight. If you can't get it into that temperature zone, leave it at room temperature for 3 to 4 hours, then refrigerate for the remaining 8 to 9 hours.

DAY 2

Mix the dough: In the bowl of a stand mixer fitted with the dough hook, mix the biga on medium speed until it's a smooth dough, 5 to 10 minutes. It should feel strong and well developed. Add the malt powder and salt and continue to mix until it is uniform. Start adding the water, a little at a time, allowing the dough to come together before the next addition. You should end up with a strong, well-hydrated dough.

Bulk ferment the dough: Oil the wide, shallow container. Place the dough inside it and mark the top of the dough on the outside of the container using a marker or piece of tape. Make your best estimate and mark where the dough will be once it's doubled in size.

Cover with a tea towel or plate and let the dough bulk ferment for 1½ to 2 hours, until it reaches the second mark, indicating that it has doubled in volume.

 Divide and shape the dough: Flour your work surface well and gently flip the dough out onto it. Sprinkle another layer of flour over the top of the dough. Using your bench scraper, cut the dough into 10 rectangles of roughly the same size. Be gentle when handling the dough, to keep as much air encased inside as possible.

Rest the dough: Heavily flour a wooden board or inverted sheet pan and transfer each portion of dough onto it. Cover with a tea towel and allow to rest for 1 hour.

Bake the ciabatta: Arrange a rack in the middle of the oven. Place a pizza stone on the rack. Preheat the oven to 480°F / 250°C.

Sprinkle the surface of a baker's peel with rice flour and gently transfer one or two pieces of ciabatta to the peel, then transfer them onto the hot pizza stone in the oven. Repeat with the remaining ciabatta, working in batches if necessary to avoid overcrowding the stone.

Bake the ciabatta for 15 to 20 minutes, until golden brown, fully puffed, and very light when you pick them up. Transfer them to a rack to cool completely.

Roman-Style Pizza

MAKES ONE 900-GRAM PIZZA

The first time I had this pizza was at my friend Gabriele Bonci's pioneering place, Pizzarium, in Rome. It seriously blew me away. The texture is unbelievable: a perfectly crisp pillow of air, made possible, in part, by a small amount of diastatic malt, which turbocharges yeast activity in the dough. The following recipe was given to me by Giuliano Pediconi, head baker at Molino Paolo Mariani.

BIGA

BAKER'S %	WEIGHT	INGREDIENT
100%	244g	Bread flour
50%	122g	Tepid water (77°F / 25°C)
1%	2g	Instant dry yeast

DOUGH

BAKER'S %	WEIGHT	INGREDIENT
151%	368g	Biga (above)
100%	244g	Bread flour
1.5%	4g	Diastatic malt powder
106%	259g	Warm water (86°F / 30°C)
4%	10g	Salt
6%	15g	Olive oil

ADDITIONAL INGREDIENTS

Neutral oil (enough to coat the inside of the bulk fermenting / proofing container)

A few handfuls of all-purpose flour (for the work surface)

Olive oil (enough to oil the pan for baking)

Sauce of your choice: tomato, béchamel, pesto, or whatever you like (for topping the pizza)

A scant few pinches of best-quality sea salt (for garnishing the pizza)

TIMING

Day 1 (afternoon or evening): Mix biga: less than 5 minutes, plus overnight fermentation

Day 2 (morning): Mix dough, bulk ferment, preshape, proof, final shape, and bake: a total of about 4 hours

EQUIPMENT

Mixing bowl, stand mixer fitted with the dough hook, flexible plastic dough scraper, wide, shallow container, marker and/or masking tape, tea towel, bench scraper, half sheet pan (13 × 18 inches / 33 × 23cm), pizza stone, pizza scissors or pizza cutter

DAY 1

Make the biga: In a bowl, combine the flour, water, and yeast and rub the ingredients together with your fingertips until the mixture clumps together and looks like wet breadcrumbs. You should have many small clumps of flour and water, not a smooth or uniform dough. If you overmix biga, it ferments too quickly.

Cover the bowl with a plate and leave it in a cool environment, ideally 53°–57°F / 12°–14°C, for 12 hours or overnight. Since most home refrigerators are colder than this (typically 41°–46°F / 5°–8°C), you can leave the biga out of the fridge for the first 3 hours of fermentation. In a warm environment, room temperature is fine. In a moderate or cold environment, you can keep the biga warm in a bowl of warm water for 3 hours, then transfer it to the refrigerator.

DAY 2

Mix the dough: In the bowl of a stand mixer fitted with the dough hook, combine the biga, flour, malt powder, and half the water and mix it on medium speed until it is smooth, 5 to 10 minutes. The dough should feel strong and well developed at this stage. Add the salt and continue to mix until it is uniform.

Now start adding the remaining water, a little at a time, allowing the dough to come together before the next addition. You should end up with a strong, well-hydrated dough that shows good resistance when you try to pull a piece away.

Next, add half the olive oil and mix until it has been absorbed into the dough. Add the remaining oil and mix again until it has been absorbed.

Recipe continues

180

Bulk ferment: Lightly oil a wide, shallow container with neutral oil. Place the dough inside it and mark the top of the dough on the outside of the container using a marker and/or a piece of tape. Now mark your best estimate of where the dough will be once it's expanded about one and a half times in volume.

Cover the container with a tea towel and allow the dough to bulk ferment for 1½ to 2 hours, until it has reached the second mark, indicating it has multiplied one and a half times in volume.

Preshape the dough: Turn the dough out onto a clean work surface. Using the bench scraper and a wet hand, tighten the dough into a ball. Let rest for 30 minutes.

Final shape: Flour your work surface with all-purpose flour. Invert the dough onto the flour and use your fingers to gently press it out to a rough oval shape that's about ½ inch / 1.25cm thick. Use the olive oil to coat the sheet pan, then transfer the dough to it. Let the dough rest for 5 minutes, allowing the gluten to relax before finally stretching it out to the full size of the pan.

Top the pizza and bake: Arrange a rack in the middle of the oven. Place a pizza stone on the rack. Preheat the oven to 430°F / 250°C.

Top the surface of the dough with the sauce of your choice, using your fingers to get it into all the crevices. Sprinkle the sauce with sea salt.

Leaving the dough in the pan, transfer it to the oven, atop the pizza stone. Bake the pizza for 15 to 20 minutes, until it is golden brown. Cut it into segments, using pizza scissors or a pizza cutter, and serve it hot.

Mixed Bag

Here are some really cool breads that I want you to know how to bake. "Mixed Bag" may be a weird name for a chapter, but the wide range of breads here doesn't fall under one specific type; various fermentation techniques and methods are used. Not everything or everyone fits into a category, but that doesn't make it, or them, any less wonderful.

English Bloomer
(aka Good Shitty Bread)

BAKER'S %	WEIGHT	INGREDIENT
100%	160g	Bread flour
100%	160g	Tepid water (77°F / 25°C)
1%	2g	Instant dry yeast

DOUGH

BAKER'S %	WEIGHT	INGREDIENT
400%	641g	Biga (above)
200%	321g	Poolish (above)
100%	160g	12-hour wheat starter (see page 73)
100%	160g	Bread flour
180%	289g	Warm water (82°F / 28°C)
6%	10g	Instant dry yeast
12%	19g	Salt

MAKES TWO 600-GRAM LOAVES

I made this bread for my love, Henrietta. She and I grew up eating bread like this in London. We both remember being so excited to hold a warm loaf, fresh out of the oven, with its crisp crust and pillowy middle.

The English Bloomer is normally made using only commercial yeast, with a quick fermentation, and it's not particularly good for you. I wanted to try and improve on it, by using pre-fermented flour, making it much better for your digestion. That is how it got the name "Good Shitty Bread."

At first, I used only pre-fermented flour, in the form of sourdough, biga, and poolish. I added only salt, yeast, and water to the mix. It was inconsistent, so I started to add a little new flour, to give the yeast army some fresh food. This fixed it, and the finished loaf is amazing (see photograph, page 184). As soon as you make and eat it, you'll recognize all the characteristics of the white bread available in every supermarket bakery, but unlike those, it's actually not shitty.

I think this is a really cool technique. Everyone understands the health benefits of making sourdough bread, how the long fermentation makes the wheat easier on digestion. This bread is based on the same principle but uses a completely different technique: a loaf made mostly of pre-ferments, resulting in a different texture and taste than sourdough. It excites me more than most things I've made in a long, long time—and I think it has potential for new and exciting roads. Please, fellow bakers, let's take it forward.

ADDITIONAL INGREDIENTS

A handful each of all-purpose and rice flours (for coating the work surface and couche)

TIMING

Day 1 (evening): Mix biga and mix poolish: a total of about 10 minutes, plus overnight fermentation

Day 2 (morning): Mix dough, bulk ferment, shape, proof, and bake: a total of about 2½ hours

EQUIPMENT

Mixing bowls, tea towels, flexible plastic dough scraper, stand mixer fitted with the dough hook, digital thermometer, bench scraper, couche (linen proofing cloth), cast-iron or enameled Dutch oven (with a flat, handleless lid), lame, cooling rack

BIGA

BAKER'S %	WEIGHT	INGREDIENT
100%	425g	Bread flour
50%	212g	Tepid water (77°F / 25°C)
1%	2g	Instant dry yeast

DAY 1

Mix the biga: In a bowl, combine the flour, water, and yeast and rub the ingredients together with your fingertips until the mixture has clumped together and looks shaggy, like wet breadcrumbs. You should have many small clumps, not a smooth or uniform dough. If you overmix biga, it tends to ferment too quickly.

Cover the bowl with a tea towel and leave it in a cool environment (ideally 53°–57°F / 12°–14°C) for 12 hours or overnight. If you can't get it into that recommended temperature zone, leave it at room temperature for 3 to 4 hours, and then refrigerate for the remaining 8 to 9 hours.

Mix the poolish: In a bowl, combine the flour, water, and yeast and mix well by hand. Use the dough scraper to scrape any excess from your fingers back into the mixture. Cover the bowl with a tea towel and let the mixture ferment at room temperature for at least 8 hours or overnight, during which time it will expand, with visible bubbles, and become fragrant.

DAY 2

Mix the dough: In a stand mixer fitted with the dough hook, combine the biga, poolish, and starter and begin to mix on low speed, gradually increasing the speed to medium, to bring it into a cohesive dough.

Turn off the mixer and add the flour and a small amount of the water. Continue to mix on low speed, adding the water in small increments, until you have added two-thirds of it. The dough will look lumpy because of the stiff biga; it will take about 5 minutes for it to come together as a smooth dough.

Add the yeast, salt, and remaining water and mix well until the water has all been absorbed. Take the dough's temperature, adjusting it as necessary by setting the bowl in a larger bowl of hot, warm, or cool water to bring it to about 82°F / 28°C. (See Controlling Temperature, page 52.)

Bulk ferment the dough: Cover the bowl with a tea towel and let the dough bulk ferment for 1½ hours, until it is roughly doubled in size. It will be full of air, have a smooth surface, and will have significantly expanded.

Divide and preshape the dough: Lightly flour your work surface with the mixture of all-purpose and rice flours. Use the flexible plastic scraper to turn the dough out onto the work surface.

Use the bench scraper to divide the dough into two equal portions. Then, using the bench scraper and a wet hand, preshape each piece into an oval and let them rest for about 20 minutes, uncovered.

Final shape: Use wet hands to gently flatten out each loaf into a roughly 8 × 12-inch / 20 × 30cm rectangle. Working from the long side, pull a strip of the dough toward you and roll it in on itself. Then pull that roll toward you and roll it back into itself. The idea is to create a tight cylinder with the dough, which will give it good shape and surface tension as it rests and bakes. This action is similar to what's used in baguette shaping, which you can see on page 194.

Lightly flour the surface of the couche with the all-purpose and rice flour mixture and gently transfer the loaf to it, arranging the folds around it to help the loaf keep its shape. Repeat the final shaping and transfer procedures with the remaining loaf. Let the loaves rest, covered with the edges of the couche, for 1½ hours, until they have expanded to about one and a half times their original size. While the loaves are resting, preheat the oven (see next step).

Preheat the oven and Dutch oven: Preheat the oven to 500°F / 260°C for at least 1 hour, with the Dutch oven inside.

Once the Dutch oven is preheated, take it out, but be careful. Use heavy-duty oven mitts or a few layers of dry tea towels when handling it. Place it on a sturdy, heatproof surface. Take the lid off and lay it down upside down, so that you can easily transfer a loaf to its surface.

Transfer a loaf to the vessel, score, and bake: Lift the edges of the couche to gently flip one loaf onto your upturned palm and forearm. Carry the loaf to the cast-iron lid and gently flip it onto the lid. Use the lame to make a few scores in the surface, then, using oven mitts or dry towels, carefully invert the pot over the lid, to cover it like a dome.

Set the Dutch oven back inside the oven and set a timer for 20 minutes.

After 20 minutes, uncover the loaf and bake for another 20 minutes. When it's done, remove it from the oven and let it cool on a rack.

Repeat the transfer, scoring, and baking procedures with the remaining loaf.

Morning Buns and Fougasse

Neutral oil (enough to coat the inside of the proofing container)

A handful each of all-purpose and rice flours, combined (for coating the work surface before dividing the dough), plus more rice flour

A few handfuls of rolled oats and/or sesame, flaxseeds, pumpkin and/or sunflower seeds, or other seeds of your choice

ADDITIONAL INGREDIENTS FOR FOUGASSE

Neutral oil (enough to coat the inside of the proofing container)

A mixture of white and black sesame seeds, coarse sea salt, crushed black pepper (to taste)

Honey (for drizzling; optional)

TIMING

Day 1 (morning): Feed starter, mix dough, and bulk ferment: a total of about 6 hours (most of which is allowing the dough to bulk ferment and proof), plus an overnight cold retard of up to 12 hours

Day 2 (morning): For morning buns: coat, divide, shape, and bake; for fougasse: preshape, coat, rest, shape, and bake: a total of about 2 hours

EQUIPMENT

Mixing bowls, digital thermometer, bowl or pitcher of warm water (for rinsing), tea towels, flexible plastic dough scraper, wide, shallow container with a lid for overnight proofing (must fit in your refrigerator), bench scraper, sheet pan lined with parchment paper, baker's peel, pizza stone, cooling rack

DAY 1

Feed the starter and mix the dough: Follow the instructions of the City Loaf Master Recipe (page 113). Coat the wide, shallow container with oil, transfer the dough into it, and put the lid on. Set a timer for 45 minutes.

Bulk ferment the dough: This is the beginning of bulk fermentation, which will take about 4 hours total, including a few folds. Letting the dough rest for 45 minutes before you fold will make it much stronger. The gluten bonds, which started to form the second you added water to the flour, will continue to develop as the dough rests.

MAKES SIX 150-GRAM BUNS OR ONE 900-GRAM LOAF

It's funny, because the Danes do love sweet buns—I mean, Danish pastries aren't called *Danish* for nothing—but every weekday morning, pretty much everyone starts the day with a fresh morning bun, warm from the oven, with butter and cheese. It's a fantastic breakfast. The crust is super light and thin, the texture is airy and open, and it has a nice complex flavor, due to the overnight bulk fermentation. Danes generally save the sweet pastries for the weekend, when they queue up in droves for boxes and boxes to share with their friends and family.

Fougasse is a French bread that is shaped to resemble wheat. I use the same dough and fermentation as morning buns, but obviously cut it into a very different shape. For a while, I have been calling it "bread for friends." I love the idea of sitting around the table, sharing a meal with your loved ones, tearing apart this intricately slashed bread. Very Joy Division.

Fougasse can have as many different toppings as you have ideas. You can dip the dough in all kinds of seeds and spices—I've even used crushed Doritos, which was awesome. I've given you a recipe for a sesame seed, salt, and pepper mix here, but feel free to change it up and keep inventing.

STARTER

BAKER'S %	WEIGHT	INGREDIENT
100%	50g	Hot water (104°F / 40°C)
100%	50g	Whole wheat flour
40%	20g	12-hour wheat or rye starter (your choice; see pages 73 and 69)

DOUGH

BAKER'S %	WEIGHT	INGREDIENTS
20%	93g	All-purpose flour
75%	350g	Bread flour
5%	23g	Whole wheat flour
80%	372g	Hot water (104°F / 40°C)
20%	93g	Freshly fed starter (above)
3%	14g	Salt

The first fold: Once the timer goes off, it's time to fold the dough. Gently lift up half of it, being careful not to tear it, and fold it in half over itself, like a book, and repeat this motion from a different angle, once or twice, until the dough offers too much resistance to be folded.

Cover it back up with the lid and set a timer once again for 45 minutes, for the second rest.

The second fold: Once the timer goes off, repeat the gentle folds as before. You should see evidence of a few air bubbles below the surface. If you don't, don't worry. It's only just the beginning of the fermentation.

Check the dough's temperature and adjust accordingly. You're about to leave the dough alone for 2½ hours, so it's important to make sure that it's nice and comfortable while it rests, so that it will properly ferment. Remember, we're going for maximum yeast activity, which happens at 86°–95°F / 30°–35°C.

Continue bulk fermentation: Now set the timer for 2½ hours, cover the container with the lid, and leave the dough alone to ferment.

Cold retard: After 4 hours or so, when the dough is nicely fermented, it's time to chill it in bulk. Fold the dough, place the lid onto the container, and refrigerate the dough overnight.

DAY 2 (FOR MORNING BUNS)

 Coat and divide the buns: Remove the dough from the fridge. Flour the work surface with a combination of all-purpose and rice flours.

Turn the dough out onto the floured work surface and gently press it down with flat hands, to make sure it is evenly distributed. Set up a sheet pan nearby, lined with parchment paper, to transfer the buns onto after they are cut.

Distribute your choice of oats and/or seeds evenly over the entire surface of the dough, pressing down gently if necessary to make sure that they adhere.

Use the bench scraper to decisively cut the dough into 6 equal pieces of 150g each. Each bun will be a slight rectangular shape. Use the bench scraper to flip each bun into your open palm, coating side down to avoid sticking, then swiftly turn each bun, coating side up, onto the prepared sheet pan to rest while you preheat the oven. There's no need for a final proof here; once they're shaped and the oven is hot enough, you can bake them.

Bake the buns: Arrange a rack in the center of the oven. Place a pizza stone on the rack. Preheat the oven to 480°F / 250°C.

Sprinkle a baker's peel with rice flour to ensure that the buns will slide easily from peel to stone. Carefully transfer the buns to the peel, working in batches if necessary, and transfer them to the hot oven.

Bake for about 20 minutes, until they are golden brown and sound hollow when tapped. Remove the buns from the oven, transfer to a cooling rack, and serve warm, ideally slathered with butter and with a slice of cheese.

DAY 2 (FOR FOUGASSE)

 Preshape, coat, rest, final shape, and bake: Remove the dough from the refrigerator. Turn it out onto a clean work surface. Preshape it into an oval.

In a wide, shallow container (or on a large plate), combine the sesame seeds, salt, and pepper and mix well so that they form a homogenous mixture. Use your bench scraper to flip the dough onto one of your open palms, then turn the dough face down into the seed mixture to coat it well on one side. Transfer to a sheet pan lined with parchment paper, seed side facing up. Let it rest for 30 minutes, uncovered, until it is relaxed and pliable.

Preheat the oven to 480°F / 250°C.

Use a flexible plastic scraper to cut 4 to 6 slits in the dough, angled outward from a center "stem." The idea traditionally is to make it look like a sheaf of wheat, but mine are more free-form. The cuts also create more surface area for browned crust.

Stretch out the dough to open each slit as you cut it and make each segment of dough about 2 inches / 5cm wide and thick.

Bake the fougasse for 15 to 20 minutes, until the surface is dark golden brown.

While it bakes, warm the honey, if serving with it, in a small pot over low heat on the stovetop, or briefly in the microwave.

Remove the fougasse from the oven and immediately drizzle it all over with the warm honey, if desired. Transfer it to a rack to cool. Serve warm with olive oil for dipping.

Divide and preshape: Sprinkle some rice flour onto your clean work surface. Use the flexible plastic scraper to ease the dough out of the bowl. Use the bench scraper to divide the dough into 3 portions of 400g each. With a wet hand and the bench scraper, preshape each portion into an oval, using swift movements with the scraper and tucking the dough underneath itself with your fingertips. Let the dough rest, uncovered, for 30 minutes.

 Final shape: Check for dryness on the surface of the dough. If it has formed a dry skin, mist the surface with water.

Use damp hands to gently flatten out a loaf into roughly an 8 × 12-inch / 20 × 30cm rectangle. Working from the long side, pull a strip of the dough toward you and roll it in on itself. Seal the resulting seam with the backs of your hands. Then pull that roll toward you, and roll it back over itself, and again seal the seam. The idea is to create a tight cylinder with the dough, which will give it good shape and surface tension as it rests and bakes. Continue pulling and rolling until you have completely rolled the dough into a tight cylinder. Don't try to lengthen the dough at this point; the goal is only to wrap a cylinder, and lengthening the dough will make it more difficult to flour the seam.

Set up a plate nearby with a well-mixed handful of rice and all-purpose flour. Spread the couche out on a sheet pan or large cutting board and dust it lightly with the flour mixture.

If the dough is stuck to the work surface, use the bench scraper to gently ease it away from the table.

Flour your nondominant hand, place it atop the baguette, and use the bench scraper to shift it off the table, inverting it into your nondominant hand. Dip the seam in flour, gently return the baguette to the work surface, and then start the rolling process.

Roll the dough all the way toward you, and then all the way back, repeating this process several times, and pressing down lightly each time to evenly extend and lengthen the baguette. The final length should be 16 to 18 inches / 40 to 45 cm. If you like, you may roll the ends into points, using a bit of extra pressure with your fingertips. Once again, dip the seam into the flour mixture and transfer the rolled-out baguette to the couche. Pull up a fold of the couche on either side of the baguette to properly support its shape. Repeat the final shaping procedures for the remaining 2 baguettes.

Let the baguettes rest for 45 minutes to 1 hour, until they have expanded and relaxed a bit.

 Score and bake the baguettes: Place a sheet pan or shallow roasting pan on the floor of the oven. Arrange a rack in the center of the oven and place a pizza stone on the rack. Preheat the oven to 500°F / 260°C.

Sprinkle a bit of rice flour onto a baker's peel. Place the transfer board alongside one baguette and use the couche to gently invert the baguette onto the board. Invert the baguette from the board onto the peel. Use the lame to make 5 even scores, straight down the center line of the baguette, very slightly offset from one another.

Transfer the dough from the peel to the pizza stone. Add about 250ml water to the pan on the oven's floor, taking care to avoid exposing your skin directly to the resultant steam, which can burn.

Repeat with the remaining two baguettes.

Bake the baguettes for 20 to 25 minutes, until the crust is dark golden brown. Remove the baguettes and let them cool on a rack. They are best eaten the day they are baked.

Bagels

MAKES TEN 120-GRAM BAGELS

My experience with bagels in London comes from two little shops on Brick Lane, in the East End, which have been there forever and have had queues out the door for as long as I can remember. I don't think their appeal is too much to do with the bagel; it's more about the warm salt beef (called corned beef in the US) that they serve in the sandwich. At Tartine, I used to make bagels for fun, so we could eat them, and to teach myself.

I've created loads of different recipes and fermentation techniques along the way, trying to achieve the perfect bagel. I'm not sure I've got it, but these are pretty awesome and easy to make at home. They're just the right texture: chewy and dense and not dry; the sourdough works as a kind of flavor enhancer.

BIGA

BAKER'S %	WEIGHT	INGREDIENT
100%	111g	Bread flour
50%	56g	Tepid water (77°F / 25°C)
1%	1g	Instant dry yeast

STARTER

BAKER'S %	WEIGHT	INGREDIENT
100%	50g	Hot water (104°F / 40°C)
100%	50g	Whole wheat flour
40%	20g	12-hour wheat or rye starter (your choice; see pages 73 and 69)

DOUGH

BAKER'S %	WEIGHT	INGREDIENT
30%	168g	Biga (above)
100%	560g	Bread flour
50%	280g	Tepid water (77°F / 25°C)
10%	56g	Freshly fed starter (above)
3%	17g	Salt
1%	6g	Instant dry yeast
10%	56g	Olive oil
10%	56g	Malt syrup

ADDITIONAL INGREDIENTS

Neutral oil (enough to coat the inside of the proofing container)

A handful of all-purpose flour (for dusting the proofing tray)

50g malt syrup (for the bagel boiling water)

A few handfuls of sesame, poppy, or other seeds; coarse salt; dehydrated onion or garlic; or other toppings, as desired (for garnish)

TIMING

Day 1 (afternoon or evening): Mix biga: less than 5 minutes, plus overnight fermentation

Day 2 (morning): Feed starter, mix dough, bulk ferment, divide, shape, and proof: a total of 6 hours, plus an overnight cold retard of up to 12 hours

Day 3 (morning): Boil and bake: a total of 2 hours

EQUIPMENT

Mixing bowls, tea towels, digital thermometer, flexible plastic dough scraper, bowl or pitcher of warm water (for rinsing), stand mixer fitted with the dough hook, bench scraper, sheet pan, large pot, parchment paper, and slotted spoon

DAY 1

Mix the biga: In a bowl, combine the flour, water, and yeast and rub the ingredients together with your fingertips until the mixture looks shaggy, like wet breadcrumbs. It shouldn't be a smooth or uniform dough. If you overmix biga, it tends to ferment too quickly.

Cover the bowl with a tea towel and leave it in a cool environment (ideally 53°–57°F / 12°–14°C) for 12 hours or overnight. If you can't get it into that zone, leave it at room temperature for 3 to 4 hours, and then refrigerate it for the remaining 8 to 9 hours.

DAY 2

Feed the starter: Follow the instructions of the City Loaf Master Recipe (page 113). Set a timer for 45 minutes.

Mix the dough: In the bowl of a stand mixer fitted with the dough hook, mix the biga on its own for up to 5 minutes, until it is smooth. Add the remaining dough ingredients and mix on medium speed until smooth, 5 to 10 minutes. The dough should feel strong and well developed at this stage.

Bulk ferment the dough: Coat the inside of a mixing bowl or other container with oil, place the dough in it, and cover with a tea towel. Let the dough bulk ferment for 3 to 4 hours, until it has risen to about two and a half times its original volume

Divide the dough and shape the bagels: Turn the dough out onto your work surface and use the bench scraper to cut it into 10 portions of 120g each.

Roll each piece into a ball using the dough balling technique: Flour your dominant hand and tap off the excess. Get one portion of dough in front of you and apply light pressure to the top of it as you use your fingers and thumb to form a kind of circular basket around the dough. Roll it in circles; the dough should be a bit sticky on the bottom as you're pressing lightly on it while rolling; that friction and sticking on the work surface will help the dough come together in a ball. As you roll the dough, your fingers should be tucking it underneath itself to help form a ball. Roll until the dough has a nice, taut surface and a round shape. Repeat with the remaining dough pieces.

Let the bagels rest for 5 minutes under a damp tea towel.

While they rest, heavily dust a sheet pan with the all-purpose flour. Once you have fully shaped the bagels, they will proof on the sheet pan and the flour will keep them from sticking.

Use your fingers to make a hole in the center of each bagel. Hang a bagel by the hole, on one of your index fingers, then use both index fingers to gently spin and stretch the bagel hole, until it is about 1 inch / 2.5cm across. Place the shaped bagel onto the floured sheet pan and repeat this process with the remaining bagels.

Proof the bagels: Let the bagels proof in a warm spot for 1 hour, covered with a damp tea towel, until you can see bubbles beneath the surface. You'll know they're properly proofed when you poke a bagel with your finger and it leaves an imprint on the surface. If the dough springs back quickly, it's not yet ready; give it 15 more minutes and try again.

Cold retard: Leave the bagels covered with the damp tea towel and refrigerate them overnight, up to 12 hours.

DAY 3

Boil and bake bagels: Preheat the oven to 400°F / 200°C.

Bring a large pot of water to a boil and add the 50g malt syrup. Set up a sheet pan lined with parchment, and if topping, a plate or tray of any topping ingredients.

Gently drop the bagels, one at a time, into the water. Don't overcrowd the pot or they won't cook evenly. Boil each bagel for 30 seconds on each side, turning them with a slotted spoon and transferring them to the plate with the toppings and/or prepared sheet pan when they're done. Be sure to bring the water back up to boiling between batches.

Once all the bagels have been boiled (and topped, if applicable), bake them, topping side up, for 8 to 10 minutes, until golden brown. Eat them fresh, however you'd like. Or if eating later, I'd suggest slicing them in half, toasting them, and slathering on a mountain of cream cheese. No judgment here.

English Muffins

MAKES SIX 80-GRAM MUFFINS

Before they were *English* muffins, these lovely little breads were known as *tea* muffins. They were invented centuries ago, to be warmed and buttered and served in posh houses for afternoon tea. After World War II, they pretty much disappeared from the UK: Britain was broke, and no one was lounging around eating muffins and drinking tea.

English muffins really need to be made fresh, and they're cooked in a skillet or on a griddle, rather than baked in an oven. They survived in US diners, where everything is made on the griddle. They really should be called USA muffins now. These are crisp on the outside, from being cooked in a skillet, chewy on the inside, and with a slightly sweet flavor from the wheat. They're best when toasted and slathered in butter.

BIGA

BAKER'S %	WEIGHT	INGREDIENT
100%	41g	All-purpose flour
50%	21g	Warm water (86°F / 30°C)
0.35%	1g	Instant dry yeast

STARTER

BAKER'S %	WEIGHT	INGREDIENT
100%	20g	Hot water (104°F / 40°C)
100%	20g	Whole wheat flour
40%	8g	12-hour wheat or rye starter (your choice; see pages 73 and 69)

DOUGH

BAKER'S %	WEIGHT	INGREDIENT
100%	207g	All-purpose flour
80%	165g	Warm water (82°F / 27°C)
30%	62g	Biga (above)
10%	21g	Freshly fed starter (above)
3%	6g	Sugar
5%	10g	Olive oil
2.5%	5g	Salt
0.5%	1g	Instant dry yeast

ADDITIONAL INGREDIENT

A handful of all-purpose flour (for the work surface)

A handful of finely ground cornmeal (for coating the muffins)

TIMING

Day 1 (morning or afternoon): Mix and ferment biga, feed starter, mix and ferment dough, divide, and shape: a total of about 6½ hours (most of which is allowing the dough to bulk ferment and proof), plus an overnight cold retard of up to 12 hours

Day 2 (morning or afternoon): Cook muffins: about 40 minutes total

EQUIPMENT

Mixing bowls, tea towel, digital thermometer, bowl or pitcher of warm water (for rinsing), flexible plastic dough scraper, bench scraper, couche (linen proofing cloth), sheet pan, cast-iron skillet

DAY 1

Mix the biga: In a bowl, combine the flour, water, and yeast and rub the ingredients together with your fingertips until the mixture looks shaggy, like wet breadcrumbs. Cover the bowl with a tea towel and let the biga sit at room temperature for 4 hours.

Feed the starter: When the biga has been fermenting for about 3 hours, feed your starter, following the instructions of the City Loaf Master Recipe (page 113). Set a timer for 45 minutes.

Mix and ferment the dough: When the starter has rested for 45 minutes, in a bowl, combine the flour, water, biga, starter, and sugar and mix until combined. Let this mixture rest for 15 minutes, then mix in the oil, salt, and yeast. If necessary, scrape down the insides of the bowl with the dough scraper to make one mass of dough. Cover the bowl with a tea towel and let it sit in a warm place for 1½ hours, until the dough is doubled in size and looks bubbly and light under the surface.

Recipe continues

Divide, shape, and coat the dough: Use the flexible dough scraper to ease the dough out onto a clean work surface and use the bench scraper to divide the dough into 6 portions of 80g each.

Roll each piece into a ball using the dough balling technique: Flour your dominant hand and tap off the excess. Get one portion of dough in front of you and apply light pressure to the top of it as you use your fingers and thumb to form a kind of circular basket around the dough. Roll it in circles; the dough should be a bit sticky on the bottom as you're pressing lightly on it while rolling; that friction and sticking on the work surface will help the dough come together in a ball. As you roll the dough, your fingers should be tucking it underneath itself to help form a ball. Roll until the dough has a nice, taut surface and a round shape. Repeat with the remaining dough pieces.

Press each dough ball flat with your palm to form puck-shaped muffins. Set up a plate with the cornmeal and carefully dip both sides of each muffin into the cornmeal, so that they are coated.

Cold retard: Set up a couche on a sheet pan or large plate and transfer each muffin to the couche, arranging the folds around each one to support and protect it. Gently cover the couche with a tea towel and cold retard the muffins in the refrigerator for 8 hours or overnight (up to 12 hours).

DAY 2

Cook the muffins: Remove the muffins from the fridge and let them sit at room temperature for about 20 minutes.

Heat a dry cast-iron skillet over medium-high heat for about 5 minutes. Gently transfer 2 or 3 muffins to the skillet and let them cook for about 3 minutes, then flip them and let them cook for 3 minutes on the other side, until they are browned and slightly puffed. Repeat with the remaining muffins. Let them cool for a few minutes, then split with a fork (which will preserve the holes in the crumb) and toast, or serve them as is.

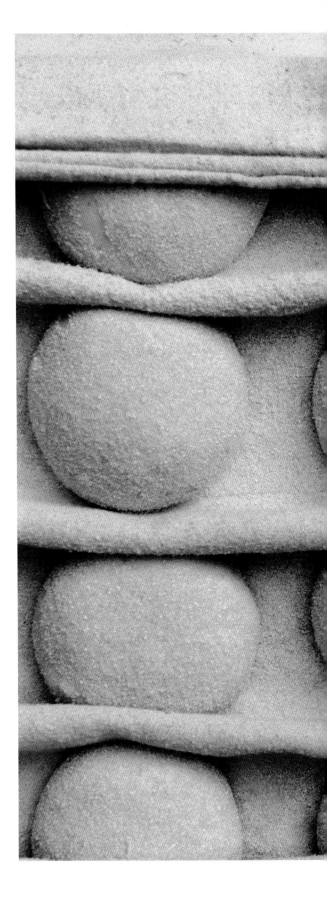

Beer Bread

MAKES TWO 900-GRAM LOAVES

We designed this bread for Barr, a restaurant in the Noma family. Barr is more of a beer place than a wine restaurant, so I thought we'd make it a threesome of rye, white bread, and beer. It's filthily good, quite a dark bread, with both sourdough and caramelized sugar notes, a crisp crust, and a tender crumb.

SCALDED RYE

BAKER'S %	WEIGHT	INGREDIENT
100%	79g	Rye flour
100%	79g	Boiling water

BREAD MASH

BAKER'S %	WEIGHT	INGREDIENT
100%	93g	Super Seed Rye Bread (page 82) or other rye bread
70%	65g	Dark stout

STARTER

BAKER'S %	WEIGHT	INGREDIENT
100%	104g	Hot water (104°F / 40°C)
100%	104g	Whole wheat flour
40%	42g	12-hour wheat or rye starter (your choice; see pages 73 and 69)

DOUGH

BAKER'S %	WEIGHT	INGREDIENT
100%	789g	Bread flour
65%	513g	Hot water (104°F / 40°C)
5%	39g	Malt syrup
15%	118g	Freshly fed starter (above)
20%	158g	Scalded rye (above)
3%	24g	Salt
20%	158g	Bread mash (above)

TIMING

Day 1 (morning or evening): Make rye scald and bread mash: a total of 30 minutes, plus overnight soaking

Day 2 (morning): Feed starter, autolyse dough, mix dough, bulk ferment, preshape, proof, and final shape: a total of about 6 hours (mostly bulk ferment and proof), plus an overnight cold retard of up to 12 hours

Day 3 (morning): Preheat oven, transfer dough to Dutch oven, score, and bake: a total of 3 hours

EQUIPMENT

Medium and large mixing bowls, spatula or wooden spoon, digital thermometer, bowl or pitcher of warm water (for rinsing), flexible plastic dough scraper, tea towel, bench scraper, two bannetons (proofing baskets), cast-iron or enameled Dutch oven (with a flat, handleless lid), lame, cooling rack

DAY 1

Make the scalded rye: Place the rye flour in a heatproof medium bowl, pour the boiling water over it, and mix with a spatula or wooden spoon until all the water has been evenly absorbed into the flour. Let it cool to room temperature, then cover and refrigerate overnight.

Make the bread mash: Slice the rye bread very thinly and place it in a shallow mixing bowl or other container. Pour the beer over the slices, covering them completely. Let the mixture soak overnight, covered, in the refrigerator.

DAY 2

Feed the starter: Follow the instructions in the City Loaf Master Recipe (page 113). Set a timer for 45 minutes.

Autolyse the dough: In a bowl, combine the bread flour, 474g of the water, and the malt syrup and mix until no dry flour remains. Cover the dough and wait until the timer for the starter has gone off.

Mix the dough, starter, rye scald, and bread mash: When the starter is ready and you've given the dough at least 20 minutes to rest after mixing, scrape the starter and scalded rye into the bowl with the resting dough. Use your other hand to gently massage the starter and scalded rye into the dough. Add the remaining water and the salt and continue to mix the dough by hand until the water has been absorbed and the salt is dissolved.

Break up the bread mash by hand, and add half of it to the dough. Work it in by hand until it is incorporated. Add the remaining mash and continue to mix.

Bulk ferment, preshape, and proof: Follow the instructions of the City Loaf Master Recipe (page 114).

Final shape: Follow the instructions of the City Loaf Master Recipe (page 115) :

Cold retard: Follow the instructions of the City Loaf Master Recipe (page 115).

DAY 3

Preheat the oven and Dutch oven, score, and bake: Follow the instructions of the City Loaf Master Recipe (page 115).

Cheese Loaf

MAKES TWO 600-GRAM LOAVES

Now, I might sound a little stupid here, but I'm going to tell you this story anyway. Way back at the beginning of my baking career, when I visited Wild Flour Bread, they had two cheese breads on the menu every day. They were amazing, and very addictive, and often before I knew it, I'd eaten a whole bloody loaf before I even got home.

Anyway, I was a novice baker, and I just couldn't work out how they made these breads so very cheesy. They were incredible and incomprehensible to me. Well, as I learned, the answer is: you just take your dough and chuck a shitload of cheese into it.

This bread is not really like Wild Flour's cheese bread, but all the same, this is a shout-out to all you cool people in Freestone, California. It's a bread that you can snack on without needing butter or anything else, and it's cheesy as all hell. Some of the cheese dissolves into the dough, but there are still recognizable pieces of cheese as well. Feel free to experiment with other types of cheese; at Wild Flour, they made a goat cheese version that was amazing.

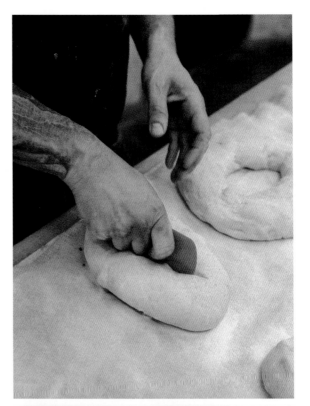

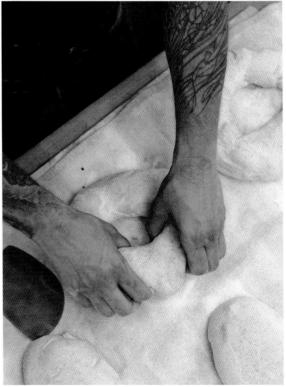

STARTER

BAKER'S %	WEIGHT	INGREDIENT
100%	70g	Hot water (104°F / 40°C)
100%	70g	Whole wheat flour
40%	28g	12-hour wheat or rye starter (your choice; see pages 73 and 69)

DOUGH

BAKER'S %	WEIGHT	INGREDIENT
40%	203g	Bread flour
40%	203g	All-purpose flour
20%	102g	Whole wheat flour
80%	406g	Hot water (104°F / 40°C)
18%	91g	Freshly fed starter (above)
2.5%	13g	Salt
20%	102g	Aged Cheddar cheese
8%	41g	Gouda cheese
8%	41g	Smoked Gouda cheese

ADDITIONAL INGREDIENTS

A handful of rice flour (for coating the couche)

A handful of all-purpose flour (for dusting tops of loaves before final shaping)

About 2 tablespoons olive oil or melted butter (for brushing the just-baked bread)

TIMING

Day 1 (morning): Feed starter, mix dough, and bulk ferment: a total of about 5 hours (most of which is allowing the dough to bulk ferment), plus an overnight cold retard of up to 12 hours

Day 2 (morning): Shape, proof, and bake: a total of about 1 hour

EQUIPMENT

Mixing bowls, digital thermometer, flexible plastic dough scraper, bowl or pitcher of warm water (for rinsing), couche, tea towels, bench scraper, sheet pan, parchment paper, pastry brush, cooling rack

DAY 1

Feed the starter: Follow the instructions of the City Loaf Master Recipe (page 113). Set a timer for 45 minutes.

Autolyse the dough: Follow the instructions of the City Loaf Master Recipe (page 114), using 330g of the water. Let the dough rest until the starter is ready.

Chop the cheese: Cut each type of cheese into ⅓-inch / 1cm cubes.

Mix the dough, starter, reserved water, salt, and cheese: When the starter is ready and you've given the dough at least 20 minutes to rest after mixing, scrape the starter into the bowl with the dough. While holding the bowl still with one hand, use your other hand to gently massage the starter into the dough. Add the remaining 76g hot water, half of it at a time, and continue to mix by hand until it has all been incorporated. Next, add the salt and continue to mix by hand until it is distributed and dissolved in the dough.

Add the cheese cubes and continue to mix until they are distributed. It may seem like too much cheese at first, but once it's incorporated into the dough, it will be more balanced.

Take the dough's temperature. In a cold climate, it should be around 88°F / 31°C. In a hot climate, it should be around 80°F / 27°C. You want to aim to keep it at that temperature throughout its whole bulk fermentation (which starts in the next step). If it's too cold, set the bowl in a larger bowl of hot water to warm it up. If it's too warm, do the same, using cool or ice water.

Bulk ferment and fold: Follow the instructions of the City Loaf Master Recipe (page 114).

Cold retard: Once the dough has bulk fermented for about 4 hours and is light and bubbly, cover it with a tea towel or place it in a container with a lid, and transfer it to the refrigerator for an overnight cold retard.

DAY 2

Preshape, final shape, and proof: Turn the dough out onto a clean work surface. Use your bench scraper to divide it into two equal portions. Use the bench scraper and a wet hand to preshape each one into a ball.

Set the couche on the sheet pan and sprinkle liberally with rice flour. Transfer the loaves to the couche and arrange it around them to support their structure. Let them rest for 20 minutes.

Dust the top of each loaf with the all-purpose flour, then use your fingertips to create a hole in the center of each loaf. Continue to gently expand the holes until they measure about 4 inches / 10cm in diameter.

Line a sheet pan with parchment paper and transfer the loaves to it. Let them proof, uncovered, for 20 minutes, until they are slightly relaxed and expanded.

Bake the loaves: While the loaves proof, preheat the oven to 480°F / 250°C.

Bake the loaves for 20 to 25 minutes, until golden brown.

Brush them with the oil or melted butter as soon as you take them out of the oven. Let them cool for a few minutes on a rack, then serve warm.

If the bread has cooled completely before serving, reheat it in the oven for about 5 minutes at 350°F / 175°C before serving.

Baguettes

MAKES THREE 400-GRAM LOAVES

This might be a bit controversial, but here goes:

Being a baker and going to Paris, the home of the baguette, I was deeply disappointed by how bad most of the baguettes I tried were. I'm sorry, Paris, but I got the feeling they were made without love.

This is the baguette I've been developing for many years. It has a mixture of pre-ferments for flavor and texture, and yeast for lifting power. It's what I imagine a French baguette to be: a bread with a crisp, thin crust and a light, open, airy, honeycomb-ish crumb.

At the bakery, I made it every day, but I only made enough so that I would sell out in a couple of hours, because that is when it's at its best. If ever I have friends or peers visit me, in the golden hour when baguettes come out of the oven, I make sure to give them one hot, with loads of butter.

POOLISH

BAKER'S %	WEIGHT	INGREDIENT
100%	125g	All-purpose flour
100%	125g	Tepid water (77°F / 25°C)
0.5%	0.5g	Instant dry yeast

DOUGH

BAKER'S %	WEIGHT	INGREDIENT
100%	500g	All-purpose flour
50%	250g	Poolish (above)
25%	125g	12-hour wheat starter (page 73)
60%	300g	Tepid water (77°F / 25°C)
3%	15g	Salt
0.5%	2.5g	Instant dry yeast

ADDITIONAL INGREDIENTS

A few handfuls each of all-purpose and rice flours (for coating the work surface and couche and sealing the seam)

TIMING

Day 1 (evening): Mix poolish: less than 5 minutes, plus overnight fermentation

Day 2 (morning): Mix dough, preshape, final shape, score, and bake: a total of 4½ to 5 hours

EQUIPMENT

Mixing bowls, flexible plastic dough scraper, tea towel, digital thermometer, bench scraper, spray bottle of water, couche (linen proofing cloth), sheet pan or shallow roasting pan, pizza stone, transfer board, baker's peel, lame, cooling rack

DAY 1

Mix the poolish: In a bowl, combine the flour, water, and yeast and mix well by hand. Use the dough scraper to scrape any excess from your fingers back into the mixture. Cover with a tea towel and let the mixture ferment overnight at room temperature, during which time it will expand, with visible bubbles, and become fragrant.

DAY 2

Mix the dough, part 1: In a bowl, combine the flour, poolish, starter, and 225g of the water by hand. Scrape the excess off your fingers back into the bowl, and scrape down the insides of the bowl so that the dough is in one mass. Cover the bowl with a tea towel and let it rest for 20 minutes.

Mix the dough, part 2: Add the salt and yeast to the dough and drizzle a small amount of the remaining 75g water into the dough. Use a damp hand to massage in the water, salt, and yeast. Once that water has been incorporated, drizzle and massage in more water, and continue this process until all the water has been incorporated.

Bulk ferment the dough: Take the dough's temperature. It's not crucial to keep the dough very warm in order for fermentation to occur, since the instant yeast is a bit of a powerhouse on its own. As long as the dough is at 81°F / 27°C, it will take about 1½ hours to properly ferment. If your environment is closer to room temperature, 75°F / 24°C, it will take about 2 hours.

You will know that the dough is ready to divide and preshape when you can see that it is about one and a half times its original size, and you can see evidence of air pockets at the surface. When you pinch and pull a piece of dough away from the mass, you should feel air bubbles bursting beneath your fingertips.

Recipe continues

Mashed Potato Buns

MAKES TEN 90-GRAM BUNS

During the early stages of the pandemic, when no one could travel, Noma opened its gardens to the people of Copenhagen, as a burger pop-up. Obviously, they got slammed. I mean, who doesn't want to sit in that beautiful place and eat the best burger ever?

Originally, they were getting the buns from another burger place, but the numbers kept increasing and they couldn't keep up. So René Redzepi asked if I could design a potato roll for them. I spoke to my friend and amazing baker Matt Jones, my old colleague from Tartine, who helped me with this recipe.

Very quickly, I realized that this recipe would not work for the Noma burger pop-up (which has now become a permanent restaurant called POPL), because the amount of potatoes I'd need to mash would be insane. By the end of the pop-up, we were hand-shaping 2,800 buns a day. It was nuts, so I changed the recipe—from fresh potatoes to potato flour—but this version is really good and worth the mashing on a smaller scale. It's soft and sweet and tastes like a baked potato; it's amazing.

MASHED POTATOES

—	300g	Starchy (baking) potatoes

STARTER

BAKER'S %	WEIGHT	INGREDIENT
100%	20g	Hot water (104°F / 40°C)
100%	20g	Whole wheat flour
40%	8g	12-hour wheat or rye starter (your choice; see pages 73 and 69)

DOUGH

BAKER'S %	WEIGHT	INGREDIENT
50%	175g	Bread flour
40%	140g	All-purpose flour
10%	35g	Whole wheat flour
23%	81g	Reserved potato water
12%	42g	Freshly fed starter (above)
15%	53g	Egg
5%	18g	Sugar
3%	11g	Salt
1.5%	5g	Instant dry yeast
12%	42g	Butter
85%	300g	Mashed potatoes (above)

ADDITIONAL INGREDIENTS

Neutral oil (enough to coat the inside of the proofing container)

A handful of all-purpose flour (for flouring the dough)

1 egg, beaten together with a splash of water and a pinch of salt

TIMING

Day 1 (evening): Cook and mash potatoes, feed starter, and mix dough: a total of about 2 hours, plus an overnight cold retard of up to 12 hours

Day 2 (morning): Divide, shape, proof, and bake buns: a total of 2½ to 4½ hours

EQUIPMENT

Large pot, skewer or paring knife, tongs or slotted spoon, mixing bowl, fork, digital thermometer, flexible plastic dough scraper, warm bowl or pitcher of water (for rinsing), tea towels, stand mixer fitted with the dough hook, wide, shallow container (must fit in your refrigerator), bench scraper, sheet pan, parchment paper, pastry brush, cooling rack

Recipe continues

DAY 1

Cook and mash the potatoes: Scrub and rinse the potatoes to make sure the skins are very clean. If the potatoes are really large, cut them into quarters, and if they're medium-sized, cut them in half. Place them in a large pot and add enough water to cover them by 3 inches / 7.5cm. You won't need to salt the water, since the dough will be properly salted and excess salt in the potatoes will interfere with fermentation in the dough.

Bring the water to a boil and cook the potatoes until they are tender but not falling apart, approximately 15 to 20 minutes. You can test for doneness by piercing a potato with a skewer or paring knife, which should pass through a well-cooked potato with no resistance.

You will be adding some of the potato cooking water to the dough, so don't dump it down the drain. Strain the potatoes and reserve the water. Transfer the water to a container to cool.

While the potatoes are still warm, crush them with the back of a fork, skins and all, to create a semismooth mashed potato mixture. Let the potatoes cool completely to room temperature. Don't try to use warm potatoes in the dough.

Feed the starter: While the potatoes cool, feed the starter, following the instructions of the City Loaf Master Recipe (page 113). Set a timer for 40 minutes.

Mix the dough, part 1: When the starter is ready, transfer 42g of it to a stand mixer fitted with the dough hook. Add both flours, the reserved potato water, egg, and sugar and mix on medium-low speed until combined. If necessary, scrape down the insides of the bowl with a flexible plastic scraper to make a single mass. Cover the dough with a tea towel and let it rest for 20 minutes.

Mix the dough, part 2: Add the salt and yeast to the dough and mix on medium speed until the dough comes together, about 5 minutes. You should see and hear it slapping against the bowl, which is a sign of good gluten development. The dough should offer strong resistance when you try to pull a piece away from the mass. This is an important step for building dough strength, so don't rush the mixing or you'll end up with a weak final dough.

Add the butter and potatoes: With the mixer on medium speed, add the butter and continue to mix until the dough is smooth and the butter has all been absorbed.

Next, add the mashed potatoes, a quarter at a time, making sure they're well distributed in the dough.

Cold retard: Spread the dough out in an oiled plastic container, cover with a lid or plastic wrap, and refrigerate overnight.

DAY 2

Divide, shape, and proof dough: Take the dough from the fridge and turn it out onto the work surface. Flour the top of the dough. Use a bench scraper to divide the dough into 10 portions of 90g each.

Roll each piece into a ball using the dough balling technique: Flour your dominant hand and tap off the excess. Get one portion of dough in front of you and apply light pressure to the top of it as you use your fingers and thumb to form a kind of circular basket around the dough. Roll it in circles; the dough should be a bit sticky on the bottom as you're pressing lightly on it while rolling; that friction and sticking on the work surface will help the dough come together in a ball. As you roll the dough, your fingers should be tucking it underneath itself to help form a ball. Roll until the dough has a nice, taut surface and a round shape. Repeat with the remaining dough pieces.

Line a sheet pan with parchment paper and evenly space the dough balls on it. Let the dough proof in a warm place, covered with a tea towel, for 2 to 4 hours, until the dough is full of air and each bun has doubled in size. A finger poked into the side of the bun should leave its mark without springing back.

Egg wash and bake: Preheat the oven to 390°F / 200°C.

Use a pastry brush to brush each bun with the egg wash.

Bake the buns for 10 to 12 minutes, until they are golden brown. Remove them from the oven and let them cool on a rack before slicing and serving. The buns will feel light and fluffy and will be jammed with a delicious potato flavor.

Kathleen Weber's Rosemary and Lemon Bread

MAKES TWO 1-KILOGRAM LOAVES

This is a variation on the most famous bread made at Della Fattoria (in Petaluma, California), where I got my start as a baker. After you have been working at Della for a while, you are totally over this bread. They make bloody hundreds of them a week, and you need to chop a ton of rosemary on a daily basis. We never had enough, so we used to drive around town, nicking rosemary from everywhere and anywhere we could find it. I'm sure the poor bakers who are working there still have to do this. So this goes out to you rosemary choppers and the local gardeners wondering about your stunted rosemary bushes.

But it is really here as a tribute to my original mentor, the lady who started my baking career, Kathleen Weber. I've made the dough formula my own but the method I learned from Kathleen. This recipe uses a beautiful technique that adds a spoonful of a flavored oil to the dough. In final shaping, it is worked to the top of the crust, which makes the bread pop up into a crown. It's a bit tricky to master at first, but we have included a video so you can see how it's done.

The base ingredients and the method are quite similar to the City Loaf Master Recipe (page 113), but with a lower hydration (60%, versus 75% in City Loaf), which yields a stronger dough that can hold up better to the flavored oil.

You can use any flavored oil, whatever you can think of. Lately I've been thinking about using sesame oil and sesame seeds. I haven't got round to it yet, but maybe one day you'll see it on my Instagram.

STARTER

BAKER'S %	WEIGHT	INGREDIENT
100%	104g	Hot water (104°F / 40°C)
100%	104g	Whole wheat flour
40%	42g	12-hour wheat or rye starter (your choice; see pages 73 and 69)

DOUGH

BAKER'S %	WEIGHT	INGREDIENT
50%	500g	Bread flour
50%	500g	All-purpose flour
75%	750g	Hot water (104°F / 40°C)
20%	200g	Freshly fed starter (above)
2.5%	25g	Salt

ROSEMARY LEMON OIL

BAKER'S %	WEIGHT	INGREDIENT
100%	25g	Olive oil
25%	6g	Rosemary leaves, finely chopped
—	—	Grated zest of ¼ lemon

ADDITIONAL INGREDIENTS

A handful each of all-purpose and rice flours (for coating baskets)

TIMING

Day 1 (morning): Feed starter, mix dough, bulk ferment, mix oil, preshape, and final shape: a total of about 8 hours (most of which is allowing the dough to bulk ferment), plus an overnight cold retard of up to 12 hours

Day 2 (morning): Preheat oven, transfer dough to Dutch oven, score, and bake: a total of 2½ to 3 hours

EQUIPMENT

Medium and large mixing bowls, digital thermometer, flexible plastic dough scraper, bowl or pitcher of warm water (for rinsing), tea towels, bench scraper, two bannetons (proofing baskets), cast-iron or enameled Dutch oven (with a flat, handleless lid), lame, cooling rack

DAY 1

Feed starter, mix dough, bulk ferment, and preshape: Follow the instructions of the City Loaf Master Recipe (page 113).

Make the rosemary lemon oil: While the dough is bulk fermenting, in a small bowl, stir together the oil, rosemary, and lemon zest and set aside.

 Final shape: Follow the instructions of the City Loaf Master Recipe (page 115). Use a bench scraper to get one loaf in front of you. Use a soup spoon to transfer about half of the rosemary lemon oil to the center of the dough's surface. Quickly pull and gather all the edges of the loaf into one hand, rolling them together and pressing the edges to seal the oil in.

Scrape or brush away any excess flour on the work surface; you want the dough to slightly stick to the surface for this next part.

Turn the dough over so that the seam is now facing down. Use your hands, cupped around either side of the loaf, to start gently shaping it back into a round, applying light pressure to both sides as you turn and shape the loaf, so that the oil on the bottom of the loaf gets shimmied up the center of the loaf, ending up visibly close to the surface. Once you can see the oil through the surface of the loaf, stop shaping. Use the bench scraper to invert the loaf into a floured proofing basket. Repeat with the other loaf.

Cold retard: Follow the instructions of the City Loaf Master Recipe (page 115).

DAY 2

Preheat the oven and Dutch oven, score, and bake: Follow the instructions of the City Loaf Master Recipe (page 115). When scoring the loaves, use the lame to create a starburst pattern right on top of where the visible oil is, so that it is released from the dough.

Superiority Burger Vegan Cornbread

MAKES A 12-INCH CORNBREAD

I don't know if this is bread or cake, but I love cornbread. I also love Brooks Headley, his food, and his New York restaurant, Superiority Burger. He has kindly shared this recipe.

BATTER

BAKER'S %	WEIGHT	INGREDIENT
100%	420g	All-purpose flour
119%	500g	Finely ground cornmeal
3%	12g	Baking powder
3.5%	14g	Baking soda
40%	170g	Sugar
2%	8g	Salt
238%	1kg	Soy milk
14%	60g	Cider vinegar
71%	300g	Olive oil

TIMING

Mix and bake: a total of about 30 minutes

EQUIPMENT

12-inch cast-iron skillet, parchment paper, two mixing bowls, wooden spoon, whisk, spatula

Preheat the oven: Preheat the oven to 375°F / 190°C. Line a 12-inch cast-iron skillet with parchment paper.

Mix the batter: In a bowl, combine the flour, cornmeal, baking powder, baking soda, sugar, and salt and mix well. In a separate bowl, whisk together the soy milk, vinegar, and oil.

Use a spatula to gently fold the wet ingredients into the dry ingredients. Transfer the batter to the prepared pan.

Bake: Bake for about 20 minutes, until golden brown and cooked through. According to Brooks, "Slightly under[cooked] is better than slightly over." Remove it from the oven and serve hot, warm, or cool.

Fresh Bread in a Skillet

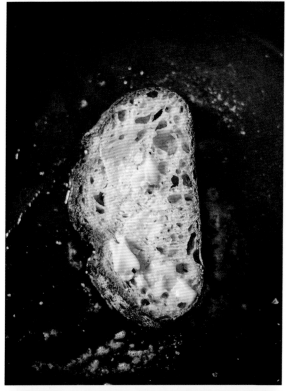

HOWEVER MUCH YOU WANT

This is my favorite way to eat fresh bread: cooked in a skillet. This is more of an explanation than a recipe. You want to sear it in a hot pan so that the outer crumb is crisp and caramelized and the center becomes custardy. It's a textural and taste delight.

TIMING

A few minutes

EQUIPMENT

Cast-iron skillet, tongs or spatula

INGREDIENTS

Thick slices of freshly baked bread

Enough fat (butter, olive oil, bacon or chicken fat) to coat both sides generously

Salt and freshly ground black pepper

Slather the bread with butter or other fat and season it well with salt and pepper. Heat the skillet over high heat and, when it's good and hot, sear the bread. Once it's caramelized, flip it and do the other side.

Eat it hot.

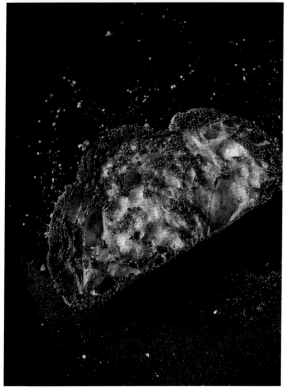

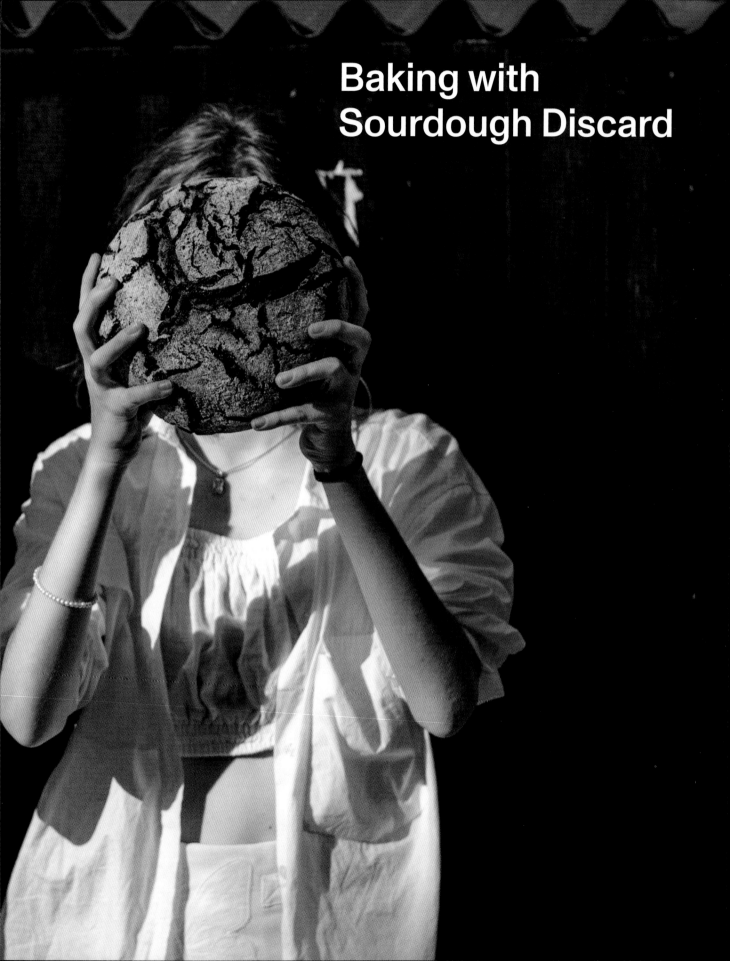

Baking with
Sourdough Discard

220

This chapter actually started with my old friend James, who said, "Rich, you've got to put in a chapter on waste starter. I hate chucking it out." I know a lot of home bakers feel weird about it. Okay, so how to answer the questions: "Is it wasteful to throw it away? What can I do with my leftover sourdough starter?"

The truth is, I don't worry about my leftover starter. My farm of yeast and bacteria have got all they can out of it and are now in a new pasture. The leftovers go into the compost, and back to the earth. I honestly think of it as being used up, spent; it's a waste product.

But that's *not* to say it can't be used. There are tons of things I could have added into a discard recipe chapter, and trust me, Laurie tried to make it happen. But pancakes, biscuits, and all that? This is my bread book, and I asked myself, *Is my pancake batter recipe going to blow your mind?* Of course not, no way. If you want recipes like that, there are thousands of them online.

I've only got three recipes here. If you feel let down by my effort, please forgive me, I'm sorry. Rather than give you recipes that just exist to use up old starter, I'm giving you recipes for breads that are made amazing by it. The Crumpets are leavened with baking soda, and the discarded sourdough adds moisture and a lot of flavor. There's still enough yeast power in the discard to make the Danny Lievito Discard Crackers full of bubbles. And the Cracked Rye Bread is really suited to using a more sour starter, so the discard is a perfect match.

Sourdough Crumpets

MAKES EIGHT 65-GRAM CRUMPETS

Crumpets are small griddle breads that are dense and chewy and full of bubbles from the leavening effect of baking soda. They're typically made with flour and warm water, but this recipe uses sourdough discard, which is well fermented flour and water; it's the ideal switch. If you're planning to make these, just accumulate a few days' worth of discard in the refrigerator.

This *very* English recipe actually comes from a Frenchie, my great friend and total legend Cannelle Deslandes. She worked with me at Hart and I love her. Cannelle designed these crumpets, which are perfect, and she has kindly let me share her recipe here.

DOUGH

BAKER'S %	WEIGHT	INGREDIENT
100%	520g	Sourdough discard
1.1%	6g	Salt
1.3%	7g	Baking soda
1.5%	8g	Sugar

ADDITIONAL INGREDIENTS

About 3 tablespoons cold butter (for greasing the ring molds and melting in the skillet)

Mix the dough: In a bowl, combine all the dough ingredients.

Cook the crumpets: Working in batches, coat the insides of the ring molds with butter and melt a tablespoon of it in a cast-iron skillet over medium heat. When it foams and subsides, set the ring molds down in the skillet and fill them each about half to two-thirds full with dough.

Let the crumpets cook for 3 to 5 minutes, until bubbles appear at the top. Slip the spatula under one of the rings and quickly and decisively turn it. Cook on the second side for 1 minute. Keep a close eye on the heat; cast-iron pans get very hot and the crumpets can easily burn. Continue to add small amounts of butter to the pan between batches.

Remove the rings from the pan and carefully dislodge the crumpets. Toast them whole, if desired, or serve hot from the pan, with butter.

Danny Lievito Discard Crackers

INGREDIENTS

Any amount of discarded mature lievito madre (aka Danny Lievito; page 272)

Salt

Preheat the oven to 350°F / 175°C.

Place the discard on a sheet of parchment paper and roll it out to a 2mm thickness, about the thickness of three credit cards stacked together. Brush it with water and season the top well with salt.

Use the pizza cutter or knife to gently cut divisions into the dough to form individual crackers. Now prick the dough all over to keep it from puffing up as it bakes.

Carefully transfer the crackers, on the parchment, to a sheet pan.

Bake the crackers for about 20 minutes, until browned, fragrant, and crisp. Let them cool to room temperature and serve. Store leftovers in an airtight container.

YIELD WILL VARY

I'm not a big cracker eater—I'd rather eat bread with my cheese—but there are times when a cracker is just the thing, and this recipe was a wonderful discovery. These crackers are light and crisp and like a water biscuit. They're really simple to make, and they keep for ages in an airtight container. For this recipe, you have to use the starter discard for panettone, lievito madre, or as we call it, Danny Lievito (see page 272). Other discards are too wet for this recipe and would require additional flour.

Danny Lievito also has no salt, so I just add salt as I roll it out thin.

By the end of your panettone tests, and all the Danny Lievito feeds, you'll be able to make a hell of a lot of crackers. You could get pretty crackered out, fast, but they do also make great gifts.

TIMING

Roll out dough and bake: a total of about 40 minutes

EQUIPMENT

Parchment paper, rolling pin, pastry brush, pizza cutter or knife, sheet pan

Cracked Rye Bread

MAKES ONE 900-GRAM LOAF

If you go to Germany, you'll find this bread in every bakery. In California, I would always see bakers making a variation on this bread, which I found to be such a mystery. It's very good-looking and rises beautifully, causing cracks all over the top (hence the name). I couldn't believe that it was made from only rye flour, and no wheat. I needed to learn how to make it.

Once I got to Denmark, the German baking legend Michael Schulze visited me at the Noma test kitchen and was more than happy to show me how he did it. Based on what he taught me, I have devised my own somewhat streamlined method, forgoing Michael's inclusion of toasted ground bread and using a multiday collection of discarded rye starter.

I used to make this bread with a starter just fed the day before, and you can get great results that way. But: rye bread likes a really *sour* sourdough starter. I wondered, *What if I just saved discarded rye starter over a number of days and built the bread from that?*

Now, I'm sure you think I'm a hypocrite, or ridiculously forgetful, after my rant against keeping sourdough in the fridge. Bear with me; this is a necessary exception. Over a number of days, the starter from day 1 will become deeply acetic and vinegary. It will get basically rank, unless you store it in the cold. By adding fresh discard every day for 5 days, and keeping it cold, you can make a rye bread that is a real showstopper.

DOUGH

BAKER'S %	WEIGHT	INGREDIENT
100%	328g	Whole rye flour
100%	328g	Rye starter discard
70%	230g	Hot water (104°F / 40°C)
4%	13g	Salt

ADDITIONAL INGREDIENTS

A handful of rye flour (for proofing basket)

A handful of rye flour or sesame seeds (for coating the loaf)

TIMING

Mix dough, ferment, and bake: a total of about 4 hours

EQUIPMENT

Mixing bowl, flexible plastic dough scraper, fine-mesh sieve, banneton (proofing basket), tea towel, cast-iron or enameled Dutch oven (with a flat, handleless lid), transfer board, digital thermometer, cooling rack

Mix and shape the dough: In a large bowl, combine all the dough ingredients and use your hands to mix it all together thoroughly but gently to form a thick dough with no dry streaks of flour remaining. Scrape the excess dough from your hands back into the bowl. Wet your hands and use a light but decisive touch to shape the dough into a rounded loaf. This is your finished dough.

Prepare the basket and dough for fermentation: Put a handful of rye flour into a fine-mesh sieve and shake a modest amount into the proofing basket to lightly coat it. This is important: don't use too much flour, which can form a seal on the surface of the dough and keep it from expanding and cracking as it ferments.

Before you place the dough in the proofing basket, either use the sieve to lightly dust the top of the dough with rye flour, again taking care not to go overboard, or scatter sesame seeds on a clean plate or work surface and gently roll the top of the loaf in the seeds, applying just enough pressure to make them adhere.

Ferment the dough: Gently set the loaf into the basket, cover it with a tea towel, and set it aside in a warm place (82°F / 28°C) to ferment for 2 to 3 hours. If you're in a cold room and need to warm it up, place the basket inside a dry bowl and place that bowl into a larger bowl of hot water. If you're in a hot environment, it could proof faster than 2 to 3 hours.

When it's ready to bake, the top of the loaf will show cracks.

Bake the loaf: Preheat the oven to 425°F / 220°C for at least 1 hour with your Dutch oven inside.

Once the Dutch oven is preheated, take it out, but be careful. Use heavy-duty oven mitts or a few layers of dry tea towels when handling it. Place it on a sturdy, heatproof surface. Take the lid off and lay it down carefully, upside down.

Invert the loaf onto the transfer board, and then invert the loaf from the transfer board onto the lid. Carefully invert the pot over the dough, to cover it like a dome.

Set the Dutch oven back inside the oven and set a timer for 30 minutes.

After 30 minutes, uncover the loaf and bake for another 30 minutes, or until the internal temperature of the loaf is 203°F / 95°C. Remove the bread from the oven and carefully transfer it to a rack to cool for several hours before slicing.

Cracked rye will keep for about 1 week at room temperature, wrapped in brown paper. You may also wrap it tightly in plastic and freeze it for up to 6 months.

Sweet Breads

Everyone who knows me knows I don't really make a lot of sweet breads. I originally came up with the breads in this chapter for those of you with a sweet tooth, but it was a real revelation developing them; I fell back in love with all the tastes and textures I hadn't been into since I was a kid.

I've taken my knowledge as a bread baker, using sourdough and all the different fermentation techniques, to enhance what would usually be various quick yeasted sweet buns and breads. You'll see, for example, in the brioche recipe, I wanted to take it somewhere new, not just a variation on the classic brioche ingredients. I asked myself, *How can I make it better?*

In all the following recipes, I am continuously asking myself that question, and I think you're going to love the results.

Brioche Master Recipe

SCALDED RYE

BAKER'S %	WEIGHT	INGREDIENT
100%	38g	Rye flour
100%	38g	Boiling water

STARTER

BAKER'S %	WEIGHT	INGREDIENT
100%	50g	Hot water (104°F / 40°C)
100%	50g	Whole wheat flour
40%	20g	12-hour wheat or rye starter (your choice; see pages 73 and 69)

DOUGH

BAKER'S %	WEIGHT	INGREDIENT
50%	151g	All-purpose flour
50%	151g	Bread flour
40%	121g	Eggs
30%	91g	Freshly fed starter (above)
25%	75g	Scalded rye (above)
16%	48g	Tepid water (77°F / 25°C)
15%	44g	Sugar
11%	33g	Milk powder
2%	6g	Salt
1%	3g	Instant dry yeast
25%	75g	Softened butter
12.5%	38g	Neutral oil

MAKES ONE 800-GRAM LOAF OR EIGHT 100-GRAM ROLLS

When I started out as a baker, I used to think brioche was easy. *You just chuck it in the mixer, chill it, bake it. Not much skill. Any old pastry chef can make it.*

I've found that this is not actually true. Good brioche is something else, in technique and in the whole experience of eating it. The eggs in the dough can create a cake-like texture and dry mouthfeel, but the best brioche transcends that: it should taste luxuriously rich and buttery but paradoxically light in texture.

When mixing brioche, you have to really pay attention. Make sure the dough has good gluten strength before you add the fat. And you need to keep the ingredients cold; otherwise, you run the risk of overheating the dough, which will make it ferment way too fast and overproof at the beginning of the process, leaving you with a sad, underperforming dough. All the details matter.

When I started thinking about putting a brioche in this book, I did a lot of work developing the recipe, looking at various quantities of butter, eggs, and all the other ingredients. But I wanted to push it even further. How could I make it more delicious?

I started toying with whole-grain flour. Although the flavor was great, the texture never quite worked; it was always a little too heavy.

Finally I came up with the answer: scalded rye. It really brings out beautiful flavor without compromising the soft, light texture of a brioche bun. As mentioned in the recipe for Perfect Sandwich Bread (page 172), the scalded rye acts as a starch, which means the dough can take a lot more hydration. It brings a complexity, adding something that you can't quite put your finger on.

ADDITIONAL INGREDIENTS

Softened butter (enough to coat the inside of the loaf pan, if making a loaf)

1 egg, beaten together with a splash of water and a pinch of salt

TIMING

Day 1 (afternoon): Scald rye, feed starter, mix dough, and proof: a total of about 3 hours (most of which is allowing the dough to proof), plus an overnight cold retard of up to 12 hours

Day 2 (morning): Shape, final proof, and bake: a total of about 2½ hours for buns or up to 4½ hours for a loaf

Mixing bowls, spatula or wooden spoon, digital thermometer, flexible plastic dough scraper, bowl or pitcher of warm water (for rinsing), stand mixer fitted with the dough hook, tea towels, loaf pan ((5 × 9 inches / 13 × 20cm; if making a loaf), sheet pan lined with parchment paper (if making buns), spray bottle of water, pastry brush, cooling rack

DAY 1

Make the scalded rye: Place the rye flour in a heatproof medium bowl, pour the boiling water over the flour, and mix well with a spatula or wooden spoon until all the water has been evenly absorbed into the flour. Let the mixture cool to room temperature.

Feed the starter: Follow the instructions of the City Loaf Master Recipe (page 113). Set a timer for 45 minutes.

 Mix the dough, part 1: Once the starter is ready, in the bowl of a stand mixer fitted with the dough hook, combine both flours, the eggs, starter, scalded rye, water, sugar, and milk powder. Start the mixer on low speed and increase the speed to medium, mixing until the dough is smooth and cohesive, about 3 minutes. Let the dough rest for 20 minutes.

 Mix the dough, part 2: Add the salt and yeast and mix the dough again on medium speed for 5 to 8 minutes. The dough will start to move as one cohesive unit, balled up around the hook. It will be ready for the butter when it's very strong, showing good resistance when you try to pull a piece away from the mass. The gluten needs to be at maximum strength before you start adding all the butter.

Gradually mix the butter in, a quarter of it at a time. After each addition, mix the dough until the butter is incorporated, then add the next quarter, and repeat until it all has been incorporated. Next, add in the oil and mix until incorporated. You will have a silky, glossy, smooth dough.

Proof and cold retard the dough: Let the dough proof in the stand mixer bowl, covered, for 1½ hours at room temperature, until it has expanded to about one and a half times its original size. Gently punch it down, cover the bowl with a tea towel, and transfer it to the fridge to proof overnight, up to about 12 hours.

DAY 2

Shape and proof the dough: Turn the chilled dough out onto your work surface, gently punching it down to release the excess gases. From here, you can choose your shape: a loaf or individual buns.

→ **For a brioche loaf:** Butter the loaf pan well. Gently shape the dough into an oval and transfer it to the buttered pan. (For a more decorative loaf, divide the dough into 3 equal portions, roll each one into a ball, and nestle them together in the loaf pan.) Let it proof at room temperature for at least 2 hours and up to 4 hours, until it has doubled in size. Keep an eye on the loaf, and if it starts to dry out, mist it with water from a spray bottle.

→ **For brioche buns:** Divide the dough into 8 portions of 100g. Roll each piece into a ball using the dough balling technique: Flour your dominant hand and tap off the excess. Get one portion of dough in front of you and apply light pressure to the top of it as you use your fingers and thumb to form a kind of circular basket around the dough. Roll it in circles; the dough should be a bit sticky on the bottom as you're pressing lightly on it while rolling; that friction and sticking on the work surface will help the dough come together in a ball. As you roll the dough, your fingers should be tucking it underneath itself to help form a ball. Roll until the dough has a nice, taut surface and a round shape. Repeat with the remaining dough pieces.

Space them far apart from one another on the sheet pan lined with parchment paper. Let them b proof at room temperature for about 2 hours, until more than doubled in size. Keep an eye on the buns, and if they start to dry out, mist them with water from a spray bottle.

Egg wash and bake the dough: Preheat the oven to 355°F / 180°C.

Use a pastry brush to brush the egg wash over the top of the loaf or the top of each bun.

→ **For the loaf:** Place the loaf in the oven and immediately reduce the temperature to 320°F / 160°C. Bake for 40 minutes, until the internal temperature is 203°F / 95°C. Remove the loaf from the oven and turn it out onto a rack to cool.

→ **For the buns:** Place the buns in the oven and bake for 10 to 12 minutes, until golden brown and shiny and the internal temperature is at least 203°F / 95°C. Remove them from the oven and let them cool briefly before serving.

Babka
(Dark Chocolate Hazelnut or White Chocolate Pumpkin Seed)

MAKES ONE 1.4-KILOGRAM LOAF

I put a babka in this book because one of my editors, Susan, asked for it. It seemed like a good idea to keep her happy.

I asked my brilliant pastry chef, Talia Richard-Carvajal, to make me something different. Why make just another babka? Talia developed a classic dark chocolate hazelnut version, and also came up with the idea of a white chocolate pumpkin seed filling. It's so, so good spread on everything, but in babka, it's sublime. Either way, take the filling of your choice, twist it into the dough, then bake it and soak it with vanilla syrup and butter when it comes out of the oven. Susan, I hope you love it.

DOUGH

—	800g	Brioche Master Recipe (page 232)

WHITE CHOCOLATE PUMPKIN SEED FILLING

BAKER'S %	WEIGHT	INGREDIENT
100%	100g	Pumpkin seeds, toasted
50%	50g	White chocolate, chopped
5%	5g	Neutral oil
2.5%	2.5g	Salt
50%	50g	Softened butter

DARK CHOCOLATE HAZELNUT FILLING

BAKER'S %	WEIGHT	INGREDIENT
55%	55g	Dark chocolate (70% cacao)
50%	50g	Softened butter
5%	5g	Neutral oil
65%	65g	Hazelnut praline paste*
15%	15g	Powdered sugar
15%	15g	Cocoa powder
5%	5g	Ground cinnamon

* Hazelnut butter can be substituted, but you'll want to increase the powdered sugar to 30g (30%).

VANILLA SYRUP

BAKER'S %	WEIGHT	INGREDIENT
100%	144g	Sugar
38%	55g	Water
—	1	Vanilla bean, split

ADDITIONAL INGREDIENTS

150g white chocolate chips (if making white chocolate filling)

150g dark chocolate chips (if making dark chocolate filling)

Softened butter (enough to coat the inside of the loaf pan)

100g clarified butter, melted (for brushing on the baked babka)

TIMING

Day 1 (afternoon): Scald rye, feed starter, mix dough, and proof: a total of about 3 hours (most of which is allowing the dough to proof), plus an overnight cold retard of up to 12 hours

Day 2 (morning): Make filling, fill and shape babka, chill, final proof, and bake: a total of about 4½ hours

EQUIPMENT

Mixing bowls, spatula or wooden spoon, digital thermometer, stand mixer fitted with the dough hook, tea towels, blender or food processor (if making white chocolate version), small saucepan, whisk (if making dark chocolate version), rolling pin, long loaf pan (12 × 4 × 4 inches / 30 × 10 × 10cm), cooling rack, pastry brush

DAY 1

Scald the rye, feed the starter, mix the dough, proof, and cold retard overnight: Follow the instructions of the Brioche Master Recipe (page 233).

DAY 2

→ **For the white chocolate pumpkin seed filling:** In a blender or food processor, combine the pumpkin seeds, white chocolate, oil, and salt and blend until the mixture is smooth. Add the butter and blend until combined. Transfer the mixture to a bowl and keep at room temperature until ready to use.

→ **For the dark chocolate hazelnut filling:** In a small saucepan, combine the chocolate, butter, oil, and praline paste. Whisk them together and gently melt over medium-low heat. Whisk in the powdered sugar, cocoa powder, and cinnamon until well combined, then remove the mixture from the heat and transfer it to a bowl. Keep at room temperature until ready to use.

Roll, fill, and chill the babka: Turn the chilled dough out onto your work surface, gently punching it down to release the excess gases, and roll the dough out into a 12 × 8-inch / 30 × 20cm rectangle a scant ¼ inch / 5mm thick.

Spread your chosen filling in a thin layer over the surface of the dough and sprinkle the chocolate chips evenly over the filling. Roll the dough tightly into a log, making sure there are no pockets of air as you roll. Chill the rolled dough for 1 hour in the fridge, loosely covered.

Twist and proof the babka: Butter the loaf pan. Remove the dough from the fridge and use a sharp knife to cut it decisively in half lengthwise. Twist the two halves of the dough around each other, tuck the ends underneath themselves, and lay the babka into the prepared pan.

Let it proof in a warm (75°–86°F / 24°–30°C) place for about 2 hours, until the babka has doubled in size and looks swollen.

Bake the babka and make the syrup: Preheat the oven to 365°F / 185°C.

Bake the babka for 20 to 30 minutes, until it reaches an internal temperature of 203°F / 95°C.

While the babka is baking, make the vanilla syrup. In a small saucepan, combine the sugar and water. Scrape in the vanilla seeds and add the pod. Bring the mixture to a boil. Keep the syrup warm until needed.

Brush and cool the babka: When the babka is done, remove it from the oven and immediately turn it out of the loaf pan and onto a cooling rack. Turn it right side up and brush it heavily with the clarified butter.

Allow it to cool slightly before brushing it with the warm vanilla syrup. Serve warm.

Brunsviger
(Danish Caramel Brioche)

EQUIPMENT

Mixing bowls, wooden spoon, digital thermometer, flexible plastic dough scraper, bowl or pitcher of water water (for rinsing), stand mixer fitted with the dough hook, tea towels, rolling pin, half sheet pan (13 × 18 inches / 33 × 46cm), small saucepan, whisk, spatula

DAY 1

Scald the rye, feed the starter, mix the dough, proof, and cold retard overnight: Follow the instructions of the Brioche Master Recipe (page 233).

DAY 2

Shape and proof the dough: Butter the half sheet pan well. Turn the chilled dough out onto your work surface, gently punching it down to release the excess gases, and roll the dough out to a 9 × 6-inch / 23 × 15cm rectangle. Gently transfer it to the prepared pan and let it proof, covered, in a warm (75°–86°F / 24°–30°C) place, until it has doubled in size, approximately 1 to 2 hours. When you press a finger into the dough, it should spring back slightly.

(You may notice that we call for proofing this dough in a warm place, whereas in the Brioche Master Recipe, page 233, it is proofed at room temperature. This is because the brunsviger is shaped into a rectangle with much more surface area, so the dough cools down more quickly than in the master brioche recipe.)

Make the brunsviger sauce: While the dough is proofing, in a small saucepan, whisk all the brunsviger ingredients together and gently melt them, while continuing to whisk, over medium-low heat. Keep the mixture lukewarm until ready to use.

Top and bake the brunsviger: Preheat the oven to 365°F / 185°C.

When the dough is proofed, dip your splayed fingers into flour, and press them deep into the surface of the dough to make cylindrical indentations that go almost to the bottom of the pan. It will look a little bit like a focaccia. Continue to do this until the whole brioche is covered with depressions.

Reheat the sauce, whisking to ensure it remains homogenous, and pour it over the whole top of the brioche. Using a spatula, work quickly to spread it across the entire surface.

Transfer immediately to the oven and bake for 15 to 25 minutes, depending on your oven, until the brunsviger reaches an internal temperature of 194°F / 90°C.

Remove the brunsviger from the oven and allow it to cool slightly before removing it from the pan and cutting it into rectangles with a sharp bread knife to serve.

MAKES AN 800-GRAM HALF SHEET PAN
(13 × 18 INCHES / 33 × 46CM)

Before I had my bakery in Denmark, one of the team at Noma asked me if I would please make a brunsviger, René Redzepi's favorite cake, for his birthday. I replied that I couldn't make cake; I'm a bread guy and really didn't want to make something half-standard, not even knowing what it actually was. It wasn't until later—when I found out it was a bread, not a cake—that I thought, *Shit, I could have made that.*

Now, unless you're Danish, the name of this fantastic sweet bread won't mean much to you, as it didn't to me. I put the recipe in here because it's amazing: it's really a brioche, oozing with dark, decadent caramel. It's a total winner.

DOUGH

—	800g	Brioche Master Recipe (page 233)

BRUNSVIGER SAUCE

BAKER'S %	WEIGHT	INGREDIENT
100%	160g	Butter
48%	77g	Light muscovado sugar
38%	61g	Dark muscovado sugar
22%	36g	Malt syrup
1%	1.6g	Salt
—	—	Grated zest of ½ orange

ADDITIONAL INGREDIENTS

Softened butter (enough to coat the half sheet pan)

A handful of all-purpose flour (for keeping fingers dry while dimpling dough)

TIMING

Day 1 (afternoon): Scald rye, feed starter, mix dough, and proof: a total of about 3 hours (most of which is allowing the dough to proof), plus an overnight cold retard of up to 12 hours

Day 2 (morning): Shape, final proof, make sauce, and bake: a total of about 2½ hours

Milk Bun Master Recipe

MAKES TEN 80-GRAM BUNS

This is a recipe I developed in Copenhagen. I wanted a dough that was crazy tender but without the richness of a brioche. Milk powder makes the bread soft and light without the additional liquid. The protein contributes to the lightly structured crumb, and the milk sugars are concentrated and caramelized for an appealing sweetness and nicely bronzed crust.

This dough is incredibly versatile. It's often the starting point for a lot of my sweet bread experiments. You can use it any number of ways. To give you a few ideas:

→ Baked in a loaf pan, it makes for a great Japanese-style milk bread.

→ Swap out around 20% of the all-purpose flour for different whole-grain flours; rye and einkorn both work really well.

→ Throw in some cooked bacon and cheese (around 25–30% of the total dough weight) for a great savory bun or loaf.

→ With some candied orange, raisins, and fennel seeds added into the dough, you can make a lovely sweet loaf or bun. Add around 25–30% of the total dough weight in candied fruit, or about 3% in spices.

STARTER

BAKER'S %	WEIGHT	INGREDIENT
100%	50g	Hot water (104°F / 40°C)
100%	50g	Whole wheat flour
40%	20g	12-hour wheat or rye starter (your choice; see pages 73 and 69)

DOUGH

BAKER'S %	WEIGHT	INGREDIENT
50%	160g	Bread flour
50%	160g	All-purpose flour
13.5%	43g	Sugar
10%	32g	Milk powder
40%	128g	Tepid water (77°F / 25°C)
16%	51g	Eggs
30%	96g	Freshly fed starter (above)
2%	6g	Salt
1%	3g	Instant dry yeast
25%	80g	Softened butter
12.5%	40g	Neutral oil

ADDITIONAL INGREDIENTS

Neutral oil (enough to coat the inside of the proofing container)

1 egg, beaten together with a splash of water and a pinch of salt

TIMING

Day 1 (morning): Feed starter, mix dough, and bulk ferment: a total of about 3 hours (most of which is allowing the dough to bulk ferment), plus an overnight cold retard of up to 12 hours

Day 2 (morning): Divide, shape, proof, and bake: a total of 2 to 4 hours

EQUIPMENT

Mixing bowls, digital thermometer, flexible plastic dough scraper, bowl or pitcher of warm water (for rinsing), tea towel, stand mixer fitted with the dough hook, proofing container, sheet pan, parchment paper or silicone baking mat, pastry brush, cooling rack

Recipe continues

DAY 1

Feed the starter: Follow the instructions of the City Loaf Master Recipe (see page 113). Set a timer for 45 minutes.

Mix the dough, part 1: Once the starter is ready, in the bowl of a stand mixer fitted with the dough hook, combine both flours, the sugar, milk powder, water, eggs, and starter and mix on medium speed to combine. The mixture will look wet at this point. Let it rest for 30 minutes.

Mix the dough, part 2: Add the salt and yeast and mix the dough thoroughly on medium speed until it is completely smooth and very strong, around 10 minutes. Don't rush this step, which will make the dough strong enough to absorb all the butter.

Now add half (40g) of the butter and mix the dough until it is fully incorporated. Add the remaining 40g butter and mix again until it is fully incorporated. Be patient!

Now add the oil, half at a time. Allow the first half to be completely absorbed before adding the rest. Make sure all the fat is properly mixed in. Ideally, the dough shouldn't be too warm (not higher than 82°F / 28°C).

Bulk ferment and cold retard the dough: Transfer the dough to an oiled container large enough to hold double its size and allow it to bulk ferment at room temperature for 45 minutes to 1 hour, until the dough begins to look bubbly and the volume has slightly increased. Cover with a tea towel and refrigerate overnight, up to 12 hours.

DAY 2

Divide, shape, and proof the dough: Cut the dough into 10 portions of 80g each.

Roll each piece into a ball using the dough balling technique: Flour your dominant hand and tap off the excess. Get one portion of dough in front of you and apply light pressure to the top of it as you use your fingers and thumb to form a kind of circular basket around the dough. Roll it in circles; the dough should be a bit sticky on the bottom as you're pressing lightly on it while rolling; that friction and sticking on the work surface will help the dough come together in a ball. As you roll the dough, your fingers should be tucking it underneath itself to help form a ball. Roll until the dough has a nice, taut surface and a round shape. Repeat with the remaining dough pieces.

Space them evenly with ample room between them on a sheet pan lined with parchment paper or a silicone baking mat.

Let the buns proof in a warm place (75°–85°F / 23°–29°C) for at least 2 hours and up to 4 hours, until they have doubled in size and do not spring back when you poke a finger into the side of one.

Egg wash and bake the buns: Preheat the oven to 330°F / 165°C.

Use a pastry brush to brush the egg wash over the top of each bun.

Bake the buns for 10 to 12 minutes, until golden brown and the internal temperature is at least 205°F / 96°C. Let them cool on a rack for a few minutes before serving.

Danish Hveder

MAKES TWELVE 66-GRAM BUNS

Now, I can't even pronounce this word. It sounds like something close to the word *villa*, but really nothing like *villa*. That's how Danish is: hard. I'm sorry to every Dane for being absolutely rubbish at your language.

    This bread is a big deal in Denmark. It's basically a soft bun (in this case, a variation on the Milk Bun, page 239), scented with a lot of cardamom. Eaten toasted, with butter, it is pretty special. It's made once a year, for a few days in May, and every bakery in the country gets slammed with orders for it. With the team and space I had at Hart, we just couldn't make enough, and we'd sell out within hours. We worked our arses off and made a few thousand every day and it still wasn't enough. Crazy.

DOUGH

WEIGHT	INGREDIENT
800g	Milk Bun Master Recipe (page 239)
9g	Ground cardamom

ADDITIONAL INGREDIENTS

1 egg, beaten together with a splash of water and a pinch of salt

60g clarified butter, melted (for brushing the finished hveder)

TIMING

Day 1 (morning): Feed starter, mix, and bulk ferment: a total of about 3 hours (most of which is allowing the dough to bulk ferment), plus an overnight cold retard of up to 12 hours

Day 2 (morning): Divide, shape, proof, and bake: a total of 2 to 4 hours

EQUIPMENT

Mixing bowls, digital thermometer, flexible plastic dough scraper, bowl or pitcher of warm water (for rinsing), tea towel, stand mixer fitted with the dough hook, proofing container, sheet pan, parchment paper, pastry brush, cooling rack

DAY 1

Feed starter and mix dough: Follow the instructions of the Milk Bun Master Recipe (page 240), which will take you through the addition of the oil to the dough.

Add the cardamom: After the oil is fully incorporated, add the cardamom and mix just until it is well distributed. Don't overmix it or you'll risk tearing the dough and weakening the gluten.

Bulk ferment and cold retard the dough: Follow the instructions of the Milk Bun Master Recipe (page 240).

DAY 2

Divide, shape, and proof the buns: Cut the dough into 12 portions of 66g each.

    Roll each piece into a ball using the dough balling technique: Flour your dominant hand and tap off the excess. Get one portion of dough in front of you and apply light pressure to the top of it as you use your fingers and thumb to form a kind of circular basket around the dough. Roll it in circles; the dough should be a bit sticky on the bottom as you're pressing lightly on it while rolling; that friction and sticking on the work surface will help the dough come together in a ball. As you roll the dough, your fingers should be tucking it underneath itself to help form a ball. Roll until the dough has a nice, taut surface and a round shape. Repeat with all the remaining dough pieces.

    Line a sheet pan with parchment paper and arrange the buns in three rows of four columns, leaving about a ½-inch / 1cm gap between them.

    Let them proof in a warm room for 2 to 4 hours, until the buns are wobbly, doubled in size, and do not spring back when you poke a finger into the side of one. The buns will be touching each other, which is what you want.

Egg wash and bake the buns: Preheat the oven to 365°F / 185°C.

    Use a pastry brush to brush the egg wash over the top of each bun.

    Bake the buns for 14 to 18 minutes, until they are golden brown and the internal temperature is at least 205°F / 96°C.

    Transfer the buns to a cooling rack and brush them with the clarified butter. Serve warm.

Chocolate Milk Buns

MAKES TWELVE 60-GRAM BUNS

These started off as chocolate brioche buns, but after testing and testing them, I still wasn't happy; they were too dense and heavy. I switched from brioche to the fluffier milk bun dough, and it makes them so much better. I also added scalded rye, because rye marries really well with the chocolate.

They are light buns with a deep chocolate taste. If you use great-quality chocolate here, it will make all the difference. If you haven't already eaten the buns straight out of the oven, cut them in half, toast and butter them, and maybe add a thin slice of chocolate or some jam on top. You can also sandwich them around good ice cream for a killer dessert.

SCALDED RYE

BAKER'S %	WEIGHT	INGREDIENT
100%	30g	Rye flour
100%	30g	Boiling water

STARTER

BAKER'S %	WEIGHT	INGREDIENT
100%	50g	Hot water (104°F / 40°C)
100%	50g	Whole wheat flour
40%	20g	12-hour wheat or rye starter (your choice; see pages 73 and 69)

MILK BUN DOUGH

BAKER'S %	WEIGHT	INGREDIENT
50%	105g	Bread flour
50%	105g	All-purpose flour
18%	38g	Brown sugar
10%	21g	Milk powder
8%	17g	Cocoa powder
40%	84g	Warm water (86°F / 30°C)
16%	34g	Beaten eggs
30%	63g	Freshly fed starter (above)
30%	63g	Scalded rye (above)
2%	4g	Salt
1%	2g	Instant dry yeast
25%	52g	Softened butter
12.5%	26g	Neutral oil
25%	52g	Dark chocolate chips
15%	33g	Milk chocolate chips
10%	22g	White chocolate chips

ADDITIONAL INGREDIENTS

Neutral oil (enough to coat the inside of the proofing container)

1 egg, beaten together with a splash of water and a pinch of salt

TIMING

Day 1 (morning): Scald rye, feed starter, mix dough, and bulk ferment: a total of about 3 hours (most of which is allowing the dough to bulk ferment), plus an overnight cold retard of up to 12 hours

Day 2 (morning): Divide, shape, proof, and bake: a total of 2 to 4 hours

EQUIPMENT

Mixing bowls, spatula or wooden spoon, digital thermometer, flexible plastic dough scraper, bowl or pitcher of warm water (for rinsing), tea towel, stand mixer fitted with the dough hook, proofing container, sheet pan, parchment paper or silicone baking mat, pastry brush, cooling rack

Recipe continues

DAY 1

Make the scalded rye: Place the rye flour in a heatproof medium bowl, pour the boiling water over the flour, and mix well with a spatula or wooden spoon until all the water has been evenly absorbed into the flour. Let the mixture cool to room temperature.

Feed the starter: Follow the instructions of the City Loaf Master Recipe (page 113). Set a timer for 45 minutes.

Mix the dough, part 1: In a stand mixer fitted with the dough hook, combine both flours, the brown sugar, milk powder, cocoa powder, water, eggs, starter, and scalded rye and mix on medium speed to combine. The mixture will look wet at this point. Let it rest for 30 minutes.

Mix the dough, part 2: Add the salt and yeast and mix the dough thoroughly on medium speed until it is completely smooth and very strong, around 10 minutes. Don't rush this step, which will make the dough strong enough to absorb all the butter. You should see and hear it slapping against the inside of the bowl as one cohesive mass.

Add half (26g) of the butter and mix the dough until it is fully incorporated. Add the remaining 26g butter and mix again until it is fully incorporated. Be patient! The dough should be strong, smooth, and shiny.

Now add the oil, half at a time. Allow the first half to be completely absorbed before adding the rest. Make sure all the fat is properly mixed in. Ideally, the dough shouldn't be too warm (not higher than 82°F / 28°C). Add the chocolate chips and mix just until well incorporated.

Bulk ferment and cold retard the dough: Transfer the dough to an oiled container large enough to hold double its size and allow it to bulk ferment at room temperature for 45 minutes to 1 hour, until the dough begins to look bubbly and the volume has slightly increased. Cover with a tea towel and refrigerate overnight, up to 12 hours.

DAY 2

Divide, shape, and proof the dough: Cut the dough into 12 portions of 60g each.

Roll each piece into a ball using the dough balling technique: Flour your dominant hand and tap off the excess. Get one portion of dough in front of you and apply light pressure to the top of it as you use your fingers and thumb to form a kind of circular basket around the dough. Roll it in circles; the dough should be a bit sticky on the bottom as you're pressing lightly on it while rolling; that friction and sticking on the work surface will help the dough come together in a ball. As you roll the dough, your fingers should be tucking it underneath itself to help form a ball. Roll until the dough has a nice, taut surface and a round shape. Repeat with the remaining dough pieces.

Space them out evenly on a sheet pan lined with parchment paper or a silicone baking mat.

Let the buns proof in a warm place (75°–85°F / 23°–29°C) for at least 2 hours and up to 4 hours, until they have doubled in size and do not spring back when you poke a finger into the side of one.

Egg wash and bake the buns: Preheat the oven to 330°F / 165°C.

Use a pastry brush to brush the egg wash over the top of each bun.

Bake the buns for 10 to 12 minutes, until golden brown and the internal temperature is at least 205°F / 96°C. Let cool for a few minutes on a rack before serving.

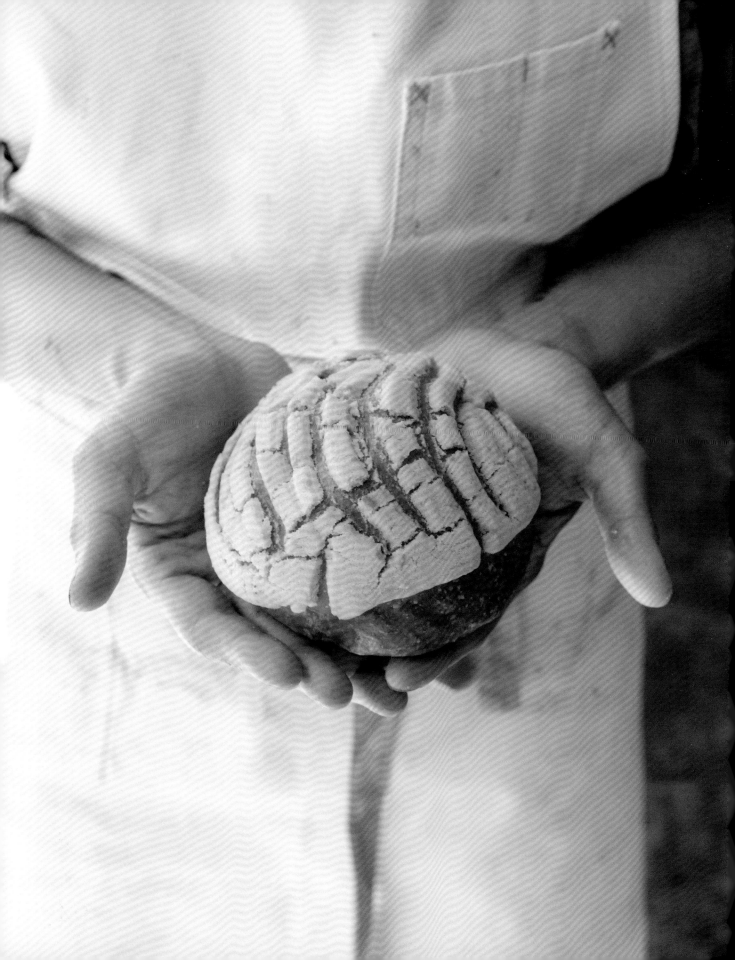

Conchas
(Plain or Chocolate)

MAKES EIGHT 100-GRAM PIECES

I started making conchas years ago, after visiting Mexico for the first time. My friend and excellent chef Rosio Sanchez often does pop-ups with other chefs at her taco restaurant in Copenhagen, Hija de Sanchez, and she invited me to collaborate with her.

My first thought was to do a Doritos burrito, but amazing as that would have been, for sure, it didn't really showcase my bread. Instead, we made what we called a "Dirty Concha," which was a concha stuffed with pickled vegetables, crispy cheese, and carnitas (slow-cooked pork and spices). It was amazing. Lots of love to you, luv, Rosio.

Conchas are typically a sweet bread, often eaten for breakfast, with a lovely, light, almost shortbread-like topping.

These conchas are not vegetarian. Like a lot of food in Mexico, they contain pork fat. It's in both the dough and the topping, which gives them an incredible umami depth and richness. If you are vegetarian, you can switch out the lard for butter and the recipe will work just as well.

STARTER

BAKER'S %	WEIGHT	INGREDIENT
100%	60g	Hot water (104°F / 40°C)
100%	60g	Whole wheat flour
40%	24g	12-hour wheat or rye starter (your choice; see pages 73 and 69)

DOUGH

BAKER'S %	WEIGHT	INGREDIENT
50%	167g	All-purpose flour
50%	167g	Bread flour
13.5%	45g	Sugar
10%	33g	Milk powder
16%	53g	Eggs
30%	100g	Tepid water (77°F / 25°C)
30%	100g	Freshly fed starter (above)
2%	7g	Salt
1%	3g	Instant dry yeast
12.5%	42g	Softened butter
12.5%	42g	Neutral oil
12.5%	42g	Lard

PLAIN TOPPING

BAKER'S %	WEIGHT	INGREDIENT
100%	55g	Lard
100%	55g	All-purpose flour
10%	5g	Cornstarch
60%	33g	Powdered sugar

OR CHOCOLATE TOPPING

BAKER'S %	WEIGHT	INGREDIENT
100%	55g	Lard
90%	50g	All-purpose flour
10%	6g	Cocoa powder
10%	6g	Cornstarch
60%	33g	Powdered sugar

ADDITIONAL INGREDIENT

Neutral oil (enough to coat the inside of the proofing container)

Recipe continues

TIMING

Day 1 (morning): Feed starter, mix dough, and bulk ferment: a total of about 3 hours (most of which is allowing the dough to bulk ferment), plus an overnight cold retard of up to 12 hours

Day 2 (morning): Divide, shape, mix topping, proof, and bake: a total of 2 to 4 hours

EQUIPMENT

Mixing bowls, digital thermometer, flexible plastic dough scraper, bowl or pitcher of warm water (for rinsing), tea towel, stand mixer fitted with the dough hook, proofing container, sheet pan, parchment paper, concha cutter or paring knife, cooling rack

DAY 1

Feed the starter and mix the dough: Follow the instructions of the Milk Bun Master Recipe (page 240), adding the lard after the butter and oil.

Bulk ferment and cold retard the dough: Follow the instructions of the Milk Bun Master Recipe (page 240).

DAY 2

Divide and shape the dough: Follow the instructions of the Milk Bun Master Recipe (page 240).

Mix the topping: Choose your topping, either plain or chocolate. In a small bowl, combine all the topping ingredients and use your hands to mix them into a smooth paste.

Proof the buns: Let the buns proof in a warm place (75°–85°F / 23°–29°C) for at least 2 hours and up to 4 hours, until they have doubled in size and do not spring back when you poke a finger into the side of one. As soon as you have started the proofing, roll out the topping and top the buns (next step).

Roll out the topping: Divide the topping into 8 equal portions. Roll each portion into a ball and flatten the ball out into a disk with your hands, using a bit of flour if needed to keep the topping from getting too sticky.

Lay one disk over the top of each bun. Use a concha cutter to incise lines or a crosshatch pattern into the topping.

Bake the buns: Preheat the oven to 330°F / 165°C.

Bake the buns for 10 to 12 minutes, until the topping looks dry and slightly cracked and the internal temperature is at least 205°F / 96°C. Let cool on a rack for a few minutes before serving.

Cardamom Buns

MAKES TWELVE 120-GRAM BUNS

In Scandinavia, people are crazy about cardamom buns. They're usually much drier than I'd like. Through testing, I've found that the secret to making a bun that's much moister is underproofing the dough. Normally, baking something that's underproofed is nothing but disappointing, but in this case, it's the way to go. A slightly underproofed center lets the dough hold on to this sticky, gooey texture that you really want in a cardamom (or cinnamon) bun.

This is essentially a cinnamon roll with cardamom, whereas the cardamom-intensive Danish Hveder (page 243) is an only slightly sweet soft roll that should be served toasted and buttered.

STARTER

BAKER'S %	WEIGHT	INGREDIENT
100%	60g	Hot water (104°F / 40°C)
100%	60g	Whole wheat flour
40%	24g	12-hour wheat or rye starter (your choice; see pages 73 and 69)

DOUGH

BAKER'S %	WEIGHT	INGREDIENT
50%	204g	All-purpose flour
50%	204g	Bread flour
13.5%	55g	Sugar
10%	41g	Milk powder
16%	65g	Eggs
35%	143	Warm water (86°F / 30°C)
30%	122g	Freshly fed starter (above)
2%	8g	Salt
1%	4g	Instant dry yeast
25%	102g	Butter
12.5%	51g	Neutral oil

CARDAMOM SUGAR

BAKER'S %	WEIGHT	INGREDIENT
100%	252g	Sugar
6.5%	16g	Ground cardamom
1%	3g	Salt

CARDAMOM SCHMEAR

BAKER'S %	WEIGHT	INGREDIENT
100%	200g	Softened butter
50%	100g	Cardamom sugar (above)

CARDAMOM SYRUP

BAKER'S %	WEIGHT	INGREDIENT
100%	71g	Cardamom sugar (above)
40%	29g	Water

ADDITIONAL INGREDIENTS

60g softened butter (for coating the muffin tins)

A pinch of ground cardamom (for garnish)

TIMING

Day 1 (morning): Feed starter, mix dough, and bulk ferment: a total of about 3 hours (most of which is allowing the dough to bulk ferment), plus an overnight cold retard of up to 12 hours

Day 2 (morning): Divide, shape, proof, and bake: a total of about 2 hours

EQUIPMENT

Mixing bowls, digital thermometer, flexible plastic dough scraper, bowl or pitcher of warm water (for rinsing), tea towel, stand mixer fitted with the dough hook, proofing container, two standard 6-cup (or one standard 12-cup) muffin tins, pastry brush, rolling pin, palette knife, pizza cutter, small saucepan, cooling rack

DAY 1

Feed the starter, mix the dough, bulk ferment, and cold retard: Follow the instructions of the Milk Bun Master Recipe (page 240). This is the same dough, only with a slightly lower hydration percentage that makes it easier to handle, which is important for the shaping process.

Recipe continues

Make the cardamom sugar: In a bowl or other container, combine the sugar, cardamom, and salt and mix well. Cover and set aside.

DAY 2

Make the cardamom schmear: In a small bowl, combine the butter and 100g of the cardamom sugar and mix until the sugar is well incorporated. Keep this mixture at room temperature so that it will spread easily across the dough.

Shape the buns: Use the pastry brush to brush the insides of the muffin tins with the softened butter.

Turn the chilled dough out onto your work surface. While the dough is still cold, use the rolling pin to roll it out into a 22 × 10-inch / 55 × 25cm rectangle a scant ¼ inch / 5mm thick.

Using a palette knife, small spatula, or butter knife, spread the schmear in an even layer over the dough, working quickly so that the dough doesn't warm up. Sprinkle 100g of the cardamom sugar in an even layer over the schmear.

With a short side of the dough facing you, fold the dough in half by bringing the top edge down to meet the bottom edge. Use the rolling pin to roll it out to a 16 × 10-inch / 40 × 25cm rectangle. It should now be about ¾ inch / 2cm thick and will be horizontally oriented.

Use a pizza cutter or sharp knife to cut 12 long strips from the dough. Hold each end of one strip in your hands and twist it on itself in opposite directions, then roll it onto itself to make a snail shape. Tuck the loose ends underneath to keep the strip from unraveling while baking and place it into the prepared muffin tin. Repeat with the remaining 11 strips.

Proof the buns: Let the buns proof in a warm place for 1 hour, until they have expanded to about one and a half times their original size. If you poke your finger into the dough, it should leave an impression but still spring back slightly. The dough is underproofed at this point, which will result in a moister baked bun.

Make the cardamom syrup: While the buns proof, in a small saucepan, combine the remaining 71g cardamom sugar and the water. Heat the mixture over high heat until it comes to a boil, then remove from the heat and let it cool to room temperature.

Bake the buns: Preheat the oven to 365°F / 185°C.

Bake the buns for 10 to 12 minutes, until they are deep golden brown and the internal temperature is at least 208°F / 98°C.

While they are still warm, invert the buns onto a cooling rack. Brush them with the cardamom syrup and garnish with ground cardamom. Serve warm.

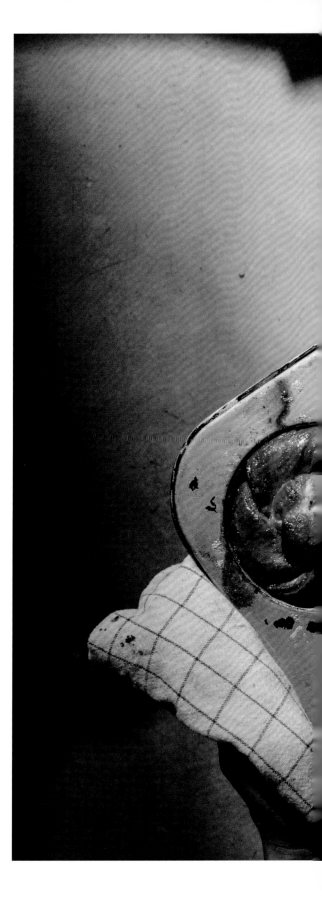

Cinnamon Buns

CINNAMON SUGAR

BAKER'S %	WEIGHT	INGREDIENT
100%	106g	Sugar
6.5%	7g	Ground cinnamon
1%	2g	Salt

CINNAMON SCHMEAR

BAKER'S %	WEIGHT	INGREDIENT
100%	115g	Softened butter
100%	115g	Cinnamon sugar (above)

ADDITIONAL INGREDIENT

60g softened butter (for coating the cake pan)

TIMING

Day 1 (morning): Feed starter, mix dough, and bulk ferment: a total of about 3 hours (most of which is allowing the dough to bulk ferment), plus an overnight cold retard of up to 12 hours

Day 2 (morning): Divide, shape, proof, and bake: a total of about 2 hours

EQUIPMENT

Mixing bowls, digital thermometer, flexible plastic dough scraper, bowl or pitcher of warm water (for rinsing), tea towel, stand mixer fitted with the dough hook, proofing container, 10-inch / 25cm round cake pan or 9-inch / 23cm square baking dish, palette knife, pastry brush, rolling pin, cooling rack

DAY 1

Feed the starter, mix the dough, bulk ferment, and cold retard: Follow the instructions of the Milk Bun Master Recipe (page 240). This is the same dough, only with a slightly lower hydration percentage that makes it easier to handle, which is important for the shaping process.

Make the cinnamon sugar: In a bowl or other container, combine the sugar, cinnamon, and salt and mix well. Cover and set aside.

MAKES EIGHT 121-GRAM BUNS

In searching for the best recipe for cinnamon buns, I've learned that the quality of the cinnamon is super important. The difference between freshly ground cinnamon and the dusty stuff you might have had lying in your cupboard for years is huge. Use the best and freshest you can get your hands on. And like the Cardamom Buns (page 253), these, too, benefit from a little underproofing.

STARTER

BAKER'S %	WEIGHT	INGREDIENT
100%	50g	Hot water (104°F / 40°C)
100%	50g	Whole wheat flour
40%	20g	12-hour wheat or rye starter (your choice; see pages 73 and 69)

DOUGH

BAKER'S %	WEIGHT	INGREDIENT
50%	153g	All-purpose flour
50%	153g	Bread flour
13.5%	41g	Sugar
10%	31g	Milk powder
16%	49g	Eggs
35%	107g	Warm water (86°F / 30°C)
30%	92g	Freshly fed starter (above)
2%	6g	Salt
1%	3g	Instant dry yeast
25%	77g	Butter
12.5%	38g	Neutral oil

Recipe continues

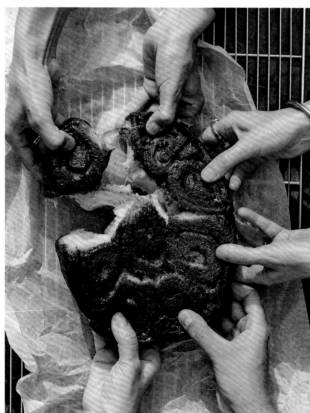

Make the cinnamon schmear: In a small bowl, combine the butter and cinnamon sugar and mix until the sugar is well incorporated. Keep this mixture at room temperature so that it will spread easily across the dough.

Preshape the dough: Turn the chilled dough out onto your work surface. While the dough is still cold, use the rolling pin to roll it out into a 16 × 12-inch / 40 × 30cm rectangle about ¼ inch / 5mm thick.

Using a palette knife, small spatula, or butter knife, spread the schmear in an even layer over the dough, working quickly so that the dough doesn't warm up.

With a long side of the rectangle facing you, roll it into a long log, starting from the top edge and rolling tightly to avoid leaving any air pockets. Transfer the log to the fridge to chill for 30 minutes.

Final shape and proof the buns: Use the pastry brush to brush the insides of the cake pan or baking dish with the softened butter, making sure to get into the corners and edges.

Remove the log from the fridge and use a sharp knife to cut it crosswise into 8 equal-sized pieces. Arrange the pieces in the prepared pan, leaving ¼ inch / 1cm space between them. Let the buns proof in a warm place for 1 hour, until they have expanded to about one and a half times their original size. If you poke your finger into the dough, it should leave an impression but still spring back slightly. The dough is underproofed at this point, which will result in a moister baked bun.

Bake the buns: Preheat the oven to 365°F / 185°C.

Bake the buns for 15 to 17 minutes, until they are deep golden brown and the internal temperature is at least 208°F / 98°C.

While they are still warm from the oven, invert the buns onto a cooling rack, watching out for any hot butter that might splash out from the pan. Serve warm.

Cinnamon Raisin Bread

MAKES ONE 800-GRAM LOAF

Anyone who knows me well as a baker knows that I have had issues with putting fruits and any other stuff into my bread. I always thought it was too easy.

I'd say, "Of course it's going to taste delicious if it's packed full of fruits, or sugar and spices, or cheese, or whatever."

It's silly, I know. Who cares how easy it is to make something delicious? If it's delicious, that's that. I need to get over myself. There are a few breads in this book with fruits and cheese and other things added, so maybe I have.

This recipe was inspired by Wendy Williams, a great baker, friend, and former colleague. She used to make us raisin bread at Hart for breakfast on cold, dark mornings. We have actually changed Wendy's recipe quite a bit, but I just wanted to mention her because she is an amazing human, and her cinnamon bread and kindness made those mornings much better.

SCALDED WHOLE WHEAT

BAKER'S %	WEIGHT	INGREDIENT
100%	66g	Whole wheat flour
120%	80g	Boiling water

STARTER

BAKER'S %	WEIGHT	INGREDIENT
100%	50g	Hot water (104°F / 40°C)
100%	50g	Whole wheat flour
40%	20g	12-hour wheat or rye starter (your choice; see pages 73 and 69)

DOUGH

BAKER'S %	WEIGHT	INGREDIENT
80%	195g	Bread flour
20%	49g	Whole wheat flour
75%	183g	Hot water (104°F / 40° C)
5%	12g	Honey
45%	109g	Raisins
33%	80g	Freshly fed starter (above)
60%	146g	Scalded whole wheat flour (above)
2.2%	5g	Salt
0.3%	1g	Instant dry yeast
5%	12g	Softened butter
5%	12g	Olive oil
1.5%	4g	Ground cinnamon

ADDITIONAL INGREDIENT

Butter (enough to coat the inside of the loaf pan)

TIMING

Day 1 (morning): Scald whole wheat flour, feed starter, soak raisins, mix dough, ferment, shape, and proof: a total of about 8 hours (most of which is allowing the dough to bulk ferment and proof), plus an overnight cold retard of up to 12 hours

Day 2 (morning): Preheat oven, score, and bake: a total of about 1½ hours

EQUIPMENT

Sheet pan, mixing bowls, fork or wooden spoon, digital thermometer, flexible plastic dough scraper, bowl or pitcher of warm water (for rinsing), stand mixer fitted with the dough hook, tea towel, bench scraper, loaf pan (5 × 9 inches / 13 × 20cm), lame, cooling rack

DAY 1

Toast and scald the whole wheat flour: Preheat the oven to 355°F / 180°C.

Spread the flour in an even layer on a large sheet pan and toast it for 20 to 30 minutes, stirring occasionally so it toasts evenly. You'll know it's done when it is light golden brown and smells nutty and delicious. Let the flour cool slightly, then transfer it to a heatproof bowl.

Pour the boiling water over the flour, mixing vigorously with a fork or wooden spoon until it is fully incorporated.

Recipe continues

Toasting the flour draws out all its natural moisture, so if some of the flour remains dry after mixing in the water, you can add a little more water to make a homogenous paste. Set the mixture aside to cool. It should be at room temperature when you mix it into the dough.

Feed the starter: Follow the instructions of the City Loaf Master Recipe (page 113). Set a timer for 45 minutes.

Autolyse the dough: In a stand mixer fitted with the dough hook, combine both flours, 122g of the water, and the honey and mix just until combined. Scrape down the sides of the bowl if necessary and let the dough rest for 45 minutes.

Rinse and soak the raisins: While the starter feeds and the dough autolyses, cover the raisins in clean water and agitate them slightly to dislodge dirt and impurities. Pour off the water and repeat this procedure twice, then cover the raisins again with clean water and let them soak for 30 minutes. Drain off the water and set the raisins aside. This may seem like a minor step, but the soaking time is important: if you don't soak the raisins long enough, they'll be too dry and will pull a lot of moisture from the dough, which will affect the fermentation. If you oversoak the raisins, they will absorb too much water and will become mushy and break apart in the dough.

Mix the dough: Add the starter and the scalded whole wheat flour to the dough. Using the dough hook, mix the dough on medium speed until it's strong and well developed, about 5 minutes.

Add the remaining 61g hot water and continue to mix the dough until the water is well incorporated. Add the salt and yeast and mix until they're both dissolved and distributed. Add the butter, mix until incorporated, then add the olive oil and mix until it's also fully incorporated.

Add the cinnamon and raisins and continue to mix the dough until it is homogenous and strong. You should feel good resistance when you try to pull a bit of dough away from the mass. If the dough feels weak, meaning that there's no resistance, continue to mix the dough for another few minutes to develop the gluten strength.

Bulk ferment the dough: Take the dough's temperature, which should ideally be 82°–86°F / 28°–30°C. Set the bowl in a larger bowl of warm or cool water, if necessary, to warm it up or cool it down. Cover the bowl with a tea towel and let it ferment in a warm place for 2 to 3 hours, until it is light and bubbly.

Preshape and proof the dough: To preshape the dough, follow the instructions of the City Loaf Master Recipe (page 114). Let the dough rest for 20 minutes.

Final shape and proof the dough: Coat the loaf pan with butter, making sure to get into all the corners.

Using a wet hand and your bench scraper in unison, tighten the loaf into an oval and carefully transfer it to the prepared pan. Let it proof, uncovered, at room temperature for 1 to 2 hours, until it has doubled in size in the pan.

Cold retard: Cover the pan with a tea towel and place it in the fridge overnight, up to 12 hours.

DAY 2

Score and bake the dough: Take the dough out of the fridge. Preheat the oven to 425°F / 220°C.

Just before putting the dough in the oven, use a lame to score a straight line into the loaf, from one end of the pan to the other. Bake it for 50 to 60 minutes, covering the top with a piece of foil if it starts to get too dark, until the internal temperature is 208°F / 98°C. As soon as it comes out of the oven, turn it out onto a rack and let it cool completely before slicing.

Hot Cross Buns

MAKES TWELVE 60-GRAM BUNS

These buns are traditionally eaten at Easter, although the warm spice and citrus flavors remind me of winter.

Hot cross buns have an emotional connection for me. I didn't realize this until I moved to the US and couldn't get them. I missed them. There *were* some terrible versions available in the US, with dreadful things like lemon cream as the cross (messed up, I know). It was then I started making them for myself, my family, and friends. In the end, it became a yearly tradition. I love making and eating them, toasted with tons of butter. Thanks to Ross Sneddon for helping with the cross recipe.

These days they sell them year-round in the UK, which kind of spoils them for me. I love the thrill of looking forward to things.

TEA AND FRUIT

BAKER'S %	WEIGHT	INGREDIENT
20%	60g	Water
0.5%	2g	Black tea leaves
20%	60g	Dark stout
25%	75g	Raisins, rinsed
15%	45g	Candied orange
15%	45g	Dried apricots

STARTER

BAKER'S %	WEIGHT	INGREDIENT
100%	50g	Hot water (104°F / 40°C)
100%	50g	Whole wheat flour
40%	20g	12-hour wheat or rye starter (your choice; see pages 73 and 69)

DOUGH

BAKER'S %	WEIGHT	INGREDIENT
50%	150g	All-purpose flour
50%	150g	Bread flour
40%	120g	Tea / stout soaking liquid (above)
11%	33g	Sugar
10%	30g	Milk powder
16%	48g	Eggs
30%	90g	Freshly fed starter (above)
2.5%	8g	Salt
1.5%	5g	Instant dry yeast
25%	75g	Softened butter
12.5%	38g	Neutral oil
0.5%	2g	Ground ginger
0.5%	2g	Ground cinnamon
0.5%	2g	Ground cloves

SIMPLE SYRUP

BAKER'S %	WEIGHT	INGREDIENT
100%	100g	Sugar
40%	40g	Water

CROSS GARNISH

BAKER'S %	WEIGHT	INGREDIENT
100%	44g	All-purpose flour
90%	40g	Water
20%	9g	Butter
10%	5g	Olive oil
3%	1g	Simple syrup (above)
3%	1g	Salt

ADDITIONAL INGREDIENT

Neutral oil (enough for coating the proofing container)

TIMING

Day 1 (morning): Brew tea and soak fruit, feed starter, mix dough, and bulk ferment: a total of about 3 hours (most of which is allowing the dough to bulk ferment), plus an overnight cold retard of up to 12 hours

Day 2 (morning): Divide, shape, proof, and bake: a total of about 4½ hours

Recipe continues

EQUIPMENT

Mixing bowls, digital thermometer, strainer, flexible plastic dough scraper, bowl or pitcher of water water (for rinsing), stand mixer fitted with the dough hook, proofing container, tea towel, sheet pan, parchment paper, whisk, pastry piping bag, small saucepan, pastry brush

DAY 1

Make the tea and soak the fruit: In a kettle, heat the water to 194°F / 90°C. Set the tea leaves in a heatproof bowl and pour the hot water over them. Let the tea infuse for 5 minutes, then strain out the tea leaves and weigh the water. If it's less than 60g, supplement with additional water. Add the stout and raisins. Cut the candied orange and apricots into raisin-sized pieces and add them to the tea and stout mixture. Let the fruit soak for 45 minutes to 1 hour.

Feed the starter: While the fruit soaks, follow the instructions of the City Loaf Master Recipe (page 113). Set a timer for 45 minutes.

Mix the dough, part 1: Drain the fruit, reserving the soaking liquid and fruit separately. Weigh the liquid and top it off with water if it's less than 120g.

In a stand mixer fitted with the dough hook, combine both flours, the soaking liquid, sugar, milk powder, eggs, and starter and mix to combine on medium speed. The mixture will look wet at this point. Let it rest for 30 minutes.

Mix the dough, part 2: Add the salt and yeast and mix the dough thoroughly on medium speed until it is completely smooth and very strong, around 10 minutes. Don't rush this step, which will make the dough strong enough to absorb all the butter. You should see and hear it slapping against the inside of the bowl as one cohesive mass.

Add half of the butter and mix the dough until it is fully incorporated. Add the remaining butter and mix again until it is fully incorporated. Be patient! The dough should be strong, smooth, and shiny.

Now add the oil, half at a time. Allow the first half to be completely absorbed before adding the rest. Make sure all the fat is properly mixed in. Ideally, the dough shouldn't be too warm (not higher than 82°F / 28°C). Add the reserved soaked fruit and the ground spices and mix just until they are well incorporated.

Bulk ferment and cold retard the dough: Transfer the dough to an oiled container large enough to hold double its size and allow it to bulk ferment at room temperature for 45 minutes to 1 hour, until the dough begins to look bubbly and the volume has slightly increased. Cover with a tea towel and refrigerate overnight, up to 12 hours.

DAY 2

Divide, shape, and proof the dough: Cut the dough into 12 portions of 60g each.

Roll each piece into a ball using the dough balling technique: Flour your dominant hand and tap off the excess. Get one portion of dough in front of you and apply light pressure to the top of it as you use your fingers and thumb to form a kind of circular basket around the dough. Roll it in circles; the dough should be a bit sticky on the bottom as you're pressing lightly on it while rolling; that friction and sticking on the work surface will help the dough come together in a ball. As you roll the dough, your fingers should be tucking it underneath itself to help form a ball. Roll until the dough has a nice, taut surface and a round shape. Repeat with the remaining dough pieces.

Arrange the buns on a sheet pan lined with parchment paper or a silicone baking mat, with each bun just touching the next one.

Let the buns proof in a warm place (75°–85°F / 23°–29°C) for 2 to 4 hours, until they are doubled in size and do not spring back when you poke a finger into the side of one.

Make the simple syrup, make the cross garnish, and bake the buns: Preheat the oven to 355°F / 180°C.

In a small saucepan, combine the sugar and water and heat over medium heat to melt the sugar, then bring the mixture to a boil and remove it from the heat. Don't let it reduce beyond the boil or else the syrup will be too thick and will weigh down the buns.

Now, make the cross garnish. In a small bowl, whisk together all the ingredients for the cross garnish, and transfer it to a piping bag. Cut a tiny hole in the end of the bag, a scant ⅛ inch / 2mm wide. Starting at the end of a row of buns, at one end of the first bun, pipe a single line through the center of all the buns in one direction, then rotate the pan 90 degrees and repeat the piping, so you have a cross piped onto each bun.

Bake the buns for 10 to 12 minutes, until the internal temperature is 205°F / 96°C, taking care not to overbake them.

As soon as the buns come out of the oven, brush them with the simple syrup. Let them cool completely. Hot cross buns are best served sliced and toasted, with butter.

Panettone

An Introduction to Panettone

"The angels started singing when I ate my first slice of panettone."

I don't remember every kind word or compliment, but this comment from a customer was such a lovely thing to say, super poetic, and it stayed with me.

When you make a beautifully risen panettone, there is *nothing* like it in the world. It's an Italian traditional bread, incredibly special, and the subject of obsession by bakers there and around the world. The texture is extraordinarily light, like bread meets candy floss (or what Americans call cotton candy). The flavors are an elegant balance of sweet, buttery richness, and fruity, citrusy notes. It's incredibly rewarding, and absolutely worth the effort, but: panettone is the most challenging thing I've ever learned to bake. Once you've made an active panettone starter, which takes 10 days to begin with, it's a 3-day process: the Lievito Madre (page 272) is mixed into a first dough, which is then fermented for 12 hours, then mixed into a second dough, then shaped, proofed, baked, and hung upside down to cool overnight.

For me, learning to successfully make panettone involved years of experiments, and a lot of failures. I asked many, many questions of many, many people and often didn't get straight answers. What I did get, I didn't always understand. Some of the recipes I tried were translated badly or missing key information. I thought I'd never get it right. It drove me crazy.

But now I've got somewhere, and I want to share what I've learned to date, and ideally help you skip through much of the trial and error. I am by no means an expert—I've got a lot more learning to do—but I can teach you what I know and help you start on your own panettone path.

The Rules of Panettone

RULE ONE: USE THE RIGHT STARTER—A LIEVITO MADRE (AKA DANNY LIEVITO)

In my earliest panettone attempts, I thought I could use my wet sourdough bread starter. That didn't work, so I started to experiment, like adding sugar to train the culture, thinking that the yeast and bacteria would get used to living in a sweeter environment.

After many failures, I knew that was not the way. The way is the way: I needed to learn the ins and outs of the traditional panettone starter, called lievito madre. I'm not one to name my starter, but Talia, my pastry chef, came up with the name "Danny Lievito," after the actor Danny DeVito, and it stuck. From here on, I will refer it to as Danny.

My whole career, I've been used to working with a wheat sourdough starter, which is characterized by an abundance of lactic acid, which has a kind of yogurt-y smell. Danny is acetic acid forward and, through different methods of feeding, is a completely different beast. Once matured, Danny has a lovely white wine smell to it. (Directions on how to start and maintain Danny begin on page 272.)

There are two takes on how to store it: either tightly wrapped in a cloth or submerged in water. I have played around with both, and at the moment, I'm keeping mine in water. (When I asked the Italian baker who taught me to keep it in water why it works, he said, "Water is life." Hard to argue with that.)

RULE TWO: USE THE RIGHT FLOUR

Because there's so much fat in the dough, panettone requires a strong, high-protein flour, which will provide enough structure for the dough to rise properly over the long period of fermentation. To make panettone, you can buy specific panettone flour, which I do, and I highly recommend you do, too. If you can't get it, you'll need to find a really strong bread flour, with a 15% or 16% protein content, like Manitoba.

Before being sold, panettone flour has been aged for between three and six months, which slows its enzymatic activity, meaning that it's ideal for a long, slow fermentation. If you're using a strong bread flour, plan ahead: buy it in summer for making panettone in winter.

As a matter of practicality, I start my Danny with high-protein bread flour and continue to feed it with that on a daily basis, because a starter needs fresh flour, full of enzymatic activity. The day I start to make panettone, I switch to using panettone flour, which is more expensive and not necessary for the daily feeding of Danny.

RULE THREE: CONTROL THE ACIDITY

Monitoring and controlling the acidity of the dough is essential to panettone success. Acidity has a major effect on gluten development. A pH of 4.1 is the sweet spot, where the gluten is at its strongest and most flexible. It can stretch to accommodate the rise over the long fermentation, trapping the gases that create a light and airy panettone crumb, without breaking under the pressure of those gases.

Dough 1
Danny 120g

Dough 1
200g H20

Dough 1
100g Yolk

Dough 1
120g Sugar

Dough 1
120g Butter

Dough 1
400g Flour

Once I began understanding and controlling the acidity of my starter, using a pH meter, everything started working out better. So go get yourself a pH meter; they're not expensive.

(As a brief refresher, the lower the number on the pH scale, which runs from 0 to 14, the more acidic it is. Battery acid is 0, lemon juice or vinegar is 2, black coffee is 5, and water is 7, meaning it's neutral. Anything above 7 is increasingly basic, but, really, anything above 4.5 is not useful for our panettone purposes.)

RULE FOUR: CONTROL THE TEMPERATURE AND WATCH THE TIME

Timing and temperature control are important in any sourdough baking endeavor, but especially so with panettone. Don't get creative with the Danny feeding schedule, don't let your first or second dough overheat, and don't let the dough ferment much longer than the recommended times. The closer you can stick to the suggested times and temperatures, the better chance you will have of baking a properly risen panettone.

PANXIETY

After years of baking, I've learned to work intuitively. I classed panettone as just another bread and thought I would have it down. Maybe I could be a panettone wizard, too.

It's just another sourdough, right?

It soon became clear, as I racked up failure after failure, that the answer was no.

At Tartine, when I started making whole-grain breads, I did a lot of experimentation, throwing different things together until, fuck me, they worked, through intuition and luck. I'd thought I could break the rules with panettone, just like I had before, but you can't break the rules until you understand them.

I spent three years at Tartine trying to make decent panettone, sometimes three times a week, with no luck. It became a running joke among the other bakers, to the point where I would come into work, and in the proofer would be my dough, which hadn't risen at all, and there were notes taped to the proofer saying things like, "Morning, Rich. Fuck you. Love, Panettone."

Most bakers have anxiety every time they mix panettone. We started calling it panxiety. To this day, baking panettone can still sometimes freak me out. The proportions of the ingredients don't seem to make sense; it's truly mental. The dough has such a high ratio of egg yolks and butter to flour. It's delicate, and prone to breaking. To get it right, you must follow some basic rules. I wish I had those rules in front of me when I started trying to make panettone, though maybe I would have tried to outthink them from the start. Anyway, for your first time, and maybe every time, follow the rules, which are here for you.

Tools for Making Panettone

pH Meter: Monitoring the acidity of the starter (called lievito madre, or, as we call it, "Danny Lievito") is essential for getting this finicky dough to ferment and rise correctly, and the only way to do that (unless you're a natural-born panettone whisperer) is with a pH meter.

Electric Bread Proofer: It's essential that panettone dough be proofed at 80°F / 27°C for 12 hours, and the easiest way to keep it at a consistent temperature is with an electric proofing box/cabinet. You can get countertop versions for home use.

Panettone Molds: These are sturdy, disposable, ovenproof corrugated cardboard or paper casings with round bottoms, sold in various sizes. I use a 1-kilo size.

Hanging Skewers: Because the structure of a freshly baked panettone is so delicate and full of air, like a soufflé, it will start to collapse in on itself as it cools. You can prevent this by piercing it along the bottom surface with thin skewers and hanging it upside down. There are special two-prong skewers you can buy for this purpose, but you can also use two multipurpose bamboo skewers.

Making a Lievito Madre

(aka Danny Lievito)

MAKES ONE 240-GRAM BATCH

This is the starter we use to make panettone in the Christmas season, and we also use it year-round in laminated pastries, which keeps it fed and cared for when we're not producing panettone. I start it with rye because the fiber in the flour helps kick-start fermentation faster than with white flour, which you'll eventually switch to. (Start with whole wheat flour, if you can't get hold of rye.)

TIMING

About 10 days, one feeding on most days

EQUIPMENT

Small bowl, medium container with lid (for proofing), stand mixer fitted with the dough hook

DAYS 1 TO 3

BAKER'S %	WEIGHT	INGREDIENT
100%	100g	Rye (or whole wheat) flour
100%	100g	Warm water (86°F / 30°C)

In a small bowl, combine the flour and water and mix by hand to form a homogenous dough. Transfer it to a clean container, cover, and set aside at room temperature until it is doubled in bulk and bubbly, about 72 hours, or 3 days. This is your "Baby Danny," referred to as such throughout this section.

DAY 4

BAKER'S %	WEIGHT	INGREDIENT
100%	200g	Baby Danny
50%	100g	Bread flour

Today, Baby Danny will become stiffer, with the addition of flour but no water.

In a stand mixer fitted with the dough hook, combine Baby Danny and the flour and mix well. Transfer it to a clean container, cover, and set aside at room temperature until it is doubled in bulk and bubbly, about 24 hours.

DAY 5

BAKER'S %	WEIGHT	INGREDIENT
100%	100g	Baby Danny
100%	100g	Bread flour
45%	45g	Warm water (86°F / 30°C)

In a stand mixer fitted with the dough hook, combine the Baby Danny, flour, and water and mix to form a homogenous dough. Transfer it to a clean container, cover it, and set aside at room temperature for 24 hours, until the next feeding.

DAYS 6 AND 7

Repeat Day 5 ingredients and method.

DAY 8

BAKER'S %	WEIGHT	INGREDIENT
100%	100g	Baby Danny
100%	100g	Bread flour
40%	40g	Warm water (86°F / 30°C)

Starting on Day 8 (and for Days 9 and 10), you'll slightly decrease the hydration, from 45% to 40%. You'll also start storing Danny in water, so be sure to squeeze out the excess water each subsequent day before feeding it new flour and water.

In a stand mixer fitted with the dough hook, combine the Baby Danny, flour, and water and mix to form a homogenous dough. Remove it from the mixer and roll it into a tight ball.

Transfer Danny to a clean container, which should be deep enough to fit the dough with room to expand above and below. What you don't want is a too-large container that lets Danny bob around like an apple in a tub of water at a Halloween party.

Fill the container with 86°F / 30°C water, enough to cover the dough. This warm water will give an initial boost to the yeast. The water will eventually cool, which is fine.

At this stage, you should start to notice Danny rising to the top of the water, within 3 or 4 hours of having been fed. That's a clear sign that there is plenty of good, active, and healthy yeast in Danny.

DAYS 9 AND 10

Repeat Day 8 ingredients and method.

Two-Part Daily Storage Feeding

(Keeping Danny Happy, Fed, and Alive)

Now that your Danny Lievito has been well established, you can drop the "Baby" and switch to this twice-daily feeding routine that will keep it full of active, healthy yeast. Each day you'll see that Danny has floated to the top of the water, showing that it's fully alive. The part that's outside the water will have formed a dry crust. When you remove the dough from the water and pull off the crust, it will reveal the soft starter underneath. After that, you will squeeze out the excess water before feeding.

TIMING

Two feedings, 3 to 4 hours apart

EQUIPMENT

Stand mixer fitted with the dough hook, container for holding Danny, electric bread proofer (or another means of keeping water at 86°F / 30°C for 3½ hours)

DAILY STORAGE FEEDING: PART ONE

BAKER'S %	WEIGHT	INGREDIENT
100%	100g	Danny Lievito (page 272)
100%	100g	Bread flour
40%	40g	Warm water (80°F / 27°C)

Remove Danny from the water, pull off the dry crust, and squeeze out the water. In a stand mixer fitted with the dough hook, combine 100g of Danny with the flour and water and mix to form a homogenous dough that shows good resistance when pulled. Roll it into a rectangle, then into a tight spiral (see page 276). Make a large crosswise score across the top (see page 277). Discard the unfed starter (this is *not* the fully matured starter I suggest using for crackers and the like in Baking with Sourdough Discard (page 219).

Transfer the freshly fed mixture to a clean container, which should be large enough to fit the dough with some room to expand above and below, plus room for enough water to cover it. Fill the container with 86°F / 30°C water, covering the dough. It's important to keep the water at 86°F / 30°C for the next 3½ hours, which you can do by continuing to replace it with fresh 86°F / 30°C water, or by using an electric bread proofer, whatever suits you. Note that when you actually *make* the panettone, you will need a proofer, so you'll want to think about getting one.

Danny should rise to the top of the water within 3 or 4 hours of having been fed, which is a clear sign of healthy yeast activity. After 3½ hours, feed it again, as below:

DAILY STORAGE FEEDING: PART TWO

BAKER'S %	WEIGHT	INGREDIENT
100%	100g	Danny Lievito
100%	100g	Bread flour
40%	40g	Warm water (80°F / 27°C)

Remove Danny from the water, pull off the dry crust, and squeeze out the water. In a stand mixer fitted with the dough hook, combine 100g of Danny with the flour and water and mix to form a homogenous dough that shows good resistance when pulled. Roll it into a tight ball. Discard the unfed starter.

Transfer the mixture to a clean container, which should be large enough to fit the dough with room to expand above and below, plus enough water to cover it. Fill the container with *cool* water (59°–65°F / 15°–18°C), covering the dough.

Transfer the container to a cool place (59°–65°F / 15°–18°C) for 20 hours.

Sugar Bath, or Bagnetto

This is a technique that I learned from the Italian bakers who have helped me make better panettone. Giving your Danny a 20-minute soak in a sugar bath, especially after it has been refrigerated for a week, is useful for sloughing off dead yeast and bacteria cells, and for eliminating some of the acetic acid that accumulated in the dough overnight, which, if excessive, can inhibit the growth of the yeasts that are essential to good fermentation.

INGREDIENTS

1 quart / 1 liter tepid water (72°F / 22°C)
5g sugar

In a large bowl or other container, combine the water and sugar, stirring until the sugar is dissolved.

Cut Danny into four pieces and use your hands to gently squeeze out the air bubbles. Transfer the pieces to the sugar bath and submerge them. Let them sit for 20 minutes.

Danny will sink at first but should float within 20 minutes. That's an indication that it's been "cleaned" by the sugar bath and is ready to be fed as per Real Talk: Managing Your Danny on a Schedule That Works for You (at right).

If it doesn't float after 20 minutes, feed it using the Two-Part Daily Storage Feeding (page 275) and give it a sugar bath the following day.

If it floats after 20 minutes, you're good. If it still doesn't float after 20 minutes, repeat the same steps each day until you get it to float after 20 minutes.

Once you get the float, give it 3 days of the Two-Part Daily Storage Feeding before using it to make panettone.

Real Talk: Managing Your Danny on a Schedule That Works for You, or, Feeding Danny Once Per Week, for People Who Aren't Total Panettone Maniacs and Have Normal Lives

If you've made it this far, you're more likely than not all in on panettone, but even total panettone maniacs may not be into the idea of feeding Danny twice a day every day.

So here's some good news: when you're not actively producing panettone, you *can* feed your Danny just once a week, using the following method:

ONCE PER WEEK DANNY FEEDING

BAKER'S %	WEIGHT	INGREDIENT
100%	100g	Danny Lievito (page 272)
100%	100g	Bread flour
40%	40g	Warm water (80°F / 27°C)

Remove Danny from the water, pull off the dry crust, and squeeze out the water. In a stand mixer fitted with the dough hook, combine 100g of Danny with the flour and water and mix to form a homogenous dough that shows good resistance when pulled. Roll it into a tight ball.

Transfer the mixture to a clean container, which should be large enough to fit the dough with room to expand above and below, plus enough water to cover it. Fill the container with cool water (59°–65°F / 15°–18°C), covering the dough.

Transfer the container to the refrigerator.

Every 7 days, pull it out of the fridge, give it a sugar bath (see Sugar Bath, or Bagnetto, at left), and then follow the Two-Part Daily Storage Feeding (page 275) before returning it to the fridge for another week.

Three days before you want to make panettone, take Danny out of the fridge, give it a sugar bath, and put it on a regular feeding schedule using the Two-Part Daily Storage Feeding method for the next 3 days.

Three Danny Lievito Feeds

To Actually Start Making the F***ing Panettone Already

This is it! You've established a healthy Danny, and now it's time to embark on the true hero's journey: making panettone. This is the time to switch from bread flour to panettone flour (see page 268).

To promote maximum yeast development, it's crucial to feed your Danny three times, at 3½-hour intervals, and keep it warm (86°F / 30°C) between feedings.

The discarded portions of Danny from this next step are too valuable to be thrown away. Turn them into the crackers (see page 224) in the discard chapter. Save the discarded part from the third feeding to carry over; this is your new Danny.

BAKER'S %	WEIGHT	INGREDIENT
100%	200g	Danny Lievito (page 272)
100%	200g (per feeding)	Panettone flour
40%	80g (per feeding)	Warm water (80°F / 26°C)

TIMING

Three feedings, 3 to 4 hours apart

EQUIPMENT

Stand mixer fitted with the dough hook, container for holding Danny, electric bread proofer (or another means of holding dough and water at 86°F / 30°C), pH meter

FIRST FEEDING

Remove Danny from the water, remove the dry crust, squeeze out the excess water, and transfer 200g of it to the bowl of a stand mixer fitted with the dough hook.

Add the flour and water and mix with the dough hook to form a homogenous dough that shows good resistance when pulled. Roll it into a tight ball.

Place Danny into a clean container large enough to hold at least triple the bulk of the dough. Cover it with 86°F / 30°C water and place it in an electric bread proofer (at 86°F / 30°C) for 3 to 4 hours, until the volume of Danny has roughly tripled in size, using your best visual estimate.

NOTE

While you're waiting for the fermentation after the first feeding, use the time to make Citrus Paste (page 291) and scale out all the ingredients needed for Classic Panettone: First Dough (page 284) and Classic Panettone: Second Dough (page 287) so that everything has time to chill and is ready to be added to the mixer. Store all the scaled ingredients in the fridge, clearly labeled for "first dough" and "second dough."

SECOND FEEDING

When the dough has tripled, repeat the procedures from the first feeding (above), removing Danny from the water and squeezing out the excess, then mixing 200g of Danny with 200g flour and 80g water until the dough is homogenous and strong.

Roll Danny into a tight ball. Place it into a clean container large enough to hold at least triple the bulk of the dough. Cover it with 86°F / 30°C water and place it in an electric bread proofer (at 86°F / 30°C) for 3 to 4 hours, until the volume of Danny has tripled. Use a marker and tape to mark the top of Danny on the outside of the container. Then use your best visual estimate (or a ruler if you like) to mark subsequent levels that would indicate a tripling in volume.

THIRD FEEDING

When the dough has tripled, repeat the feeding procedures, removing Danny from the water and squeezing out the excess, then mixing 200g of Danny with 200g flour and 80g water until the dough is homogenous and strong.

Roll Danny into a tight ball again. Place it into a clean container large enough to hold at least triple the bulk of the dough. Cover it with 86°F / 30°C water and place it in an electric bread proofer (at 86°F / 30°C) for 3 to 4 hours, until the volume of Danny has tripled. Use a marker and tape to mark the top of Danny on the outside of the container. Then use your best visual estimate (or a ruler if you like) to mark subsequent levels that would indicate a tripling in volume.

CHECK THE PH

At this stage, 3 to 4 hours after the third feeding, Danny is full of yeast and quite healthy. Use the pH meter to check the acidity, which should ideally be at 4.1 or 4.2. Once it's tripled in size and has reached the desired acidity, it's time to mix the first dough (see Classic Panettone: First Dough, page 284).

A Throwdown Averted

To start improving my panettone skills, in 2017 I went to Rome to hang out with, and learn from, my friend Gabriele Bonci. He is a master and I love him. It was amazing to watch him mix panettone. He's definitely learned his craft and has the freedom to work instinctively. He always knows, by look and feel, exactly when his lievito is ready, and precisely when to add the ingredients for the panettone dough. Spending time with Gabriele was hugely helpful, and after being with him, I got somewhere with my panettone.

In 2018, my first year at Hart, René Redzepi made a social media post saying that my panettone was the best he'd ever tried. I think he was being kind. I was flattered, but it almost started a war. A few weeks later, I was contacted by the organizer of Panetthòn, an annual panettone competition in the Italian region of Veneto.

"Dear Mister Richard Bageri," the email began. "René Redzepi—on his Instagram profile—argues that you make the best panettone in the world. For that, we write you for a panettone challenge: your panettone against our Panetthòn champion. We are ready to meet you in Copenhagen in a battle of raisins and candied fruits," and it was signed by a half dozen of the contest's organizers and promoters.

I was a beginner, and they would have crushed me. And if I had, by some miracle, come out on top, I thought they might come after me, and I wasn't ready to lose my life over panettone. It was a lose-lose situation. Jokes aside, I don't care about medals or trophies; I just want to feed people really well, so I declined.

Troubleshooting Your Danny Lievito Feeds

If the pH is higher than 4.2:
Wait up to 1 more hour for the pH to get down to 4.1 or 4.2, which is the perfect amount of acidity in the dough. Don't let it go too much longer, though, or the yeasts will get tired and won't be as powerful as you'll need them to be for the long fermentation. As long as it's lower than 4.5, you can mix the dough.

If the pH is lower than 4.1 (which is very unlikely after three feeds):
A pH number lower than 4.1 means that Danny has got too acidic. Using it now will affect the gluten bonds in the dough. They will be more fragile and prone to breaking when you add the sugar, eggs, and butter.

I know this sounds like a disaster, but you'll need to give your Danny another day to sort itself out. Everything has to line up to make your panettone a success. Store your Danny in the fridge overnight, and start the next day with a sugar bath (see Sugar Bath, or Bagnetto, page 278) and the three preparatory feedings.

Classic Panettone

A total of about 30 minutes mixing time, plus 12 hours proofing

EQUIPMENT

Stand mixer fitted with the dough hook, proofing container (large enough to hold dough as it triples in size), marker, masking tape, electric bread proofer (or other means of keeping dough warm), sheet pan

MAKES ONE 900-GRAM LOAF

Now that you've invested almost 2 weeks in creating your Danny Lievito, it's time to start the three-day process of actually making panettone.

→ First Dough (below)

→ Citrus Paste (page 291)

→ Second Dough (opposite)

→ The Bake (page 292)

PANETTONE PART 1: FIRST DOUGH

In Three Danny Lievito Feeds (page 281), I advised you to scale and refrigerate all your ingredients for the first and second doughs after the first feeding. Before you start mixing, make sure that everything you've scaled out is chilled, so you can keep an eye on the dough as it mixes.

FIRST DOUGH

BAKER'S %	WEIGHT	INGREDIENT
100%	200g	Panettone flour
50%	100g	Cold water
30%	60g	Danny Lievito (page 272)
30%	60g	Sugar
30%	60g	Butter, room temperature and pliable*, diced
25%	50g	Egg yolks

ADDITIONAL INGREDIENT

Neutral oil (enough to coat the inside of the proofing container)

About 15 to 20 minutes before you start mixing, take the butter out of the fridge, so it's room temperature and pliable by mixing time, which helps it incorporate into the dough before the mass overheats.

 Mix the dough: In a stand mixer fitted with the dough hook, combine the flour, water, and Danny and mix on low speed until it just comes together. Increase the speed to medium, then mix for about 10 minutes. Don't shortcut this step because you think the dough looks well combined. Test the strength of your dough: give it a light tug. You should encounter really strong resistance, like chewing gum that you've chewed all day. If it's not feeling that strong, mix it more, up to 5 minutes longer, and test it again.

The dough does not need to look super smooth before the sugar goes in. It just needs to be very strong.

Add half the sugar and continue to mix on medium speed until the sugar is dissolved and you can no longer feel the sugar crystals when you rub the dough between your fingertips. Add the rest of the sugar and continue to mix until you can again no longer feel the sugar crystals.

Add half the butter and continue to mix until it is almost incorporated. Then add the remaining butter and continue to mix until it is completely incorporated, meaning you can't see or feel any lumps of butter in the dough.

Decrease the mixer speed to low to avoid splashing and add half the yolks. Once they have begun to mix in, increase the speed to medium and mix until the yolks are incorporated. Decrease the speed to low again, add the rest of the yolks, and continue to mix until the dough is completely smooth and homogenous.

The dough should take about 30 minutes total to mix.

Oil the inside of the proofing container and transfer the dough into it. Use a marker and tape to mark the top of the dough on the outside of the container. Then use your best visual estimate (or a ruler if you like) to mark subsequent levels that would indicate a tripling in volume.

Place the container inside an electric bread proofer and set the temperature to 81°F / 27°C. Let the dough ferment and rise for 12 hours. Note that this dough does most of its rising in the last few hours, so don't make yourself crazy checking it every hour at first, because you won't see much change until about hour 8. (See opposite for troubleshooting.)

NOTE

If you haven't already made the Citrus Paste (page 291), now would be a good time to do that.

After the dough has tripled in volume, transfer it to a sheet pan and flatten it out a bit so that it can cool quickly, which will stop it from overfermenting in the moment and keep it from overheating in the next mix. Transfer it to the fridge, but don't let it cool down too much or the butter in the dough will cause it to solidify. Once the dough has cooled to 64°F / 18°C, which should take about 30 minutes, you can start to mix the second dough (see page 287).

PANETTONE PART 2: SECOND DOUGH

Some words of reassurance and hope as you prepare to mix the second dough: This is the phase when "panxiety" typically hits. To the chilled first dough, which is already full of butter, eggs, and sugar, you're going to add a little flour, a lot more butter, sugar, and egg yolks, and then, so much fruit. You're going to ask yourself, *Does this much fat and sugar and fruit make sense? Can I put all this stuff into a bread and have it work?* I am here to tell you it can work.

Which is not to say that it isn't a finicky process, because as you surely know by now, it is.

If the second dough gets too warm, it will break (in England, we say "split") like an overheated hollandaise, and once that happens, it is fucked: game over. The best way to keep the dough cool and intact is to store all the ingredients, except for the butter, in the refrigerator until just before adding them to the dough.

Now, you may also look at the quantity and variety of highly acidic citrus fruits—candied, zested, juiced, pureed—being added to this thing, and you would be right to ask: Isn't all of this acid threatening the balance of the dough? It's true that it would be a lot easier to maintain the dough's structural integrity by dialing back the citrus, but I feel that the flavor payoff is worth the risk.

One more note about the fruit: please wash your raisins in warm water, agitate them slightly, then drain them. Repeat this a few times until the water runs clear. You'll be amazed (and probably a little disgusted) by all the dust, wax, debris, and maybe even a few tiny insects that have been hiding in those crevices. Once you've done that, transfer the raisins to a towel-lined sheet pan to dry overnight.

Recipe continues

Troubleshooting the Fermentation of Your First Dough

→ **If, after 12 hours, the dough has risen only about half as much as you'd expect:** You can increase the proofing heat a bit, up to but not over 86°F / 30°C. If it ferments for too long, more than 15 hours, it will be at risk of being too acidic, and the second dough will almost certainly split while you're mixing it.

→ **If the dough already tripled in size by hour 10, or anytime before 12 hours are up:** It's ready. Transfer it to the fridge to cool to 64°F / 18°C before the second dough.

→ **If the dough has expanded beyond triple in volume:** It will likely be too acidic. You can still make panettone from it, but it won't be primo: it likely won't rise to its full capacity as it bakes, and it will stale more quickly. An imperfect panettone is still panettone, so don't give up at this stage.

→ **If it's been 12 hours and it's clear that it hasn't risen at all:** It's likely that your starter wasn't healthy and active enough. Put it in the bin, or bake it as an experiment, and try again tomorrow, starting with putting your Danny in a sugar bath (see Sugar Bath, or Bagnetto, page 278), followed by the three feedings.

SECOND DOUGH

BAKER'S %	WEIGHT	INGREDIENT
—	—	First Dough (page 284)
100%	50g	Panettone flour, cold
110%	55g	Sugar, cold
7.5%	3.75g	Salt, cold
220%	110g	Butter, room temperature and pliable, diced*
160%	80g	Egg yolks, cold
20%	10g	Honey, cold
20%	12.5g	Citrus Paste (page 291), cold
300%	150g	Raisins, rinsed (see page 285), cold
150%	75g	Candied orange, cold, cut into raisin-sized pieces

ADDITIONAL INGREDIENTS

Grated zest and juice of 1 cold lemon

Grated zest and juice of 1 cold orange

About 30 minutes before mixing, take the butter out of the fridge, so it's room temperature and pliable by mixing time, which helps it incorporate into the dough before the mass overheats.

TIMING

A total of about 45 minutes mixing time, 3 hours for resting and shaping, and anywhere from 5 to 12 hours proofing depending on which you choose, cold or warm

EQUIPMENT

Stand mixer fitted with the dough hook, flexible plastic dough scraper, bench scraper, paper panettone mold (1-kilo size), 2 wooden skewers, electric bread proofer (or other means of keeping dough warm)

Mix the dough: In a stand mixer fitted with the dough hook, combine the first dough and flour and mix on low speed until the mixture just comes together. Increase the speed to medium-high and continue to mix until the dough is strong and smooth, 10 to 15 minutes. You should see and hear the dough slapping against the inside of the bowl as one cohesive mass.

Test the strength of your dough: give it a light tug. You should encounter really strong resistance, like gum that you've chewed all day. If it's not feeling that strong, mix it up to 5 minutes longer, and test it again.

This is when the fear sets in, but you've come this far, and you've got to persevere. You're strong, and your dough is now at its strongest point, before you start adding sugar, eggs, and butter. The friction from the mechanical mixing and the heat of the motor will heat the dough up a bit, but don't freak out—you're about to add a lot of cold ingredients.

Add half the sugar and all the salt and continue to mix on medium until the sugar and salt have dissolved and you can no longer feel the crystals when you rub the dough between your fingertips, up to 5 minutes. Add the remaining sugar and continue to mix until you can again no longer feel the sugar crystals, up to another 5 minutes.

Add half the butter, mixing until it has been incorporated and you can no longer see or feel visible butter lumps. Decrease the speed to low to avoid splashing and add half the yolks. Once they have begun to incorporate, increase the speed to medium and mix until they are fully incorporated. Next, add the remaining butter, honey, citrus paste, zest, and juice and continue to mix until they have been completely incorporated.

Decrease the speed to low again to avoid splashing, add the rest of the yolks, then increase the speed again and continue to mix until they are fully incorporated, up to another 5 minutes.

Finally, add the raisins and candied orange and mix on low speed for about 2 minutes, until all the additions are well distributed.

After you've added the fruit, the dough won't feel as strong as it did before: don't panic. It should be smooth, homogenous, and have some resistance when you tug on it gently.

At this point, the dough is finished. It should look and feel like a wet bread dough.

Recipe continues

Let it rest in the mixer bowl, covered with a tea towel, for 1 hour.

Preshape and rest the dough: Transfer the dough to a clean work surface and preshape it into a round. Let the preshaped dough rest, uncovered, for 1 hour, until it has relaxed and formed a skin.

Final shape: Skewer the panettone mold with 2 parallel wooden skewers, about 3 inches apart, as close to the base of the mold as possible.

Give the dough a final shape into a round and gently transfer it, seam side down, to the panettone mold.

Final proof: Now you have two options: a short warm proof or a cool overnight proof. At my bakery, we switched to the overnight proof to work with our schedule, but either way works and it doesn't affect the outcome.

→ **Short warm proof:** Set the mold in an electric bread proofer at 80°F / 27°C for 5 to 8 hours. At this stage it needs to rise to fill the inside of the panettone mold by two-thirds.

→ **Cool overnight proof:** Transfer the mold to a cool place (60°F / 16°C) for up to 12 hours, until it has risen to fill the inside of the panettone mold by two-thirds.

The Process from Start to Finish

As a general overview, this is what the process looks like:

→ Create Danny Lievito, which takes about 10 days.

→ Establish a regular feeding schedule for Danny; you'll feed it twice daily.

→ On the day you're ready to start making panettone, feed Danny three times, in 3½-hour intervals.

→ Mix the first dough and let it ferment for 12 hours.

→ Mix the second dough and let it ferment for 2 hours.

→ Divide and shape the dough and let it proof for 5 to 8 hours.

→ Bake the panettone for 1 hour.

→ Let it hang for 8 to 12 hours before slicing and enjoying.

Citrus Paste

This citrus paste is one of the ingredients for the second dough. It doesn't taste amazing on its own, but in combination with the sweet, rich, buttery dough, it provides a great balance. This recipe makes more than you will need for one loaf, but you can refrigerate it if you're baking again within a few days, or freeze it if you're not going to bake again for a week or longer. I use a minimum of two oranges and two lemons, because the blender won't properly puree a smaller amount of fruit.

Choose oranges and lemons with thin, unblemished skins and fruits that are heavy for their size, which indicates juiciness. If you can't get unwaxed, organic citrus, gently wash the skins before zesting the fruits or cooking them into a puree.

TIMING

45 minutes total

EQUIPMENT

Paring knife (for microwave method), microwave oven and microwave-safe bowl large enough to hold fruit (for microwave method), roasting pan (for oven method), blender or food processor, storage container

INGREDIENTS

2 oranges, rinsed well in warm water

2 lemons, rinsed well in warm water

COOK THE CITRUS

Microwave method: Make a few small cuts with a paring knife in each piece of fruit to keep it from exploding in the microwave. Place the fruit in a large microwave-safe bowl or other container, loosely covered with plastic wrap or a lid left ajar. Microwave on full power for 15 minutes.

The fruit should be uniformly very soft all over. If it still has any firm-feeling spots, return it to the microwave for 1- to 2-minute intervals, until it is all very soft.

Oven method: Preheat the oven to 355°F / 180°C. Arrange the fruit in the roasting pan and cover with the lid or foil. Roast for 1 hour, until the fruit is very soft all over.

MAKE THE CITRUS PASTE

Let the fruit cool for 15 to 20 minutes.

Cut the fruit into quarters, so it's easier to blend, then transfer it to a blender or food processor and puree until it is a coarse paste. It shouldn't be totally smooth. You might need to add a little water to get the blender going. Transfer the mixture to a clean, shallow container and refrigerate it to cool completely.

The Bake

MAKES ONE 900-GRAM LOAF

This is it!

TOPPING

BAKER'S %	WEIGHT	INGREDIENT
30%	30g	Egg whites
100%	100g	Sugar
25%	25g	Almond flour
1.5%	1.5g	Salt
1.5%	1.5g	Cornstarch

ADDITIONAL INGREDIENTS

A handful each of pearled sugar and sliced almonds (optional)

TIMING

Preparation: 15 minutes; baking: 1 hour; cooling: 8 hours

EQUIPMENT

Mixing bowl, whisk, soup spoon or pastry piping bag, spatula or pallet knife, sheet pan, digital thermometer

Preheat the oven to 300°F / 150°C.

 While the oven preheats, mix the ingredients for the topping: In a medium to large bowl, whisk together all the topping ingredients until they are well combined. Spoon or pipe the mixture over the top of the panettone and use a spatula or pallet knife to gently distribute it. Don't worry if some of the mixture drips down the sides. I like to sprinkle the top with pearled sugar and sliced almonds, so if you like, do that, too.

When the oven is at temperature, put the panettone on the sheet pan and place it into the oven to bake for 30 minutes.

As soon as you have put it in the oven, set up two chairs or a stack of books, or rig some other system by which the panettone can be immediately hung upside down by its skewers when it comes out of the oven, to keep it from deflating or collapsing.

After the first 30 minutes of baking, increase the oven temperature to 320°F / 160°C and bake for 20 minutes. Then increase the temperature to 340°F / 170°C for the final 10 minutes. Use a thermometer to check that it's done; it should have an internal temperature of at least 198°F / 92°C.

As soon as you're happy with the bake, don't waste a second between opening the oven door and flipping the panettone upside down onto your hanging station.

Let it hang for at least 8 hours or overnight, then invert, slice, and eat.

Endnote: A good panettone, made correctly, stays fresh and delicious for weeks, thanks to the curing action of a sourdough starter, along with the abundance of sugar and fat in the dough. I've eaten some panettones made by the real pros that have been up to 8 months old, stored in a plastic bag inside a cardboard box, and they still taste fresh. Mine's not quite there yet.

Baking Terms

Acetic and lactic acids: The two acids produced by lactic bacteria in a sourdough starter. Lactic bacteria in a starter convert simple sugars into acetic and lactic acids (along with alcohol and carbon dioxide). Acetic and lactic acids impart tangy flavors to sourdough bread.

All-purpose flour, or **plain flour:** Soft wheat flour, suitable for general baking use, including sourdough baking. I typically combine it with bread flour, whole wheat flour, and sometimes rye or other grain flours.

Autolyse: Pronounced "auto-lees," this is a baker's shortcut that simplifies the dough-mixing process and makes for better-rising bread.

To autolyse just means to mix your flour or water together and then let that mixture rest, anywhere from 20 minutes to several hours. This gives the flour time to properly hydrate and the gluten bonds time to form and relax. When you autolyse, you don't have to extensively mix or knead your dough, because the gluten forms by itself.

This concept was pioneered by the late professor Raymond Calvel, a bread expert and baking instructor whose experiments and research into bread-making technique helped to revive traditional French-style breadmaking in the second half of the twentieth century.

Bacteria: Certain bacteria, like the various types of lactic bacteria found in sourdough starter, are your good friends. Lactic bacteria are essential to fermentation and to flavor. They convert the simple sugars in flour into lactic and acetic acids, alcohol and carbon dioxide, all of which give sourdough bread its characteristic tangy taste, its crisp crust, and its chewy, light, and spongy crumb.

Baker's percentage: The baker's percentage is the calculation you'll need in order to write your own bread recipes, or scale up or down an existing recipe, or adjust a single ingredient within a recipe to improve your bread. (See Understanding Baker's Percentage, page 49, in the Bread Baking Techniques chapter for the specifics.)

Bassinage: This is a French term for a second addition of water to your dough, after the autolyse (see page 50). By starting with a slightly dry dough and then adding water after some mixing, you end up with a stronger dough.

Biga: A dry pre-ferment (see page 76) made with flour, water, and a small amount of commercial yeast.

Bran: The outer shell of various whole grains, rich in fiber and nutrients.

Bread flour, or **strong flour:** Flour with a medium-high protein content, typically 12%–14%.

Bulk fermentation: The term *bulk* refers to the fact that the dough is left in one solid mass; some doughs are later divided into individual loaves once the fermentation is right, and others are left to bulk cold retard (see page 55) overnight, to be shaped the following day.

Carbon dioxide: The gas that results when yeast and bacteria digest the sugars in flour during fermentation. The air pockets that make a light crumb are created mostly by carbon dioxide, with a small amount of air also coming from alcohol as it evaporates during baking.

Cold retard: A period in which your dough sits at a cooler temperature to slow the fermentation and to build up essential flavor. My ideal temperature range is 50°–54°F / 10°–12°C. This technique is an alternative to proofing (see page 56).

Crumb and crust: The interior and exterior, respectively, of bread.

Endosperm: The bulk of a grain kernel is endosperm; this is the layer between the bran and the germ, containing protein and carbohydrates. The endosperm is the only part of the grain kernel that remains after milling white flour.

Enriched dough: A dough that includes eggs, milk, butter, oil, or any other type of fat, which makes it softer and more tender. The fat coats the flour, which creates a challenge for the yeast and bacteria. This is why, when making enriched breads, I use commercial yeast along with my sourdough starter.

Enzymes: In the simplest terms, enzymes are proteins that make chemical reactions happen. In breadmaking, enzymes break complex starches down into simple sugars, which can then be digested by yeast and bacteria during the process of fermentation.

Falling Number: The Falling Number is the result of the Hagberg Falling Number Test, which measures enzyme activity in a particular flour. A device is dropped into a heated slurry of flour and water, and the number of seconds it takes to fall through that slurry is the Falling Number. The more enzyme activity in the flour, the faster the starches break down, and the faster the device falls, and the faster a dough made with that flour will ferment.

Feeding: This is the act of adding fresh flour and water to a starter to continue to feed the yeast and bacteria and maintain its viability as a leavening agent. It is also known as *refreshing*.

Fermentation: This is the fundamental process of bread-making. Most simply put, it starts when enzymes break down complex starches into simple sugars in a dough. The bacteria work with wild yeasts to break those sugars down into ethanol, carbon dioxide, and acids. This whole process leavens a dough and gives sourdough bread its great flavor and texture.

Folding: This is a process by which dough is pulled and stretched by hand. This action builds gluten strength as it causes the proteins to link together into longer chains.

Germ: The center part of a grain kernel or berry, whose job, botanically speaking, is to sprout a new plant. Wheat germ is ground with the bran and endosperm for whole wheat flour. Wheat germ is also separated, rolled, and dried to be sold … as wheat germ.

Gluten: The gluten in wheat is composed of two proteins: glutenin, which gives the dough strength, and gliadin, which gives it extensibility, or the ability to stretch. The two proteins begin to bond together during autolyse (see page 294), creating a network that can trap the carbon dioxide gas created by yeast during fermentation, which is what causes bread dough to rise. Rye and barley also contain gluten, but of different types that do not behave like wheat gluten.

Hydration, or **hydration percentage:** This is the amount of water in a dough relative to the amount of flour. When you calculate percentages in baking, the amount of flour is always considered the baseline, at 100%. The other ingredients are then given as percentages of the amount of flour. So if you had 100 grams of flour and 75 grams of water, the hydration percentage would be 75%.

Lactobacillus: This is the name of the dominant genus of bacteria that naturally occur in sourdough. They flourish under the right conditions of fermentation, converting sugar into lactic acid, acetic acid, and carbon dioxide.

Lame: Pronounced "lahm," this is a small handle to which a disposable razor blade is attached; this tool is used to slash/score/slice the tops of loaves before baking.

Leaven/levain: The English and French words, respectively, for a catch-all synonym for sourdough starter.

Lievito madre: An Italian sourdough starter, used for making panettone and other enriched breads. In my bakery, we call it "Danny Lievito" (named after the actor Danny DeVito) or, more often, just "Danny."

Milling: The act of grinding whole grains into flour.

Poolish: Poolish is a wet pre-ferment (see below), made with flour, water, and a small amount of commercial yeast.

Pre-ferment: A portion of dough that is fermented ahead of mixing the rest of the dough, to help create better texture and more flavor.

Proofing: The step after final shaping, in which dough is kept at a warm temperature of 80°–82°F / 27°–28°C, which promotes maximum yeast activity. I use this technique for breads that benefit from a quicker fermentation (e.g., milk buns, baguettes, brioche, and ciabatta). For sourdough breads, I use cold retard (see page 56) to slow the fermentation.

Scoring: The act of cutting slashes into a loaf, just before baking, to facilitate the maximum amount of rise once the dough is transferred to a hot oven. Scoring gives a baker control over how the gases will move through and out of the loaf as it bakes.

Shaping, pre- and final: A series of important steps in the process of making bread, following the bulk fermentation, in which dough is portioned and shaped to build surface tension, then shaped again and sometimes transferred to a banneton (proofing basket), couche (linen proofing cloth), or sheet pan, giving the dough outside support to facilitate a strong rise during proofing and baking.

Starter: Another term for leaven/levain, this is a pre-fermented dough that is added to a bread dough to naturally leaven it.

Whole grain: This refers to any flour that has been milled to include the whole grain (bran, endosperm, and germ), whether wheat or another grain.

Whole wheat: This refers specifically to wheat flour that has been milled to include either all parts of the wheat grain or, in some cases, just the endosperm and bran, but not the germ.

Yeast: Microorganisms that occur naturally in flour, on human skin, and in the air. When cultivated in sourdough starter and added to dough, yeast converts sugars into alcohol and carbon dioxide.

Acknowledgments

My deepest love and thanks to Karishma, Talia, and all of my wonderful team at Hart Bageri.

Ben Liebmann for being my friend and greatest champion.

René and Nadine Redzepi and all the team at Noma.

Ben and Emma, Victor, Luca, Greg and TJ, and my mum and dad, who helped with the photo shoots.

Maureen Evans for the photos and Manuel Avila for the videos. James Robinson for the website, QR codes, and feeding me Bakewell tarts.

Chad Robertson, Kathleen Weber, Gabriele Bonci, and all the bakers I've had the pleasure of hanging with.

Laurie Woolever, Francis Lam, and Susan Roxborough and the team at Clarkson Potter for getting this book in such great shape.

Matty Matheson, Lionel Boyce, and all the crew for the huge Hart love in *The Bear*.

Madeline and Sander Buitelaar, for being my guardian angels, and to Lauren Dundes, for her eagle eye in finding everything we missed.

Everyone who's been in my life over the years, all my friends and family who have made my life better and shaped me.

All the chefs who have been kind and supportive of me, those who have become my friends, and finally all the chefs who have inspired and influenced me in my career.

I love you all and thank you profoundly.

Index

G

germ, 297

gluten, 297
  in autolyse process, 294
  formation, and bassinage, 51
  and protein content, 32

grain mill, tabletop, 28

grains, whole and processed, 39
  See also pan loaves; rye breads;
    specific grains

H

half sheet or quarter sheet pan, 28

half whole wheat city loaf, 120

hand-mixed dough, 50–51, 55

honey-roasted walnut whole wheat city
    loaf, 126

hot cross buns, 263

hveder, Danish, 243

hydration, 50, 297
  second. *See* bassinage

I

ingredients
  baker's percentage, 49
  essential, 32, 35
  other ingredients, 36, 39
  scaling, 49
  See also specific ingredients

Italian ciabatta, real, 176

K

Kathleen Weber's rosemary and lemon
    bread, 214

L

lactobacillus, 297

lame and razor blades, baker's, 28, 297

leaven/levain, 297
  See also sourdough starter

Lievito madre, 297
  making a (aka Danny Lievito), 272

loaf pans, 28
  baking with, 61

local grain pan loaf, 105

M

machine-mixed dough, 51–52, 55

the magic number, 49

malt powder, diastatic, 39

malt syrup, 39

marble rye city loaf, 118

masa, 39
  in sand dollar, 143

mashed potato buns, 211

master recipes
  brioche, 232
  city loaf, 113
  milk bun, 239

measuring cups or jugs, 24

milk bun master recipe, 239

milk powder, 39

milling flour, 32, 35, 297

miso, 39
  rye, 86

mixing bowls, 24

mixing dough. *See* dough

morning buns, 189

multigrain pan loaf, pumpernickel style, 98

N

naan, 167

naked rye, 89

The Noma Guide to Fermentation (Redzepi
    and Zilber) 39

nuts
  in babka (dark chocolate hazelnut or
    white chocolate pumpkin seed), 234
  honey-roasted walnut whole wheat city
    loaf, 126
  See also seeds

O

oat bread, 146

oils, 39

ølands, 36

100% rye marble rye, 93

P

panettone, 268, 271
  the bake, 292
  citrus paste, 291
  classic panettone, 284
  making a Lievito madre, 272
  sugar bath, or bagnetto, 278
  three Danny Lievito feeds, 281
  a throwdown averted, 282
  troubleshooting your Danny Lievito
    feeds, 282
  two-part daily storage feeding, 275

pan loaves
  Ballymaloe brown yeast bread, 102
  barley bread, pumpernickel style,
    test #1, 101
  local grain pan loaf, 105
  mixing, 51
  multigrain pan loaf, pumpernickel style,
    98
  pumpernickel pan loaf, 97
  See also loaf pans

pita, 168

pizza, Roman-style, 179

pizza stones, 27
  baking with, 61

polenta bread, 151

poolish, 75, 76, 297

potatoes, 39
  mashed potato buns, 211

pre-ferments, 297
  adding to dough, 50
  types of. *See* biga; poolish; sourdough
    starter

proofing dough, 297
  alternative to. *See* cold retard process
  ambient proofing, 60
  See also bannetons; couche;
    fermentation process

protein content of flours, 32

pumpernickel pan loaf, 97
  See also barley bread, pumpernickel
    style, test #1; multigrain pan loaf,
    pumpernickel style

Q

QR codes, 46

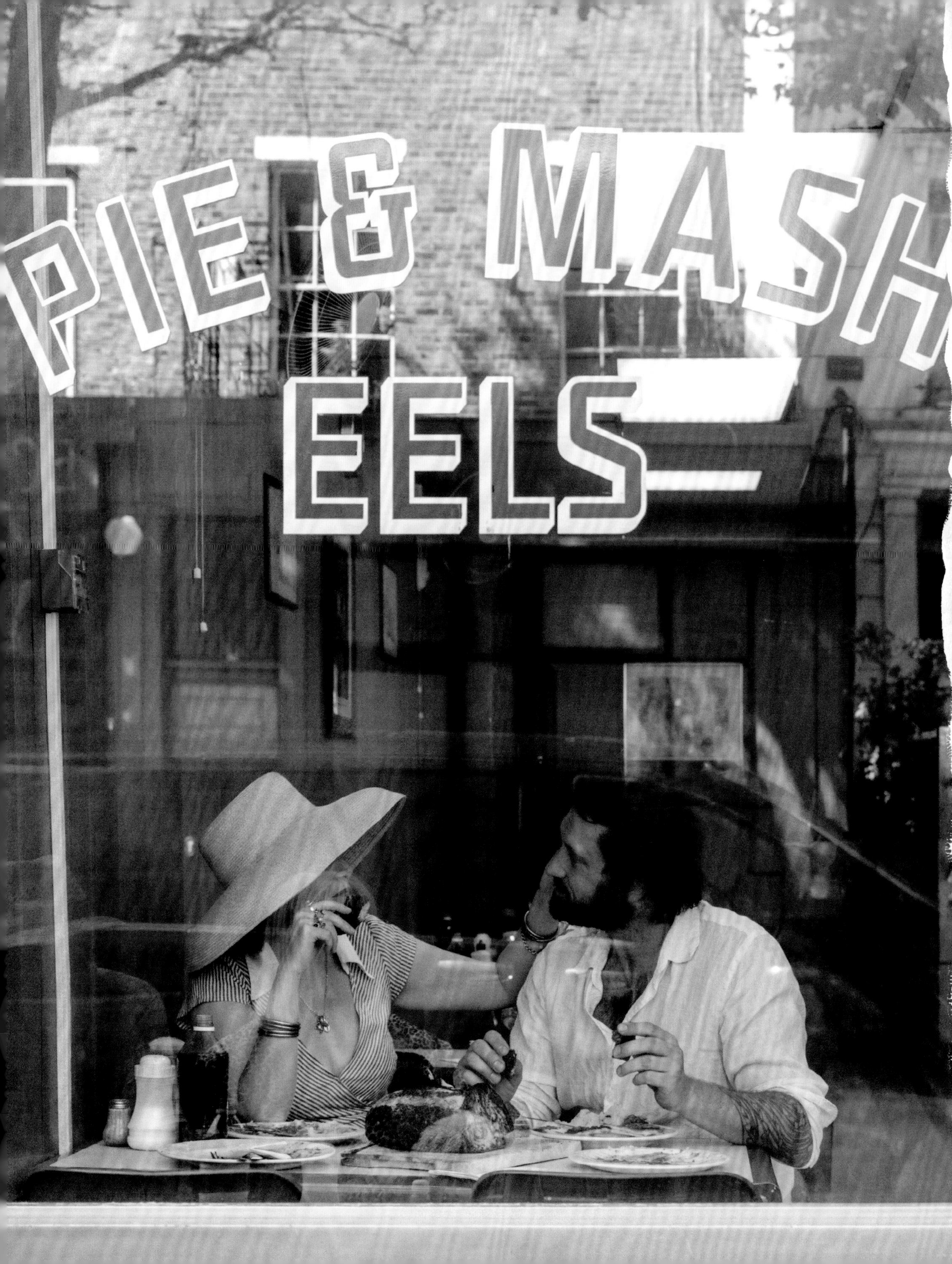
PIE & MASH
EELS